Joyce's Dislocutions

FRITZ SENN

Joyce's Dislocutions:

Essays on Reading as Translation

EDITED BY

John Paul Riquelme

The Johns Hopkins University Press

Baltimore and London

The Johns Hopkins University Press, Baltimore, Maryland 21218
The Johns Hopkins Press Ltd., London

The paper in this book is acid-free and meets the guidelines for permanence and durability of the Committee on Production Guidelines for Book Longevity of the Council on Library Resources.

Library of Congress Cataloging in Publication Data

Senn, Fritz.
     Joyce's dislocutions.

     Bibliography: p. 213
     Includes index.
     1. Joyce, James, 1882–1941—Criticism and interpre-
     tation—Addresses, essays, lectures.
     2. Joyce, James,
     1882–1941—Translations—Addresses, essays, lectures.
I. Riquelme, John Paul. II. Title.
PR6019.O9Z7946   1984   823'.912   84–777
ISBN 0–8018–3135–0

For Erlene

The editor dedicates his part in this project to the memory of

LOUIS O. MINK (1921–1983),

the Vidal de La Blache of Joyce studies

*Nom de Lieu*_(291.17) My globe goes gaddy at
geography giggle (275.F2) but only an amirican could
apparoxemete the apeupresiosity of his atlast's
alongement (132.02) with a meticulosity bordering
on the insane (173.34).
Oh Kosmos! Ah Ireland! (456.07)

Contents

Author's Preface

The essays gathered in this volume are witness to a very personal, limited, lasting concern. They are extended glosses, basically commentaries, on passages that fascinated me, and it seems that the enjoyment can be passed on. To reach tentatively for meanings and relations was a welcome, intermittent distraction from failure. That Joyce seems to have had a great understanding of, and sympathy with, failure and human shortcomings—not at all shared by the more high-minded of his critics—may well have been an additional, deeper reason for the continuous involvement. Figuring out what a text might imply was a beneficent kind of lotophagia. Under the overwhelming impact of Joycean Signipotence one's own incompetence may, at times, appear less depressing. And it was comforting to learn that our insights can be communicated to others. Joyce, whose works are *also* about loneliness, can make us overcome some of our isolation and seek each other out.

Most of us are, by ability and inclination, specialists, which is a euphemistic way to hide the inevitable limitations of those who are more like Bloom (or let me add Little Chandler) than like Odysseus or Shakespeare. What attracts me, and what I can profitably deal with, is Joyce's *Signipotence—* what words, letters, phrases, styles can bring about. At first I was interested in what *"was"* in the text, but my attention shifted more and more to what *happens* there, or what seems to happen in that interaction with our minds that we call, without knowing what it is, reading. I am occasionally impatient with those who still treat Joyce's works as things, static objects, that have certain properties, and who overlook what Joyce seems to make very difficult for us to overlook any longer, that we are concerned with processes. Of course they are never easy to grasp or name. The Western mind has had a tendency to think in terms of objects: they can be observed, arranged, ordered, classified, filed, and administered, and so they become more solid than they might be. Correspondingly, the nouns in our language are privileged (look at any index; it consists of nouns). Joyce, who could exaggerate this nominal proclivity (as in "Ithaca"), also provides some antidote. From him we could learn that inert mass is active energy.

I concentrate—aware of the hazards that physicists discovered for their own experiments—on Joycean energies (not to be distinguished, etymologically, from urges, or "workings"), dynamisms, motions, kinetics. I often wish we could counteract the nominal basis of our concepts by using more verbs. I have become very skeptical of formulas like "*Ulysses* is . . ." and would favour such metaphorical phrasings as "*Ulysses* does . . . acts . . . performs . . ." In one essential sense, there "are," for example, no "allusions" or "epiphanies," but Joyce's texts abundantly allude, or epiphanize, or manifest. Such prejudices of mine explain why I focus on reading, translating, righting, turning, weaving, processing, knowing (and *not* knowing), and doubting. Or why I keep returning to terms with prefixes that signal local changes: meta-, trans-, dis-. Verbs have the advantage of suggesting and expressing time. The time we have to spend on Joyce's works in itself becomes functional. We can learn that reading and understanding take time, and that this time (not Time) affects the reading and changes the understanding. Joyce often makes the latter part of a sentence determine an earlier part; his ends transform his beginnings.

Joyce allows the tiny part to speak up for the macrocosmic whole, and the synecdochal method has been pursued here. Ideas were usually triggered by a specific passage and developed through inductive groping. Articulation of what I thought I perceived in an increasingly intricate texture usually led to some paradox and contradiction, or to some cautious generalization. My approach is textual, pedestrian, extrapolatory—that of a Bloomian agnostic who tries to let his mind roam into parts unknown. Any resemblance to theories, especially currently relevant ones, is likely to be accidental: I have read few of them and understood none. The list of thinkers, scholars, philosophers, theorists, structuralists, et alia that I have not used, not even named, is longer and more impressive than the persuasive roll-call of reputable names that some of our colleagues manage to cram even into the shortest of their presentations.

In looking over my provisional weavings of many years ago, I was strongly tempted to undo some damages and to replace some early conceptual misses by more up-to-date apparent hits. But I refrained from such anachronistic righting. I left untouched those passages that now seem to suggest that I then believed in such things as Homeric "parallels" or even in the presence—or utility—of demiurgic beings like narrators, arrangers, catechisers, or hallucinators that, according to the best authorities, seem to haunt Joyce's prose. I did not believe in those entities even then, but was simply, and uncritically, as we all do some of the time, following terminological convenience.

All Joycean ways lead to *Finnegans Wake*. Once we have reached it, we will never be the same again, nor will the earlier works. Whatever dynamisms we discover, the *Wake* will show them magnified, in the extreme. It often appears sufficient for a demonstration just to point at *Finnegans Wake* and let the matter rest there. It is easier to use the *Wake* as proof for something we want to have proved than to know anything precise about it. So some warning is called for. *Finnegans Wake* offers unique reading rewards (at the cost of unequaled frustration); it will remain a fascination and a challenge. But while we can usually make an instructive show of select passages, we ought not to confuse the *Wake's* exemplary complaisance with our understanding of it. When I started out, some thirty years ago, in the juvenile flush of those euphoric first unravelings of meaning, I hoped that within some decades we might jointly arrive at sufficient basic understanding (at the modest level of Roland McHugh's helpful *Annotations*) that would enable us to go beyond those resistant details and to make statements of more general import and validity, perhaps even in a scholarly way. We obviously haven't. As a *Wake* reader who has done quite a bit of devoted homework, I may be entitled to say that, collectively, we have failed in a most elementary way and that we are hardly qualified to discuss *Finnegans Wake* with scholarly pretense. It is a pretense that I, for one, can no longer keep up with a straight face. (It is of course possible, and legitimate, to theorize intelligently about *Finnegans Wake* without actually having gone near it, or on the basis of what has already been written about it—but that is not my concern here.)

I am glad and somewhat puzzled to see that my own futilitarian attitude and utter resignation is not shared by other, confident *Wake* adepts, who do not seem to be dissatisfied at all. I am also fully aware that my own profound and sincere ignorance is not shared by most of my colleagues, but I usually find that when I *specifically* want to know "And what do you think *this* means?" they do not alleviate my ignorance but generally confirm it.

Joyce students—whether they pretend to understand *Finnegans Wake* or not—like to communicate and flock together and encourage each other. We could almost define Joyce by one of his most kinetic effects: he actually brings people together and turns more of them into friends than their divergent views would make it seem likely. There is a real, diverse, humane, many-minded Joyce community. I don't think it would have been possible to survive without its contacts, interchanges, the correspondence, the meetings, and the emerging friendships. Most of our ideas have been passed around in a generous attitude that is amazingly free of competition—that too is one of the meanings of "Joycean." Here I can only thank a handful of friends to whom I am indebted. (We naturally also owe a great deal to all those whose statements provoked us into articulating our disagreement.)

It was James S. Atherton who first motivated me and advised me, an amateur, to start writing about *Finnegans Wake*, which in the end resulted in almost everything else. Adaline Glasheen, in her sparkling letters, has been encouraging throughout. It was my good luck that a young Clive Hart wrote to me, and our common enthusiasm brought about some fruitful interchange and the serial publication of *A Wake Newslitter* (for which he did practically all the work). When Thomas F. Staley, of the newly founded *James Joyce Quarterly,* visited me in 1966, all kinds of vague plans included one to convene a few Joyceans we knew the following Bloomsday in Dublin, and we grandiloquently called the venture the First International James Joyce Symposium. It had some consequences that we did not then foresee. Over more than twenty years I have greatly benefited from conversations with Bernard (and later also with Shari) Benstock, taking place most often in Unterengstringen, but also in places ranging from Honolulu to Dubrovnik. Countless inquisitive, strenuous, rewarding late hours were spent with Klaus Reichert, who is so much more than a perceptive scholar and the most enlightened translator I have come across. Breon Mitchell, who started out by sharing my own interest in the German translation of Joyce, has been of great help over many years and also made it possible for me to become a visiting academic in the United States, as did Thomas E. Connolly, Morris Beja, Margaret Solomon, and Zack Bowen. My many conversations with Brook Thomas have been amongst my most stimulating experiences. I owe many fertile impulses to Hugh Kenner; we first talked shop in Buffalo in 1968, and since then at irregular intervals, but always with ample results.

It was John Paul Riquelme who first thought of collecting some articles for this volume, as a spiritual act of mercy in a bad time, and my final thanks go to him for persevering, for doing most of the editorial work and, ultimately, for believing in the value of such a revival.

Fritz Senn

Editor's Acknowledgments

In August 1982 a conversation with Louis Mink, then director of the Center for Humanities at Wesleyan University, gave me the idea to collect some of Fritz Senn's essays for an English-speaking audience. It was our great loss that Louis Mink died unexpectedly of a heart attack before the project was fully under way. It is to his memory that the editor dedicates his own part in this transatlantic endeavor.

Much of the editorial work for this volume was carried out during the editor's stay in the Federal Republic of Germany as an Alexander von Humboldt Research Fellow. I want to thank the von Humboldt Foundation in Bonn for its generous support and encouragement during my sojourn in Freiburg and Konstanz. Numerous people helped make the work easier and the results more satisfying than they otherwise would have been. Brook Thomas helped with the organization and the selection of essays at an early stage. Later, Joel Weinsheimer suggested some directions to pursue concerning theory of translation, and he provided a typewriter for a wandering editor in need. Southern Methodist University supported the project in a variety of ways. Kathleen Triplett and Irene Poole cheerfully did a great deal of typing, word-processing, and copying at short notice. Dean R. Hal Williams of Dedman College and Steven V. Daniels, chairman of the English department, arranged for an expense grant to defray clerical costs. A grant from the University Research Council at SMU enabled me to travel to Zürich to complete the editing. Page Thomas at SMU's Bridwell Library helped me obtain copies of some of the essays not readily available in the United States. In Europe, the Universitäts-Bibliotek at Freiburg University made its resources available to me. The staff of the Johns Hopkins University Press was, as always, efficient, encouraging, and helpful. I want to thank William Sisler and Jane Warth at Johns Hopkins, especially, for their guidance and suggestions. Ms. Warth's editing of the manuscript was more scrupulous and sensitive than any author or editor could expect.

The essays collected here appeared in earlier versions in various journals and collections, sometimes under different titles. Our thanks go to the following for permission to reprint: Thomas F. Staley, editor of the *James Joyce Quarterly,* in which "The Challenge: *ignotas animum,"* "Metastasis," "Dogmad or Dubliboused," and "Book of Many Turns" first appeared; the University of Pittsburgh Press, in whose volume *Approaches to "Ulysses": Ten Essays,* ed. Thomas F. Staley and Bernard Benstock (1970), "Translation as Approach" appeared under the title *"Ulysses* in Translation"; the editors of *Akzente,* in which an earlier German version of *"Transluding off the Toptic"* appeared; the Universidad de Seville, publishers of *James Joyce: A New Language: Actas/Proceedings del Simposio Internacional en el Centenario de James Joyce,* edited by Francisco Garcia Tortosa et al. (1982), in which "Dynamics of Corrective Unrest" first appeared; the University of Delaware Press, publishers of *Irish Renaissance Annual* 1 (1980), in which "Bloom among the Orators" appeared; the University of California Press, publishers of *James Joyce's "Ulysses": Critical Essays,* ed. Clive Hart and David Hayman (1974), in which "Nausicaa" appeared; Haffmans Verlag (Zürich), publishers of *Nichts gegan Joyce: Joyce Versus Nothing* (1983), in which "Dislocution" appeared as "Variants of Dislocution in *Ulysses"*; Didier Érudition (Paris), publishers of *Ulysse cinquante ans après,* ed. Louis Bonnerot (1974) (*Études anglaises* 53), in which "The Rhythm of *Ulysses"* appeared. "A Reading Exercise in *Finnegans Wake"* is reprinted from *Levende Talen* 269 (June–July 1970): 469–80. "Foreign Readings" is reprinted from *Work in Progress: Joyce Centenary Essays,* ed. Richard F. Peterson, Alan M. Cohn, and Edmund L. Epstein (Carbondale: Southern Illinois University Press, 1983). All the essays have been changed in many small ways, but only *"Transluding off the Toptic"* is substantially different from the version originally published. Dates of composition have been given at the end of each essay.

Finally, I want to thank Fritz Senn for his friendship, his help, and his hospitality recently and in the past. He was the first among my colleagues in Joyce studies to encourage me to express my ideas in print and at scholarly meetings. Over the years he has helped many other younger scholars on both sides of the Atlantic in similar ways. During our work on this volume in his home near Zürich, he provided a place for me to stay and to write. And he patiently reviewed his essays with me, explaining things I did not at first understand and putting up with my sometimes naïve suggestions for changes. This volume is the result of his willingness, apparent in every essay, to engage at length in dialogue and to take divergent positions seriously.

John Paul Riquelme

The Use of Translation and the Use of Criticism

Lesen ist schon Übersetzen und Übersetzen ist dann noch
einmal Übersetzen . . . Der Vorgang des Übersetzens
schließt im Grunde das ganze Geheimnis menschlicher
Weltverständigung und gesellschaftlicher Kommunikation
ein. (Reading is already translation, and translation is
translation for the second time. . . The process of translating comprises in its essence the whole secret of human
understanding of the world and of social communication.)—Hans-Georg Gadamer, "Wieweit schreibt Sprache
das Denken vor?" ("To What Extent Does Language Pre-
scribe Thought?")

Interlingual translation is . . . an access to an inquiry into
language itself. "Translation," properly understood, is a
special case of the art of communication which every successful speech-act closes within a given language. On the
inter-lingual level, translation will pose concentrated, vis-
ibly intractable problems; but these same problems
abound, at a more covert or conventionally neglected
level, intra-lingually.
                        —George Steiner, *After Babel*

Joyce's works consist of translation and glorify all cognate processes.
                        —Fritz Senn, *"Transluding off the Toptic"*

Fritz Senn has written and spoken against certain tendencies of critics and
theorists to appropriate Joyce's works for their own ends. Despite Senn's
justified suspicion of method and theory, many of the attitudes he expresses in
his commentaries of the past three decades tend to cohere as a critical stance.
That stance involves what can be broadly described as a method, and it raises,
though often indirectly, theoretical questions. Senn's approach is distinctive in
part because it works toward, as well as through, the raising of new questions

and the opening up of new possibilities rather than toward the answering of questions previously raised and the limiting of horizons. The approach never becomes static. It attempts to be the critic's equivalent of an act of translation. Like any other interpretive act, translation, if it is carried out coherently, involves repeated operations whose principles can be described and perhaps justified as a method, though the method never explains completely the successes and the failures of translation (or interpretation). Attempts to translate regularly invite the question of translatability, which can hardly be posed outside some theoretical frame. Senn's approach through translation results in descriptions of the reading of Joyce's texts (and of Joyce's writing them) as struggles with a foreign language. That struggle is the struggle with language itself as foreign. Through encountering and reproducing the dislocutions available through language, reader and writer are displaced from what they might otherwise take to be a normal, or neutral, position within a specific language, or within language generally speaking. By experiencing the literary text's dislocutions, the critic may come to share a region of linguistic freeplay with the author. For the particular author and the particular critic under consideration, that region—defined by the simultaneous interaction and expression of many linguistic and interpretive possibilities—is Switzerland, both biographically and figuratively.[1] By attempting to enter that region with the passport of Joyce's writings and Senn's readings, we too become foreign readers.

The road to the palace of wisdom for Joyce included not only excess but also exile, and a crucial portion of his exile's route runs through the canton of Zürich. As A. Walton Litz has persuasively argued, we can associate the three stages of the writing of *Ulysses,* initial, middle, and final, "with the three cities of Joyce's dateline: Trieste, Zürich, Paris."[2] It was in Zürich that Joyce undertook "the radical experiments in style and form that mark the intermediate chapters of *Ulysses,*" which "were the decisive events in the developments of Modernism in English literature."[3] This is a large claim, but one that is fully justified. The middle, or Zürich chapters, from Wandering Rocks through Oxen of the Sun, are, in Litz's words, "the absolutely necessary transition . . . to the world of the last chapters"[4] and also the catalyst for Pound and Eliot's transforming of *The Waste Land* into the paradigmatic poem of Modernism. Litz cites Joyce's use of so-called "spatial form" and his focus on the transformative qualities of language in the Zürich chapters as the direct and enabling antecedents for the kind of revisions Joyce made in Paris in 1921, revisions without "inherent limits."[5] We can, of course, only speculate about the various factors that merged to make possible the sort of rewriting that led eventually to the final shape of *Ulysses* and then to *Finnegans Wake.* But one of those factors is Joyce's new, and unforeseeable, sense of language based on his growing experience with languages besides English during his years on the Continent.

The biographical facts are clear enough, and widely known, but the implications have not been widely developed.[6] Having studied while in Ireland Latin and several modern languages (French, Italian, Dano-Norwegian, and German) at school, at the university, and independently, Joyce moved to the Continent in 1904 at the age of twenty-two with the intention of teaching for Berlitz in Zürich. His wanderings from city to city in Italy, Switzerland, and France have become nearly legendary for students of modern literature. Our concern here is not so much the legend as the linguistic and cultural realities of this most unusual exile. Ordinarily, when we think of expatriation, we may well imagine someone settling in a foreign culture and mastering a new language sufficiently to be considered bilingual. Joyce's expatriation, however, was more complicated. Because of his employment by Berlitz, he was able to exchange language lessons with his colleagues and thereby extend his knowledge not just of one language but of several, either simultaneously or in overlapping succession.[7] Additionally, largely by chance, he found himself from the start in a polyglot situation that did not diminish in its linguistic diversity, despite the moves from Pola to Trieste, then to Zürich, and finally to Paris, which took place over a period of fifteen years. Even before the move in 1915 to Zürich, out of exigency after the outbreak of World War I, Joyce's life in Europe was polyglot in the extreme. In Pola (now the city of Pulj in Yugoslavia), where Joyce first taught for Berlitz, he would have heard Italian, German, and Serbian spoken on the streets. And in Trieste, where he lived for the most part during the decade before the Zürich years, besides hearing the special Triestine dialect, Joyce could have heard regularly the variety of languages and accents spoken by the Greek, Austrian, Hungarian, and Italian residents of the city. This long period of gestation came to fruition once Joyce reached Zürich, where his transformed sense of language and the freedom to write provided by newfound patronage combined to enable him to undertake the work that led ultimately to *Finnegans Wake*. Having acquired either proficiency or extensive familiarity with several languages, Joyce found himself in a German-speaking but polyglot culture, in which the interplay of languages would have been a constant factor in his daily life. In normal times, Zürich is a city in which several languages are either in use (primarily German, both High- and Swiss-German) or near at hand (primarily French). Today we see the evidence of this circulation of languages in the many public signs around the city and even in the labels on products in grocery stores printed in three and occasionally four languages (German, French, Italian, and sometimes English). But during World War I, the influx of foreigners seeking a haven from the hostilities would have created an even more intensely diverse linguistic atmosphere for a polyglot artist whose reputation and energy meant involvement with many groups and projects. In this unusual, and transient, atmosphere, Joyce's transformations of English prose style became possible.

The experience of Switzerland was for Joyce not the beginning but rather an advanced stage of a process that began in Ireland and continued in Italy: the process of recognizing English as foreign and of using it in ways that would make that recognition available to others. His route starts in Ireland, because he encountered there the difference between the King's English and English as the Irish speak it. Later, in Pola and Trieste, he experienced the difference between Dante's Italian, which he had studied, and modern Italian, and he heard not just Italian, but Italian as the Triestines speak it and the Triestine dialect as foreigners spoke it. Given the linguistic circumstances of Joyce's life in Europe, it should be no surprise that a writer with his cultural and educational background could develop a sense of language usage and a practice of style that are comparable to those of the translator, even when he is writing in what is ostensibly his native language. And yet the results Joyce produced are perennially surprising. His mature style always poses problems for readers, who are asked to share in the polyglot translator's experience of language, though usually without having undergone the writer's linguistic experiences that made the style possible. The difficult, but potentially successful, communication between the artist and the ordinary citizen, which Joyce's narratives often probe, is made available to us through our performance as readers. Though we need not be polyglot to read Joyce, it is also not surprising that a polyglot reader might develop a particularly sharp sensitivity to the dynamics of Joyce's language. That sensitivity channels the reading process back toward the translating process as the style's origin and goal. In this regard, a German-speaking Swiss reader could well develop a particularly acute receptivity to Joyce's writings, for such a reader's sense of language would have been moulded by an experience with German like Joyce's with English and with Italian.[8] Not literally, but structurally, reader and writer in this case come from the same linguistic country, where the spoken vernacular and the official, written language differ starkly. By realizing within a polyglot context the difference between writing and speaking as a determining factor in the linguistic world all of us share, the Irish writer and his Swiss reader can invent strategies for revealing the dynamic, and disruptive, qualities of literary language. Once they have made these qualities available to us, we can discover the energizing connections and differences between language and cognitive processes.

The difference that is the explicit focus of many of Senn's essays is not between speaking and writing or between consciousness and language, but between languages. And in that difference lies one version of the problem of translatability. Although translation has a wide range of meanings in his essays, Senn returns regularly to translations in the narrow sense, that is, to specific attempts to find equivalents for Joyce's works in languages other than English. Senn also frequently uses the word "translation" in one of its widest contexts of meaning to name the metaphorical nature of all language usage, but especially within Joyce's writings themselves. Translation, in this regard, always involves substitution. *Metaphor* here means the uneasy equivalence between two concepts that results when we try substituting words for one another. This equivalence is uneasy because it can never be exact; there is always a residue of meaning left over or a new meaning added in the act of substitution. This failure of exact fit in metaphor, and specifically in the language of translators and critics, can give rise to compensating strategies that attempt to right the imbalance. Senn's writings are a response to the recurring failure of fit. He responds with a critical strategy that is the following out of a sequence of tropological maneuvers. These enable him to evoke the energy of Joyce's language and simultaneously to admit the inadequacy and the inevitability of the attempt to substitute, including the attempt of the translator. The sequence moves structurally from metaphor ultimately to irony through two intermediate stages that we can associate respectively with metonymy and synecdoche. Such a bald sketch cannot, of course, do justice to the subtle insights about the evocative texture of Joyce's language that Senn consistently produces. And the tropological language of contemporary cultural theorists is one that Senn would never himself use.[9] But it can help us to see that, for him, translation as the metaphorical process of language usage leads to the discovery of irony at the core of metaphor, because the attempt to produce equivalences also results in failures of fit. What looks at first like a possible equivalence turns out to be also a contrast. This failure of fit leads to yet another substitution, and so on. And that is the life of reading as substitution.

This shuttling movement between similarity and difference in the critic's writings produces energetic motions like those of the translator at work. And these motions are also, within limits, the energetic, originating motions of the style being translated. The shift from metaphor to irony proceeds through metonymy and synecdoche in the following way. The search for an equivalence results not just in one possibility but in many, which can be ranged against one another in a proliferation that cannot be adequately described as a one-to-one correspondence. Instead, the correspondence is between the original word, or concept, and the array of possibilities for rendering it in one or several languages. The producing of such an array effects a change in emphasis in the interpretation from metaphoric equivalence to metonymic juxtapositions that vie with one another as possible substitutes. We can see these metonymic juxtapositions spatially configured on the pages of Senn's essays when he sets quotations from Joyce and from Joyce's translators against one another, sometimes in page-long charts. Senn moves to metonymy in another, equally important, way in his concern with *network* in Joyce's language when he traces the possible connections between words repeated in widely scattered parts of Joyce's writings. If these connections through repetition occur regularly in our experience of reading Joyce, as Senn's commentaries confirm, then it is part of the translator's task, and the critic's, to reproduce them whenever they are relevant. In this way, the critic can help other readers, including translators, recognize the connections worth emphasizing and some possible meanings for the network.

The metonymic array of possible equivalents and the networks of connections provide an abundance of details for Senn's presentation of Joyce's writings as if they were synecdochic. Joyce's reader experiences the evocation of a larger whole that becomes perceptible in spite of, as well as by means of, the microcosmic networks of small fragments that compose it. In order to reflect this aspect of Joyce's works, Senn takes fragments, especially individual words or small groups of words, and argues for the relation of part to whole by tracing the network of links. But he includes consistently an auto-corrective component in his arguments, and that component is also a reflection of Joyce's language, especially of its dislocutory nature. The recognition of a synecdoche in response to the linkages is never adequate to explain the details fully. As in the substitutions of translators, there is always a discernible lack of fit in the suggested equivalence. By admitting that inevitable lack of perfect fit, Senn gives us yet another aspect of our experience of reading Joyce. The shift to irony, the admission that a difference always emerges along with the substitutions of metaphor and, especially, with synecdoche, is actually no shift, for this admission permeates Senn's attitudes all along. The admission is no absolute ending, no final defeat, for reader, critic, or translator. It is instead a claim that all our arguments are at best provisionally valid. That claim is always a beginning as well as an end. The provisional quality is the proof of the vitality of Joyce's style and of our responses. Because of it, the process of rereading and retranslating continues. Without it, the works would become merely a past experience and not the potentially present and engaging one that they remain.

Senn often deals with translation in the narrow sense by probing the adequacy of various renderings of Joyce's texts into Western European languages. The purpose of these investigations and of his discussion of translatability is not primarily to criticize all existing translations as, in certain recurring ways and specific instances, inadequate. His commentaries have another use, for they suggest various alternative possibilities for understanding, and also for misunderstanding, Joyce's writings. By stressing the plenitude of repetitions with a difference and of trials and errors, Senn treats translation not only as a product to be understood semantically but also as a cognitive process. This notion of translation as process is reflected in the tropological description of the method of his essays. That structure itself attempts to be the sort of self-transforming, self-generating, spiraling process we experience through Joyce's styles.

The verb "to translate" is for Senn primarily intransitive, for he uses it to refer to a process of mind that sometimes results in the written products we call translations. By ascribing the methods and goals of the translator to the act of reading Joyce's texts (and by further extension to Joyce's writing of them), Senn describes those aspects of Joyce's works that every reader, and especially every translator, struggles with: their dislocutions. This term points, generally speaking, to the disruptions of our habitual frames of reference that we experience when we read Joyce's works, most obviously *Ulysses* and *Finnegans Wake*. These disruptions are triggered by abrupt shifts, such as those that Senn claims are the distinctive characteristic of *Ulysses*. He traces these displacements in style, as well as in story, throughout Joyce's career, but especially in the sentences of *Ulysses,* which are full of potential turbulences. In the essay "Dislocution," for instance, Senn sketches the polyglot play of references in a passage of *Ulysses* in which four cultures are refracted within an Irish setting, and he suggests as well that, as in *Finnegans Wake,* the effect of the sound may be quite different from the semantic meanings otherwise communicated. By stressing disruption through the term *dislocution,* Senn counters the overemphasis on Homeric "parallels" in some critical commentaries. Instead of the one-to-one correspondences of some critics' interpretive substitutions, he finds the criss-crossing of patterns that are mutually disturbing. These disturbances occur in the narrative action, in the language viewed historically (through etymology and obsolete meanings), and in our experience of serial approaches, as in the changing of perspectives in *Ulysses* from chapter to chapter and within chapters. The dislocutory aspects of Joyce's style are transformative, for they ask us to modify the perspectives we bring with us.

Senn describes dislocution as both a "blurred trope" that points to the originality of Joyce's language and an "illustrative synonym for translation." The blurring that gives us a synonym for translation may be understood in one way as the close connection between metaphor and its ostensible opposite, irony. We need both tropes in conjunction to describe translation insofar as it involves acts of substitution that do not quite work. The difficulty for the reader, and especially for the translator, is that Joyce's texts already contain so many dislocutions, which are themselves translations. These elements have already undergone a process of substitution and transformation that we may recognize and reenact when we encounter them. The signs of that process, which the dislocutions exhibit, encourage us to understand them as part of transforming sequences. As such, they become virtually impossible to translate, for they are themselves already part of a process, one name for which is translation.

In such essays as *"Transluding off the Toptic,"* Senn presents by means of examples the nature of that process, the kinds of problems it causes translators, and the aspects of Joyce's style that engender it. This was originally a talk given to a German audience, an offshoot of Senn's work as consultant, along with Klaus Reichert, for the Wollschläger translation of *Ulysses* into

German. The difficulty for the translator, in its most general form, is to render simultaneously the Dublin surface and narrative, so important to the book, *and* the reverberations of meaning that depend on peculiarities of Joyce's style. Style and story in *Ulysses* are inextricably intertwined in a mutually modifying, internally transforming relationship that the reader experiences as a process of discovering shifting possibilities. Insofar as translations tend always to limit those possibilities, they short-circuit the process by giving us something simpler and more stable. By making available to us only one, or at best a few, of the potential results of reading *Ulysses,* the translation cuts us off partially from the book's energies. This can happen in a variety of small ways, which Senn illustrates in *"Transluding"* and elsewhere. In these situations, the words of *Ulysses* generally function simultaneously in two or more contexts of meaning; that is, they contribute to the networks that Senn often presents. Even if the translator recognizes these interlocking contexts, and many readers of English may not, there is still the problem of making that recognition available to the reader of another language. The translator may well have to decide to turn off the music, as Senn sometimes puts it, by giving a semantically correct rendering that has a different effect on the reader. Translators of other authors face many of these same problems, but usually not in the extreme forms or with the frequency of *Ulysses*. A word or sequence may have to suggest a certain state of mind, the reverie of poetic creation, for example, or it may need to evoke a grammatical indeterminacy or hesitation, which causes the reader to waver between several meanings. Or certain words may function allusively or suggest certain etymological meanings, or both, in English in ways that are unusual or even impossible in some other languages.

When Senn suggests, by calling *Ulysses* dislocutory, that it is already a translation and therefore untranslatable, he is pointing to these difficulties, and others, as aspects of English that have already been transformed and extended by Joyce. That is, the translator faces a problem different from the usual one of rendering the possibilities of English into another language, for Joyce has already extended English in radical ways, ways that were not possible before he wrote. The translator must continually find equivalents for effects that are unusual even in the language and traditions of the original. Given the number and types of transforming disruptions permeating Joyce's texts in their details and in their larger structures, the cumulative problem for the translator seems insurmountable. Yet translation as a certain kind of cognitive process is a necessary response to Joyce's writings in our act of reading itself, for, as Senn explains, processes cognate with translation are inscribed in the writing, especially in various chapters of *Ulysses*. In Proteus we encounter the possibility of wayward etymological metamorphoses, for which the act of translating is one counterpart and fulfillment. Ithaca is perhaps Senn's best example of one of the book's styles suggesting throughout a process like translation, because it invites us to render its implications in another sort of language, which we imagine to have been the original. We respond by reintroducing the emotional language that is consistently avoided in the chapter itself. Senn suggests that the untranslatability of Oxen of the Sun can stand for the difficulty of the whole book, for it is an "intratranslation," a sequence of transformations not only of linguistic usages but of complete sets of attitudes within a single chapter. In the case of Oxen, the problem of translation concerns the differences between historical periods and not just the differences between languages. Once the difficulty of recapturing the past through representation is seen as a version of the problem of translation, the issues raised by Joyce's styles merge with some of the most perplexing questions pertaining to our understanding of human culture.

At the same time that historical processes of transformation necessitate a kind of translation as we face our own past, translation is cognate with the process by which language attempts to capture the movements of mind. In this regard, Eumaeus, a chapter neglected or disdained by many critics, is important for Senn, because its style gives the impression of having "its own self-reflective consciousness." This is a style of "erratic appropriateness," of "cognitive effort," of "the elusive and frustrating striving of language toward validity."[10] Both reader and writer can share in that elusive striving. In "Foreign Readings," Senn describes the cumulative effect of the multiple dislocutions of *Ulysses*. Because of them, it is "the first consistently intra-transferential fictional work," for its chapters are like a variety of translations that together become "a conjugation of all of language's potential and all stylistic ranges."

Both dislocution and translation, as Senn uses them, refer to reading and writing, the related processes of mind through which we consume and produce a text's style. At times, those processes seem, in his descriptions, essentially associative, for they involve our traversing networks of connections that will differ according to the temperament and schooling we bring with us. But it would be a misreading to overemphasize the subjective and associative elements in these essays, as important as those elements often are, for the most important effect of the dislocutions occurs in spite of our conventional habits of mind and in spite of the associations that have been inscribed within us as predetermined channels of thinking. The reader's dislocutory procedure, which is also an ideal act of translating, is only in part a rational, associative procedure. Because it cannot account wholly for our experience, that part leads us to something else. We cannot justifiably limit our reading of Joyce to what Samuel Beckett calls the realm of the "feasible," though the sort of understanding that pertains to the feasible always plays a role in any interpretation.

The sorting out of possibly relevant implications that Senn repeatedly undertakes is necessary, though at times seemingly perverse, not because it gives us the right interpretation, but because the activity eventually transforms our ordinary position in relation to language. It does so by enabling us to realize alternatives where no possibility for choice previously existed for us. We discover that new possibility by coming to see Joyce's late texts as if they were written in a foreign language, even though we may be native speakers of English. This new relationship to the mother tongue is one important effect of Joyce's styles that few readers besides Senn have as yet fully recognized. It is arguably a central part of the legacy Joyce leaves to his most creative younger contemporary, Beckett, who writes English through the transforming process of composing in another language. By writing French and translating into English, Beckett achieves a distance from his native language that allows him to use it in startling, foreign ways. Such distance may be especially important for American readers, who often tend to assume erroneously a familiarity with Joyce's use of English by identifying contemporary American usages with the language Joyce learned in Ireland nearly a century ago. In this circumstance, the foreigner's would-be handicap of unfamiliarity turns out to be an advantage.

As Senn explains in some detail, particularly in the essay "Foreign Readings," along with the disadvantage of being uncomfortable, the foreign reader has the advantage, because the language is not familiar, of being forced to look at it very closely. The foreigner brings a different set of presuppositions to the encounter with the language, which may produce a different kind of understanding than is normally available to the native speaker. The special sort of attention and concentration that develops may create a sensitivity to the language's texture that native speakers do not have. This insight, persuasively reinforced by the examples of both Joyce and Senn, is itself foreign, for it runs counter to our usual assumption that a native speaker can deal most sensitively with the nuances of literary language. In fact, our responses to literature, and to all forms of language within our own culture, are often so habitual and conventional that it is only through some tremendous effort of the imagination in answer to an equally large challenge that we can achieve an outsider's perspective. Both Joyce and his favorite hero, Odysseus, were foreigners who learned to operate by their wits, as must the reader of Joyce's works. As Senn points out, Joyce regularly evokes the situation of the foreign observer by representing it within his narratives, frequently through the use of foreign words, or within the narration, often through startling combinations of words. With *Ulysses* the unfamiliar aspects of the style become so pronounced that they are difficult for us to overlook, though we may succeed sometimes in doing just that. The translator cannot ignore them. To the extent that we, too, learn not to, we have become foreign readers. But this is a skill we have to work to achieve; the non-native speaker can recognize and admit more readily than most readers the difficulties we all face.

We gain more in this process than just a highly sophisticated sense of the style's vivid texture and its disruptive cross-currents, for we come to recognize ourselves, as well as the style, as foreign. We discover as did Joyce and, to a lesser degree, the young Irishman Stephen Dedalus, that all the languages we speak are "acquired." One implication of Senn's commentaries, though he does not formulate it in this way, is that we come to know language per se as foreign, as different from the processes of mind with which it is sometimes naively identified. Sensitized by Joyce's disruptive language, we glimpse a horizon that is beyond language but also within us. We become foreign readers of the text of ourselves as language users through finding a new orientation toward language, one that may include a sense of ourselves as not just textual. We can understand this position, to which we are translated by Joyce's writings, in one way to be translating itself as the activity Senn calls righting. Righting is, of course, also writing. It is, on the one hand, the act of producing something new. And, on the other, it is simultaneously the attempt to rectify disruptions, to put things right. Reading as translating is always the process of crossing the shifting border between restitution and invention.

The dynamism that is the constant overstepping of borders, within a language, between languages, and between language and mind, is at its most obvious because most hyperbolic in *Finnegans Wake*. Although Senn mentions this dynamism prominently in his essays, for the most part he no longer writes directly about the details of the *Wake*. When he does, as in "Dogmad or dubliboused?", he describes what amounts to a double helix in the *Wake's* language, whose interlocking but antithetical implications give us the opportunity to stay in motion. The long essay on Nausicaa presents a similar interpretive attitude by treating that chapter as an apparently bipartite structure in which the two halves are not wholly separate. Senn derives this attitude toward the structure of metaphor as a process of interaction from his experience with *Finnegans Wake*. The *Wake* is both the inseminating beginning and the end as conclusion and as methodological basis for Senn's work on Joyce. He began as a critic by producing numerous commentaries on details of the *Wake*. But through the process of writing about it, he explored both its untranslatability and some of the grounds for that untranslatability. *Finnegans Wake* is an internally transformative text, one that is dislocutory in the highest degree, for its language is relentlessly involved in various overlapping, interlocking processes of transformation and mutual implication. A variety of borders are continually being simultaneously transgressed within its covers. To say that *Finnegans Wake* is the ultimate dislocutory text and that it is untranslatable is by no means to suggest that it is nonsense. It makes sense instead in special ways to be understood in relation to cognitive processes and not only in relation to semantics. The conclusion that Senn draws from the *Wake* is that the critic can learn a new procedure, not to write *about* it, but to write *through* it, to write in its mode, which is transformational and self-correcting. We may learn *righting* through reading the *Wake* and thereby learn to write, and not just read, through it. Righting-as-also-writing through the *Wake* is translating the *Wake*, not in the conventional sense but in an experiential one. In this way, all of Senn's commentaries, because they are written through the enabling perspective of *Finnegans Wake*, are themselves translations of the untranslatable text. Through the hindsight provided by the *Wake*, the pervasive cognitive dynamism that Joyce was in the process of discovering and representing as styles of language throughout his career becomes visible to us even in the early stories. The appearance of that dynamism even there requires the critic to rethink conventional readings of Joyce's texts from the ground up, and this is the project that Fritz Senn pursues in his essays. This project frees us *from* the pretenses of objectivity, of the natural perspective, and of the hegemony of any one language. It frees us *for* the extending of our language by realizing that new choices are now available.

In such a project, critical writing about translation ceases to be primarily an adjunct to translation and becomes a form of it. We can say of Senn's commentaries what Beckett has said about Joyce's late writing: "His writing is not *about* something; *it is that something itself.*"[11] It achieves the status of translation itself insofar as it fulfills the goals of translation, ideally considered: not just to exchange words, but to extend the language, to reach "the live value . . . of gauging, deliberating, choosing, and rejecting,"[12] and to be a running commentary on the original. *Ulysses* is such a commentary on Homer's *Odyssey.* To achieve these goals the translator allows language to be co-author of the response. The loss of sensitivity to the possibilities of style keeps many translations too thing-oriented, many theories too idea-oriented, many interpretations too theme-oriented, and many critical methods too rigid. Despite the importance of things, ideas, themes, and methods in our responses to literature, if both the response and the literature's style are imbedded in processes, our commentaries have the chance to evoke the exuberance of the style. They can restore some of the energies lost in conventional translations and commentaries by revivifying even neglected texts and parts of texts. They can send us back to the originals with an increased awareness of the style's vitality and complexity. That is the use of criticism in the mode of translation. The critic can extend the language, producing new words and combinations of words to say what only the text has been able to say before. As Senn suggests concerning his own term *dislocution,* no single neologism is sufficient. The critic's vocabulary needs constantly to be renewed if it is not to repeat previously formulated insights. The critic actually has the advantage over the translator, for no translator could reasonably devote as much attention to isolated details. The critic need not come to rest as quickly as the translator normally must. And yet, this does not mean translations must always fail. The vitality of the original may come through despite the loss of some details if the translator's sense of language, transformed by the work of translating, results in the production of something new.

A heightened sense of uncertainty, even of insecurity, because of the failure of fit in our theories and in our other explanatory schemes is the price we pay for the kind of freedom *Finnegans Wake* may help us to realize. Through dislocutions in literary language, we can come to experience one form that freedom, in all its glorious instability, may take. Without instabilities is no freedom. This type of freedom involves achieving a vision of a new horizon, however distant, where something new fuses with the workings of memory. That sight is as frustrating and as exhilarating as the glimpse Moses had on Mt. Pisgah. By attending to the energy in Joyce's language, as it translates us and turns us into translators, Fritz Senn's essays trace some of the routes of many turns that Joyce may have followed up the mountain. They challenge us, restlessly, through knowing ignorance, to recognize in Joyce's dislocutions ourselves and the writer as fellow wanderers, as strangers in a strange land.

Notes

1. In "Foreign Readings," Senn says the following about *Finnegans Wake:* "Paradoxically, the *Wake* is the most forbiddingly xenophobic of all prose works, and yet at the same time it extends a catholic welcome to all foreigners by meeting them on their own territory." Switzerland could, *mutatis mutandis*, be similarly described.

2. A. Walton Litz, "The Author in *Ulysses:* The Zurich Chapters," in *James Joyce: A New Language—Actas/Proceedings del Simposio Internacional en el Centenario de James Joyce*, ed. Francisco Garcia Tortosa et al. (Seville: University of Seville, 1982), 114.

3. Ibid.

4. Ibid., p. 119.

5. Ibid., p. 115.

6. The most detailed account of Joyce's life is, of course, Richard Ellmann's *James Joyce: New and Revised Edition* (New York and Oxford: Oxford University Press, 1982).

7. In *A Colder Eye: The Modern Irish Writers* (New York: Alfred A. Knopf, 1983), Hugh Kenner discusses briefly the effect of the Berlitz method of language instruction on Joyce's developing strategies as a writer of fiction in English (146–53).

8. In *A Colder Eye*, Kenner remarks that "Of the readers of *Ulysses* known to me, the one most at ease in what he reads is Swiss" (15).

9. In the United States, the best known practitioners of tropological literary and cultural criticism are Hayden White and Harold Bloom. White discusses the relationships between tropes and narrative in *Metahistory: The Historical Imagination in Nineteenth-Century Europe* (Baltimore: Johns Hopkins University Press, 1973), and in *Tropics of Discourse: Essays in Cultural Criticism* (Baltimore: Johns Hopkins University Press, 1978). Bloom discusses the tropology of English poetry in, among other books, *A Map of Misreading* (New York and Oxford: Oxford University Press, 1975).

10. The discussion of Eumaeus occurs in "Dogmad or dubliboused?"

11. Samuel Beckett, "Dante . . . Bruno, Vico . . . Joyce," in *Our Exagmination Round His Factification For Incamination of Work in Progress* (London: Faber and Faber, 1936), 14.

12. This ideal is expressed in *"Transluding off the Toptic."*

Conventions of Reference

Below are the abbreviations used in this volume for parenthetical references to Joyce's works and to some of the translations of *Ulysses*. Whenever the reference is clear in context only the page number is given. References to other translations of Joyce's works are provided in notes. The titles conventionally assigned to the chapters of *Ulysses* are always given without quotation marks as a reminder that they do not actually appear in Joyce's text.

Joyce's Works

CW
: *The Critical Writings of James Joyce*, ed. Ellsworth Mason and Richard Ellmann. New York: Viking Press, 1959.

D
: *Dubliners*, ed. Robert Scholes, in consultation with Richard Ellmann. New York: Viking Press, 1967; and *"Dubliners": Text, Criticism, and Notes*, ed. Robert Scholes and A. Walton Litz. New York: Viking Press, 1969.

FW
: *Finnegans Wake*. New York: Viking Press, 1939; London: Faber and Faber, 1939. Passages are identified by page and line numbers. References to the footnotes in Book II, chapter 2, include an "F" preceding the note number.

Letters I, II, III
: *Letters of James Joyce*. Vol. I, ed. Stuart Gilbert. New York: Viking Press, 1957; reissued with corrections 1966. Vols. II and III, ed. Richard Ellmann. New York: Viking Press, 1966.

P
: *A Portrait of the Artist as a Young Man*. The definitive text corrected from the Dublin Holograph by Chester G. Anderson and edited by Richard Ellmann. New York: Viking Press, 1964; and *"A Portrait of the Artist as a Young Man": Text, Criticism, and Notes*, ed. Chester G. Anderson. New York: Viking Press, 1968.

SH
: *Stephen Hero*, ed. John J. Slocum and Herbert Cahoon. New York: New Directions, 1944, 1963.

U
: *Ulysses*. New York: Random House, 1934 ed., reset and corrected 1961.

Selected Translations of Ulysses

D   Danish   *Ulysses*, paa dansk ved Mogens Boisen (Copenhagen: Martins Forlag, 1964), 5th ed. First published in 1949. Reissued in 1970 in a substantially revised form.

F   French   *Ulysse,* traduction intégrale par Auguste Morel, assisté de Stuart Gilbert, entièrement revue par Valery Larbaud et l'auteur (Paris: Gallimard, 1948). First published in 1929 by La Maison des Amis des Livres, Paris.

Go   German   *Ulysses,* vom Verfasser autorisierte Übersetzung von Georg Goyert (Zürich: Rhein Verlag, 1956). First published privately in Basel, 1927, in three volumes, but substantially revised in 1930.

Wo   German   *Ulysses,* Übersetzung von Hans Wollschläger (Frankfurt: Suhrkamp, 1976).

I   Italian   *Ulisse,* unica traduzione integrale autorizzata di Giulio de Angelis, consulenti: Glauco Cambon, Carlo Izzo, Giorgio Melchiori (Milan: Arnoldo Mondadori Editore, 1961), 4th ed. First published in 1960.

P   Portuguese   *Ulisses,* tradução Antônio Houaiss (Rio de Janeiro: Editôra Civilização Brasileira, 1966).

SP   Spanish   *Ulises,* traducción por J. Salas Subirat (Buenos Aires: Santiago Rueda, 1959), 3rd ed. First published in 1945.

SP, Valv. Spanish   *Ulises,* traducción por José Maria Valverde (Barcelona: Editorial Lumen, 1976).

SW   Swedish   *Odysseus,* oversattning av Th. Warburton (Stockholm: Albert Bonniers Förlag, 1964). First published in 1946.

I.

Reading as Translation:
Foreign Readings

1

Translation
as Approach

The process of translation involves an approach—every translator of *Ulysses* approaches the novel in his own unique way. The results, the individual translations, are approximations, not, in themselves, approaches. Readers can of course use them in their struggle with the original text, as many do whose native language is not English. At some time bilingual editions of *Ulysses* (as of many other classics) will no doubt be published abroad.

Translations can, however, also be turned into an approach—if we compare them with the original and among themselves. This is a somewhat academic exercise and really a misuse of the translations, whose purpose is not mutual comparison and which, at any rate, are not written for the study or the classroom. But it can be a rewarding exercise. It will tell us something about the nature of translation and about its limitations; on the other hand, it will oblige us to take a close look at the original, from perhaps several angles. When we speak of "translating" *Ulysses* we pretend that we know what either *translating* or *Ulysses* means when the novel means something different to every one of us and we may not have a very clear conception of what the translation of a complex work of literature amounts to or should amount to. If we had such a conception and could agree on it we would be prepared to answer the ultimate question of whether *Ulysses* can be translated at all. Joyce himself said that only the original was authentic,[1] but then he also helped and encouraged translations.

The following remarks are based on passages selected from a handful of translations of *Ulysses* into what is really an extremely narrow range of languages. They ought to be supplemented by a summary of the problems and perspectives of translators working in languages that are fundamentally different from the Indo-European ones. The aim is not to establish principles of translation, or to evaluate the existing translations, but to analyze what has actually been done by the translators and to find out, if possible, what their intentions were. Apart from each translator's skill and sensibility, the translations reflect their cultural background, the potentialities and confines of the language the translations are written in. They also represent diverse points of view, reflections in mirrors throwing back light on the original. Every translation will highlight some characteristics, either where it succeeds in re-creating a particular effect or where, sometimes by a painstaking effort, a purpose becomes manifest. Even where it fails, the comparison, by contrast, will throw some feature of the original into distinct relief. Passages that appear typically Joycean and by their complexity compel the translator to make decisions naturally deserve the greatest attention.

By necessity a comparison of this kind is concerned with details, and the details have to be separated from much of their larger context. The translations as a whole, their intrinsic artistic merit, will not be considered. Such decisive, but elusive concepts as the tone, the feel, the total impact of a translation have to be neglected as well as the question of whether a translation catches the spirit of the original, whatever that means. These aspects are essentially matters for the critic within his own language. The comparison of isolated passages, even words, with the vision sharpened, I hope, by the juxtaposition, often boils down to just a close reading which always comes dangerously close to an overreading since it cannot help being a verbalization of what are ultimately subjective impressions. Nevertheless, no valid approach can be made without, in the last resort, taking account of what is actually on the page. The translator is a close reader too, perhaps the closest there is. He is almost the only one who is professionally obliged to examine every single word. We do not grant him the selectivity of the critic; he is not allowed the luxury of omission.

Since translations are, at least quantitatively, a complete running commentary of the original, we may call them in as witnesses to help determine some puzzling questions in Joyce's text. There is particular temptation to make such use of the two translations that came into being under Joyce's supervision. In 1927 the German translation was published and announced as "vom Verfasser geprüfte Ausgabe von Georg Goyert."[2] In spite of this claim, it had to be revised at Joyce's insistence, and the second edition of 1930 bears an even prouder imprint: "vom Verfasser geprüfte definitive deutsche Ausgabe."[3] In the meantime, in 1929, the renowned French translation had come out, *Ulysse,* "traduit de l'anglais par M. Auguste Morel, assisté par M.

Stuart Gilbert. Traduction entièrement revue par M. Valery Larbaud avec la collaboration de l'auteur."[4] These formulae seem to imply something beyond a merely legal placet, and we may fancy ourselves in the fortunate position of having two authorized commentaries, all the more so since one of the co-translators and advisors, Stuart Gilbert, became the first extensive commentator of *Ulysses*. There is, however, no evidence that Joyce's supervision entailed a careful examination of every word. In the late twenties Joyce, preoccupied with *Work in Progress,* with Lucia's illness, and troubled by failing eyesight, even if he had had the inclination, could hardly have found the time and the energy that the task evidently required. We know that he relegated some of the responsibilities of the German translation to friends.[5] There are instances of the two authorized translations clearly contradicting each other. In fact the German and the French translation are the least accurate of all, which is understandable enough in view of their early origin, but clearly precludes too hasty a notion—suggested strongly in *geprüfte, definitive,* and *entièrement revue*—of Joyce providing a reliable commentary himself.[6] It is safe to say that neither the celebrated French translation nor the German one by Goyert (which has come in for severe criticism) can be adduced to settle controversial points even if, in exceptional cases, they might corroborate conclusions for which there is other evidence as well.

Translation comes into the novel as a rather minor theme. A few sparse attempts made at translating a few phrases, while not very serious, are either faulty or incomplete. Bloom comes to grief over two lines from *Don Giovanni,* for the most elementary of reasons, insufficient knowledge of the language: "What does that *teco* mean. Tonight perhaps" (180). Bloom's subjective reading "doesn't go properly." Translation often doesn't. Stephen's two renderings of a Latin misquotation, *"Descende, calve, ut ne nimium decalveris,"* are primarily facetious: "Get down, bald poll!" (40); "Down, baldynoddle, or we'll wool your wool" (243). Both versions are defective or paraphrastic and partly subjective again. Protean metamorphosis too can come near to translation: "She trudges, schlepps, trains, drags, trascines her load" (47), just as translation often results in a metamorphosis. The near-synonyms, which Stephen culls from four languages and which he mentally tries for effect, have similar meanings but different suggestiveness.

An intentionally literal, word-for-word translation of a common French phrase ("Mais c'est bien triste, ça, ma foi, oui") is, and, according to Joyce's stated view, must be, quite unconvincing: "But it is well sad, that, my faith, yes" (427).[7] The pedantic accuracy and hopeless inadequacy of this version as well as the imaginative woolliness of Stephen's earlier mock translations are extremes not unknown to most practitioners of the art.

The rapid transformations of style that go to make up the Oxen of the Sun chapter could also be taken to be a series of translations, not horizontally from one language into another, but vertically through progressive stages of the literary language, and of course into the idiom of highly individualistic writers. This is one of the reasons why translators find the Oxen of the Sun chapter particularly frustrating.

It may be significant that in the Library chapter, whose art is literature, Stephen makes a point of reading the "gorbellied works" of Saint Thomas "in the original" (205), implying perhaps that even in philosophical discourse, which, on the whole, tends to be lucid and unambiguous, there is a difference between a translation and the original. Joyce himself studied Norwegian and German in order to read two favorite authors.

In general we rarely trouble to distinguish between reading the original and reading a translation. For obvious reasons we could only sample a small fraction of the world's literature if we had no translations to fall back on. We often have no means of knowing what translations, necessarily substitutes, cut us off from, and we may forget that they do. Courses in comparative literature, for example, usually have to be conducted in only one language, on the tacit assumption that literary works can be discussed and compared in translation. Thousands of readers who do not know English have "read" *Ulysses* when in fact they have not been exposed to a single word as Joyce wrote it. It is worth pausing a moment to realize that a translation changes the whole of a literary work, with the exception of, usually, the names. What is the relation between a new, entirely changed surface and the original one? And how much of the "meaning" is thus affected? Translation presupposes that the content can be dissociated from its linguistic form. Whatever the epistemological position to be taken, we know that the presupposition can be acted on—up to a point. Communication would be difficult to attain unless in large areas of human speech expression could be changed within the same or into another language without seriously altering the meaning. On the other hand, language does not consist of simple labels for clearly defined things, actions, and relations that could be replaced and interchanged. In the highly subtle and sophisticated use of language that is called literature all the resources of language are drawn upon, including its formal qualities, and the more ambitious a writer is the more he will also integrate all those secondary functions that escape categorization and go beyond mere designation. We have come to accept as a truism that with Joyce form and content become one. If they really and completely did, translation, by its drastic change of form, would indeed be impossible. The more language approximates the condition expressed in Samuel Beckett's view of Joyce's later prose ("His writing is not *about* something; *it is that something itself*"),[8] the more it is put out of the translator's reach.

Fortunately (for the translator) this complete identification remains an ideal rather than an achievement, but even so, and even in *Ulysses*, Joyce approximates it often enough, in what has been called "expressive form," to make *Ulysses* a borderline case and to push *Finnegans Wake* out of the translator's province. The problems and difficulties encountered in *Ulysses* are not even new ones, but most of them assume a greater importance. Hardly anything can be discounted as inessential. There seems to be always more at stake.

From the early beginnings Joyce's protagonists are portrayed as unusually conscious of the value of words, and they devote much of their attention to language itself. *Ulysses* is very much concerned with language; it is even largely *about* language. Many of the book's characters join in the game. When Bloom meditates "There is a word throstle that expressed that" (93), this observation about a word cannot just be taken over into any other language. Mere probability goes against the semantic equivalent of another language expressing the same thing that Bloom has in mind. The Spanish translation, for example, cannot continue with its word for *throstle* (*zorzal*), but has to remain vague: "Hay una palabra que lo expresaba" (SP 127). Similarly, Molly's comment on the name of a congenial author: "Paul de Kock's. Nice name he has" (64), is too firmly grounded in the English language to enable reproduction. The chances are, again, that the nicety of the name—assuming for the moment that the name of an actual author must remain as it is in translation—may disappear or change its character in, say, German, Czech, or Japanese. If the translation still claims that the name is nice the reader may be led to suppose that Molly refers to its sound.

The spotlight may be turned on language in a less explicit manner: "Do ptake some ptarmigan" (175) appears among other evocations of banquet scenes in Bloom's imagination. By the mere addition of a superfluous letter the sentence has become a playful comment on an oddity of English spelling. "Nehmen Sie doch etwas Schneehuhn" (Go 199–200) remains on the level of table talk and leaves what may be the more important part of Bloom's idea out of consideration. If a spelling peculiarity is simply imitated, as in "Ptrendete un ptò di ptarmigan" (I 238), a comment on language is included, but there is little point to it in its non-English context. The word *ptarmigan* has not really been translated, but transplanted without its lexical background, and without it *ptake* is not really ptranslatable.

Ever so often, the translator has to be content with an accurate rendering of the surface. Even this he can only do if he knows what the basic meaning is, and he will often guess wrongly. The search for errors in translations, though deeply gratifying to our malevolence and a gleeful pastime of fellow translators, is perhaps the least profitable pursuit. There must be many mistakes in all translations of a book so challenging and, partly, still obscure as *Ulysses*. Small wonder that "Dunlop, Judge" (185) appears as "Dunlop, Juge" (F 182), "Dunlop, juez" (SP 221), "Dunlop, Richter" (Go 211), or "Dunlop, domaren" (SW 194)—it may take extensive research to establish if *Judge* is the profession of Dunlop or a proper name, which more recent commentators have told us that it is. That Joyce did not, apparently, notice, or point out, the misreading in either the French or the German translation would indicate that his supervision was more superficial or intermittent than it might have been. Nor did Joyce, if he really looked closely at these passages, communicate his superior knowledge to the translators when he allowed them to render "lousy Lucy" in Stephen's thoughts (215) by "die lausige Lucy" (Go 245) and "L'ignoble Lucie la pouilleuse" (F 211). The translators, not being Shakespearean scholars, turned lousy Lucy, whom they could not expect to be Sir Thomas Lucy, reasonably enough, into a girl. Errors of this kind may decrease in number as the bulk of scholarship grows, but the exposure of ignorance remains one of the translator's professional risks.

Apart from errors of fact or glaring linguistic howlers (Goyert's German version "des dunklen Arbeitszimmers" for "in a brown study"—354—was still chuckled over long after it had been corrected in the second edition[9]), however numerous, the concept of "correctness" does not apply too well to *Ulysses*. Sometimes a rather narrow view has to be taken to label a rendering "wrong." A few years ago, in a harsh attack on the German translation, the use of *bogenförmig* was objected to: "Bending archly she reckoned fat pears" (228), which reads: "Sie beugte sich bogenförmig" (Go 237).[10] As any dictionary can tell, and as the French and the Danish translations bear out (*coquette*—F 222, *kokett*—D 237), *archly* does not mean *like an arch*. The wrong translation nevertheless catches some undercurrent. Architectural expansion in space is one of the features of the Wandering Rocks chapter, which already contains "Merchant's Arch" and various other arches. *Bogenförmig* may be a wrong turn, in a chapter that is intentionally full of wrong turnings, but it archly refers to at least a remote possibility that Joyce may have had in mind. The Spanish and the Portuguese translations, incidentally, also settle for an architectural reading: *arqueadamente* (SP 264), *em arco* (P 259). This may be a case of overinterpretation at the cost of a more important basic meaning. If we call it an error, translators' errors too may serve as useful portals of discovery.[11]

The choice of a word is often not a matter of correctness but of a careful balance of various effects. To illustrate in concrete terms some of the questions involved, a word shall be presented that does not complicate the issue by too many semantic problems, that is free of ambiguities and not affected by auctorial convergences (as in the cluster made up of "Throwaway," "a throwaway," and "I was just going to throw it away") or interfered with by homonymy (such as "arch," "grave," "race," "massproduct," etc.). The word has some definite and important functions within the novel; it is moreover the "organ" assigned to a whole chapter: "Womb." Anyone undertaking a study of, say, Stephen's preoccupations, his psychology (and, for that matter, perhaps Joyce's too), his esthetics, or some theological interpretation could hardly afford to bypass the motif *womb* in *Ulysses*.

For the translator this motif is a word. It occurs some twenty times in the novel. One of the dilemmas is whether, for the sake of unity, the translator ought to stick by a given choice or whether the optimal effect of each passage is to be preferred. It is easy to state dogmatically and naively that a word like *womb* must be translated consistently by the same word wherever it occurs. So it should, but in practice this is not feasible. The French translation, for example, usually gets by with *ventre,* but has to deviate to *matrice, les limbes,* and an occasional paraphrase. In Italian the convenient word *grembo* ensures some continuity, but *ventre* as well as *utero* are substituted at times. Every vocabulary imposes its own restrictions. They seem to be particularly baffling in German.

In the Proteus chapter Stephen's speculations range from midwives via navelcords to Eve, to "belly without blemish" and on to "womb of sin" (38). In German this latter becomes "Leib der Sünde" (Go 46). Now *Leib* is not a felicitous choice; it is ambiguous and the meaning most likely to be understood here is the rather general one of *body.* The sinfulness of the flesh will be suggested to the reader rather than original sin. The misconception might have been evaded by the more unequivocal *Mutterleib,* but this pedantic composite would have been clumsily out of place. Another possibility is *Bauch;* it corresponds to *belly* and has already been used for "belly without blemish" and would be confusing. Finally there is *Schoss,* which would fit the context, even if it is predominantly figurative. It is the word that was used by the same translator to do duty for "the virgin womb of the imagination" in *A Portrait:* "im jungfräulichen Schosse der Imagination."[12] But it lacks the presence of a body. So the German vocabulary—a very rich one, on the whole—does not contain a suitable word. It might be argued that there is not really any choice, that, in keeping with the biblical tone of the passage, the Old Testament word must be taken over, which happens to be *Leib.* It also fits the relevant phrasing in the account of the Annunciation (Luke 1:44).

But *Leib* does not at all lend itself to the Protean change immediately following: "Wombed in sin darkness," where the word is made verb. *Leib* does not permit this change, nor, for that matter, would *Bauch, Mutterleib,* or *Schoss.* The womb, then, is simply refined out of existence: "In sündiger Dunkelheit." A translation that does follow the original rather closely here is the Portuguese one: "Matriz do pecado. Matrizado em pecadora escuridade" (P 43); *matriz* is not, however, the prevalent word for *womb* in *Ulisses.*

Neither *Leib* nor *matriz* are continued into the next ventral reference in Proteus: "mouth to her womb" (48). Goyert chose *Bauch:* "Mund auf ihren Bauch" (Go 58). There is some justification for this; *Leib* would have been far too general and would only have been understood to mean *body;* of the other possible words, only *Bauch* offers the necessary physical surface for a mouth. But there is no echo of "womb of sin." Nor does "Mund auf ihren Bauch" serve as a basis for the rhyming experiment to which Stephen subjects *womb:* "Oomb, allwombing tomb." The translator does not aim higher than at mere repetition, and a flat paraphrase of *allwombing:* "Bauch, allumschlies-sendes Grab." There is neither rhyme nor too much reason, but it is, as always, easier to disapprove than to suggest a satisfactory solution. The French translation uses an ingenious detour: "ventre. Antre, tombe où tout entre" (F 50). Some device is obviously called for, such as "suo grembo. Onbo, tomba omnigrembo" (I 70). "Antre: ventre" as well as "tomba: grembo" can be taken up later, in the Aeolus chapter, when Stephen recalls the rhyme: "mouth south: tomb womb" (138). The German translator has no rhyme to fall back on, but aware that Stephen here is clearly pondering on the rationale of rhymes, introduces a parallel structure: "Mund Hund: Erdmutter Gebärmutter" (Go 158), which is entirely without precedent, containing two words the reader never met before in the book, therefore not possibly a recall of an earlier thought. The physiological term *Gebärmutter* (*uterus*) is an odd choice in the context of the rather traditional sort of poetry that Stephen is imitating. The word is much more appropriate later on, in a Bloom passage, "in blutroten Gebärmüttern" (Go 266), relating to an illustration of Aristotle's *Masterpiece:* "infants cuddled in a ball in bloodred wombs" (235). Most of the other translations also become more anatomical here, using *matrices* (F 230), *uteri* (I 318), and so on.

The word *womb* has also a career in Bloom's thoughts, starting with a maternal "womb of warmth" in the Lotus Eaters chapter (86). In German it is "im warmen Leib der Wanne" (Go 100), while it is psychologically glossed over in French: "dans une chaleur d'eaux maternelles" (F 85). Bloom returns to it in the Sirens chapter: "Because their wombs. / A liquid womb of woman eyeball" (286). The German translation decides for the more clinical term (as does the French one, *matrice*): "Weil ihre Gebärmütter. / Ein feuchter gebärmütterlicher Augapfel" (Go 321). These words do not charm the ear, but in spite of their clumsiness, as associations to birth and Mrs Purefoy, they are not quite out of tone. The dark-voweled monosyllable *womb* allows Joyce more auditory scope than the translators have with equivalents like *matrice, Leib,* or *Gebärmutter.* If they take care of the sense, the sounds will not always take care of themselves. A translator might, for example, consider using *Bauch* instead of *Gebärmutter* in the above sentence, and, for the sake of the experiment, we might balance the resonant gains against the semantic losses in an otherwise unchanged rendering: "Weil ihre B*äuch*e. Ein f*euch*ter geb*auch*ter *Aug*apfel."

The hospital scene, Oxen of the Sun, above all, is dominated by the organ womb. The German translation continues with *Leib* as far as possible. "Leibesfrucht" (Go 432) is the inevitable and suitable word for *wombfruit* in the invocation (383). "Im Leibe des Weibes" (Go 441) translates "In woman's womb" (391), where *Leib* will hardly be misunderstood, though it may be distracting that *Leib* has already had to serve for the liturgical and eucharistic *my body* in the same paragraph. "Im Leibe schon wurde es geliebt" (Go

432) is a pale imitation of the heavy cadences of "Within womb won he worship" (384), in marked contrast to a strongly alliterative sequence in Portuguese: "Verso ventre vencia veneração" (P 436). Sometimes *Bauch* is preferred to *Leib,* and *Gebärmutter,* which is of course thematically appropriate, recurs twice.

The resources of the German language then proved insufficient to provide a word to cover all the uses of *womb,* and few of the words selected for each occasion fit their immediate context too well. In none of the translations examined here was it possible to preserve the thematic unity, which is so much a matter of course in the original, by one and the same word (the German and the French translators did not, of course, have a word index to trace any given motif through the entire novel). Even if some improvements look possible, the semantic distribution alone prevents the delineation of a motif that takes such a simple form in English (there are some further twists like the Shakespearean "uncared wombs"—202—which pose yet another problem). In every language at least three different nouns had to be called in; distinctions like the one between *womb* and *belly* cannot be upheld; some of the music has been silenced and odd side-effects creep in. Neither *Leib, Bauch, Gebärmütter,* nor *Schoss* (in *A Portrait*) can become as fertile a source of conception, whether literary or embryonic, as *womb.*

Fortunately, not all the words of *Ulysses* are saddled with such heavy thematic burdens. Or are they? No one would insist, ordinarily, on the exact translation of a particular word within an idiomatic phrase like "But Dignam's put the boots on it" (380). There is nothing wrong, except perhaps, a certain flatness, with "la visite chez Dignam m'a achevé" (F 374), "Ma la visita a Dignam è stata l'ultima goccia" (I 514), or "Aber Dignam das war zuviel" (Go 429). It would be idle to complain about the absence of (merely metaphorical) boots. But, out of a wide array of idiomatic possibilities, Joyce selected boots, and this at least allows the reader to recall that the late Patrick Dignam, as his son remembers, in his last mundane appearance was "bawling for his boots" (251). And it seems to be the selfsame pair of boots that Dignam's ghost singles out for particular attention in the séance parody (302). These potential memories and overtones give the sentence a different ring, a slightly humorous touch, and at least a suggestion that there is, as usual, more to it. And they help to tighten the closed world of *Ulysses* just a little bit more. It may not amount to much, but the little flutter in the reader's response was probably Joyce's aim.

A figure of speech, if taken literally, sometimes serves an ironic turn. Bloom's advice to Stephen is couched in the choicest inappropriate terms: "I wouldn't personally repose much trust in that boon companion of yours . . . , Dr Mulligan, as a guide, philosopher, and friend, if I were in your shoes" (620). The translations, "si j'étais de vous" (F 545) and "ich an Ihrer Stelle" (Go 621), being entirely neutral, fail to drive home just how much Bloom is out of touch with the reality he tries to influence: Stephen happens to be wearing, as the reader will remember, but as the reader of the translations has no cause to remember, the shoes of the very person that he is being warned against. The Italian translation, a late one, did not miss the pointed reference: "se fossi nelle sue scarpe" (I 800).

The correct, literal translation can falsify a meaning. A telling example can be taken from a passage made up of the simplest of words, in Molly's monologue. A woman who has poisoned her husband occupies Molly's thoughts:

> take that Mrs Maybrick that poisoned her husband for what I wonder . . . white Arsenic she put in his tea off flypaper wasnt it I wonder why they call it that if I asked him hed say its from the Greek leave us as wise as we were before. (744)

Not a word here that might not be translated without much effort. In fact a translator would have very little choice—there is certainly no choice whatever for the word that arouses Molly's curiosity *as a word* for the moment, the name of the poison, which has its given form in all European languages: *Arsenik, arsenico,* and so forth. But in none of these languages (with the exception of the Scandinavian ones) does the inevitable word permit the same association. And without this association Molly's interest must appear more purely philological. Molly is never, as far as we know her, curious about etymologies—though, oddly enough, the etymology of *arsenic* is revealing too: the word was assimilated to a Greek one, *arseneikon,* literally meaning *male* (due to its potency as a poison), and so also something worthy of Molly's attention, though she would not know (this remote etymological benefit is theoretically contained in the translations). But to turn Molly momentarily into a linguist makes her a different human being. The "correct" translation results in a distortion of character. To put it differently: if Molly were thinking in a language other than English, she would never bother about a word like *arsenic;* it might not even occur to her in the first place. Only in the original, not in the translations, does a word, once more, become flesh through Molly, almost literally so. The identical word in translation becomes a sterile one. Joyce's humor could hardly be called "cerebral" here; it is rather down to earth, characteristic of both Molly Bloom and the whole Penelope chapter—it goes to the bottom of things. The point that is lost in the other languages happens to be a cardinal one in the structure of the chapter. We have Joyce's word for it that its "four cardinal points are the female breasts, arse, womb and sex."[13]

The reader of the translation is indeed as wise as he was before; he will not be induced to stop and wonder "why they call it that." The translation does not condition him to look for implications and correspondences, and if he does look for them, he may be led astray. This amounts to a change in the reading process. The detail does not stimulate the reader to respond, and his concentration will be turned more to action and plot, things relatively unaffected by translation. *Ulysses* becomes thereby a more ordinary, more traditional novel.

The loss of overtones and ambiguities in translation is normally taken for granted, but the stripping of a phrase to its bare semantic bones may occasionally render it incongruous in its own context even as a piece of realism. Buck Mulligan's smooth quip "Monsieur Moore . . . , lecturer on French letters to the youth of Ireland" (214) is one that some translators can only simplify: "conférencier ès lettres françaises" (F 210), "Lektor der französischen Literatur" (Go 244), "uppfostrare i fransk litteraturen" (SW 223). This is a different characterization of George Moore. But the chief drawback of the straightforward translation is that it misrepresents the speaker too, who would probably never wish to be caught uttering as innocuous a statement as that, and one as devoid of informative content for the erudite audience that he is addressing (the French translation, by referring somewhat equivocally to Moore as a *conférencier,* at least hints at some malice). For the contraceptive undercurrent is the point of Mulligan's remark. If there were no point to it, he would keep silent. But this alternative—silence—is one that the translator is forbidden to use, and of course omission would mutilate the text even more.

When Mulligan's saying is taken up by Stephen in the hospital scene, "regius professor of French letters" (393), some translators inconsistently, but with good reason, go out of their way to reinsert the missing component: "königlicher Professor für französische Kondoms" (Go 443), "professor i preservativologi" (SW 399). There is thematic justification for limiting the meaning to literature in the Library episode and for pushing it toward contraception in the Oxen of the Sun chapter, but the correspondence between the two passages may be lost sight of (it certainly is in the Swedish translation). The link (between literature and fertility/sterility) has been severed.

The rather narrow focus employed here, which tends to reduce the whole novel to a web of small, interconnected verbal units—and fails to see the novel as a whole—largely coincides with the translator's own. Whatever his theories or ambitions, in the actual workshop the problems manifest themselves often as nothing more exalted than a choice among available words and forms. Technically, a giveaway like Bloom's tripping up over "the wife's admirers" for "the wife's advisers" (313) depends on the similarity of two words. If *admirers* and *advisers* are faithfully rendered into other languages, the resulting pairs evince a varying degree of similarity, due on the whole to common prefixes, suffixes, and endings: *admiradores/consejeros* (SP 352), *admiradores/consultores* (P 356), *beundrere/behjaelpelige* (D 320), *pretendenti/consulenti* (I 422), *beundrare/rådgivare* (SW 319), *Bewunderer/Berater* (Go 351), *courtiseurs/conseilleurs* (F 306-7). The opportunity for a slip of the tongue diminishes with the loss of phonetic proximity. The Italian and the French translators took some pains to achieve closer resemblance than would have resulted from a literal rendering; they prefer *pretendenti* and *courtiseurs* to *ammiratori* or *admirateurs* (by which *admirers* is translated in a previous occurrence, p. 309). Both *pretendenti* and *courtiseurs* are closer to the meaning *suitors*. Thus the translators, when endeavoring to provide more linguistic basis for a psychological slip, were able to push the text nearer to a Homeric analogy, Penelope's suitors, than the original—no doubt a legitimate device.

An instructive alternative solution was adopted by the Dutch translator. In an interview, he insisted on the relevance of the Freudian slip, to which the dictionary renderings, *bewonderars* and *raadgevers,* would fail to do justice—the sort of pair that would find its place in the list quoted above. In Dutch then Bloom says *zaadgevers* instead of *raadgevers.*[14] This certainly comes as close as the language will allow and is technically much more pertinent than all the other translations. But, as the translator himself pointed out, *zaadgevers* (literally *seed-givers*) bluntly overstates the sexual component and even adds another dimension. The word is, moreover, not common in Dutch, not one that would easily slip out in conversation, and for this reason as well as for its grossness it sounds odd on the lips of prudent Leopold Bloom (outside, maybe, an episode like the Circe chapter). If Bloom did use the word it might well startle the regulars of Barney Kiernan's pub a great deal.

Here, then, is a common dilemma. A straightforward, correct translation often deprives a passage of an essential function. If an artifice is resorted to, some requirements may be fulfilled, but the emphasis may shift; the passage may be distorted in other respects. In order to save the plausibility of a slip of the tongue, an unusual and strong word, *zaadgevers,* has to be put into Bloom's mouth. The insertion of *seed* also enlarges the spectrum of associations in the perceptive reader (if the reader is not perceptive a great many of the translator's efforts are wasted anyway and not even worth discussing): he might well imagine some significance where none is warranted. It has to be remembered, however, that the translation that does *not* try to re-create some particular effects can also distort the context—by default.

The increasing volume of studies of *Ulysses* will ensure that a present-day translator is very alert. Where earlier translators had to grope their way courageously in partial darkness through what they often took to be chaos, their successors, with an abundance of illumination at their disposal, can afford to choose consciously, to weigh the various advantages and sacrifices of every solution on the various levels they think relevant. Perhaps all that can be required is that the translator choose in lucid awareness of what is at stake. On the other hand, some naïve insouciance, or an intuitive grasp, might prepare the translator better to square the Joycean eccentric circles than the necessarily fearful tread of the systematic scholar. A conscious choice was plainly involved in the version *zaadgevers:* the attendant misconceptions must have appeared less weighty in the balance than the alternative sacrifices. This is a question of interpretation.

Interpretation and the translator's own views come into play whenever there is a parting of the ways, irrespective of whether the verbal complications are profound or superficially shallow. The predilection for words and language in all its coincidences, which Joyce's characters share with their author, accounts for the high percentage of riddles, double entendres, puzzles, spelling bees, and other verbal fireworks that crop up in their conversations. These outward and visible signs of the spell, the mysteriousness but also the deceptiveness of language, are a formidable challenge if they are witty; but even if they are not they oblige the translator to make decisions. Prominent among the facile punsters is Lenehan with his repertoire; and the Aeolus chapter, with its variations of rhetorical noises, is a suitable playground. A few lines sung, and quoted, from Balfe's *The Rose of Castille* (130) prompt him to force a riddle upon a rather reluctant audience:

> What opera is like a railway line? . . . *The Rose of Castille.* See the wheeze?
> Rows of cast steel. Gee! (132, 134)

Lenehan's wheezy joke, for which Stuart Gilbert has supplied the technical term, *paronomasia,*[15] is not an example of supreme wit and might deserve offhand treatment in translation if Joyce did not integrate it into the texture of the novel. The opera is a recurrent motif in the Sirens chapter, where its title is mentioned six times. The riddle is repeated in the chaotic verbiage that closes the Oxen of the Sun chapter: "With a railway bloke . . . Opera he'd like? Rose of Castille. Rows of cast" (426). In the Circe chapter it recurs twice, first intimately connected with *flower* and Bloom: "This is the flower in question. . . . You know that old joke, rose of Castille. Bloom" (455). Then it is linked to Gibraltar: "What railway opera is like a tramline in Gibraltar? The Rows of Casteele" (491).

For the translator the task can be described very simply: he should include Balfe's opera, which was popular in Ireland in the second half of the last century. If its title is not susceptible of riddling transformation, the name of another opera, preferably Irish (or known to the Dubliners of 1904) is to be substituted. It should be Spanish in content and title. And be associated with a railway line, or something equivalent. What is the equivalent of a railway line for a translator? Do we actually need an opera? Isn't it perhaps enough to have some sort of verbal resemblance? The translators give various answers.

The Danish, Swedish, and German translations take the easy way out: they retain the name of the opera, untranslated, and also the paronomastic version in italicized English: *"rows of cast steel."* This leaves the entire motif and its full significance (whatever it may be) intact, but it also puts them out of the readers' grasp. In the non-English context, Lenehan's contribution to the general amusement takes on a different color; he is credited with linguistic knowledge extending to double entendres in a foreign tongue. On the surface of it, there is the odd and somewhat anticlimactic effect of a character mustering an untypical amount of sophistication to give voice to a witticism lacking almost all sophistication.

But even the wholesale retention of its English guise cannot safeguard all the potential correspondences in the motif's further exfoliations. The Castilian rose cannot be blended with a homonymous "rose" in the Sirens chapter, nor is it possible for the equivalent of *steelyringing* to induce the name of the opera, via the rows of cast steel, in the overture of the Sirens chapter (256). In all three translations, the name of the opera *is* translated in this chapter, so that *"The Rose of Castille"* occurs alongside of "Kastiliens ros" (SW 264), and so on.

The fact that some translators took over the whole riddle in its original form, in spite of some marring effects, testifies to the importance they attributed to it, as well as to their admission of its untranslatability. They also took for granted a certain willingness of their readers to accept foreign words and phrases. This is less true within the Romance languages. There the obstacle has to be overcome by some means, and the translators' inventiveness produces interesting results.

In Italian it was possible to retain the title of the opera and to give it an entirely native reading:

> Quale opera assomiglia a una donna frigida? . . . *La Rosa di Castiglia.* . . . La Rosa casti li ha. (185)

The riddle, however, is different, it refers to a woman, not a railway line. The correspondence of the *Rose of Castille,* Irish opera in a Spanish setting, with Molly Bloom, Irish singer of Spanish origin, is stressed more than in Joyce's wording. But this emphasis also alerts us that the ingredients of the new riddle, frigidity and chastity, have changed both the temperature and the temperament. If we are to think of Molly as a Castilian rose—which the personified version rather invites us to do—*frigida* and *casti* are hardly *mots justes.*

In the French translation the opera is replaced:

> Quel est l'opéra qui ressemble à une filature? . . . *L'Etoile du Nord.* . . . Les Toiles du Nord. (132)

This preserves Lenehan's *kind* of wit, but little else. With a different opera, there is no possible connection with the snatches from Balfe's aria that went before, and we may wonder what put the thought of that particular riddle into Lenehan's mind at this instant. This, it is true, may also happen to the reader of the original who is unlikely to recognize and place " 'Twas rank and fame" (130) and to connect it with Lenehan's flash of inspiration. But the reader of the French translation does not even have the *possibility* of detecting this detail of Joycean motivation. The railway line too has disappeared, and there is no longer a rose. The missing rose causes some difficulty in the Circe chapter, where the transition from a flower to the riddle looks arbitrary: "Voici la fleur en question. . . . Vous connaissez bien cette vieille plaisanterie, les Toiles du Nord. Bloom" (F 440). And later on, still in Circe, it is difficult to infer why the riddle should recur to Bloom in connection with trams and Gibraltar:

> Quel opéra tramatique ressemble à une filature de Gibraltar? Les Toiles du Nord. (F 464)

Since there never was a railway line associated to the riddle, the otherwise clever *opéra tramatique* is unmotivated—the reader in translation will not expect much motivation in Circe, and the chapter will appear more fitful to him than in fact it might be. On the other hand, both *filature* and *toiles* in the French translation could take the alert reader, by devious paths, to Penelope's web and thus on to Molly Bloom, née Tweedy. But a reader who regards these words as valid clues and starting points for interpretative flights would be rather nonplussed if he wanted, consistently, to apply the same method to *étoile* and tie this bright particular star to other Ulyssean constellations. And, still acting on the same principle, what is he to make of the North? Wouldn't there be temptation to dig for hidden depths when Bloom and Stephen pass the North Star Hotel (613) on their way to the cabmen's shelter? If *filature* and *toile* could—theoretically—be trusted (all the more so since they imply a web, a texture, interrelatedness), *Nord* probably could not, and the reader has no guiding principle to tell him which words do deserve the interpreter's zeal.

The Spanish translation removes the riddle yet farther from the original combination. There is no longer an opera:

> Cuál es el país que tiene más hoteles? . . . Suiza. . . . La patria de Guillermo-hotel. (SP 169)

Guillermo Tell might, but hardly does, include Rossini's opera; the reference is primarily to the Swiss legendary hero (who puts in a transitory appearance among the Irish and Hibernicized heroes in one of the Cyclopean catalogues, p. 297). But William Tell does not fit into any contexts. Switzerland is, as far as *Ulysses* is concerned, a dead end. The riddle in Spanish is attuned to Lenehan's mental capacity but remains otherwise almost completely unintegrated.

Though the opera is changed in French, and in Portuguese ("Que opera é vegetal e mineral? . . . *Palhaço.* . . . Palha e aço," P 152) and dispensed with altogether in Spanish, all three translations allude to the title of the original *Rose of Castille* throughout the Sirens episode, and not to *Etoile du Nord, Palhaço* or Swiss hotels. The motif has been split up into two unrelated parts.

One consequence is again that no explanation is provided why Lenehan should introduce the opera during his vain overtures to the barmaid (264).

All the different solutions, while circumscribed by the linguistic potential, also reflect different emphases. Some translators were more intent upon a network of associations than others. The Spanish translator set store by the immediate effect alone; in the Germanic languages the motif seemed so important as to justify its total but unassimilated inclusion. This principle, carried to its logical extreme, would bring us back to the original (the reader, instead of struggling with mutilated, distorted translations, could be advised to learn the language of the original). The opposite extreme is radical change. It would be interesting to speculate upon the outcome of such a translation experiment that would rigorously apply the principle of change. *The Rose of Castille* might be replaced by *L'Etoile du Nord,* or by Switzerland and William Tell, and railway lines and cast steel by *filatures* and *toiles,* and these substitutes could be consistently adhered to so that ultimately an entirely different texture would emerge. Translation might, after all, be understood to mean more than just an exchange of words—a transference of names, places, allusions, of the whole cultural background. In some such sense *Ulysses* is such a radical translation of the *Odyssey,* from ancient Greek into modern Irish.

The pedantic insistence on the necessary distortions of every translation raises the question of their relevance. The losses may be negligible. The Dutch translator, who also settled for a different opera ("*Herodias:* hierodiejas"),[16] indicated that there are, after all, other ways to refer to Molly. So perhaps we need neither railway lines, nor Spanish operas, nor music, but just some sort of facile pun. Since values are involved, no objective answer can be given; and the proof of the translation is in the reading. There is no doubt that the implications of the motifs that were either dropped or newly introduced by the various translations have been overrated. In all probability we are not meant to take every word as a sign to be interpreted, connected with every other part of the translation. Which is, of course, exactly the point. Joyce always seems to imply, to suggest, to provide clues that we *can* take up (which is no blanket justification for every conceivable fanciful interpretation). In translation it is not possible to play the same game. The reader has fewer opportunities to read with the sort of creative cooperation that seems to be a characteristic Joycean activity.

Considered as a quotation, *"The Rose of Castille"* is not much of a problem. In the translations an opera is clearly referred to, and its title is quoted. But quotations are often much longer, and not clearly marked, shading off into numerous allusions. The translator is at a loss as soon as the same performed verbal matter that we call a quotation or, if it is more indirect, an allusion, is not available in his own language and literature. And of course it usually is not. Even where a quotation is available, the form it takes may prevent its incorporation into the translated context. For a familiar Shake-spearean tag like the one contained in "But how to get there was the rub" (613), there *is* a rendering in German, but it has never become familiar at all, and its form (the standard translation of *Hamlet* turns it into a flat and unspecific "Ja, da liegt's") makes it entirely unsuitable for a passage in the Eumaeus chapter. So there is no inkling of *Hamlet* or poetry in "Aber der Haken war nun, wie sie dahin kommen sollten" (Go 615) and consequently no feeling of the distance between the literary tradition and the marketplace. And yet, the translator no doubt recognized the allusion.

The recognition of familiar elements in new surroundings is a pleasure the reader of the translation often has to forego. When Joe Hynes, in the Cyclops chapter, being informed with the rest of the company that the victims of hanging die with an erection, comes out with a slick comment: "Ruling passion strong in death" (304), the reader is likely to be startled and amused. Whether he knows the line or simply feels it as being part of a heritage of poetic wisdom, or whether he considers *ruling passion* no more than a cliché, its sudden new application puts the barroom scene in a different light and Pope's verse[17] in turn acquires a new meaning and will never be the same again. No corresponding relationship will be set up in the translations that, with no possibility of referring to the literary tradition, content themselves with a faithful rendering of the sense. Versions like "La passion maîtresse forte encore dans la mort" (F 298) or "Lidenskab i doden" (D 311), though they might have a poetic ring, must appear more like simple elaborations of the preceding topic than as a sudden oblique sidelight, and they hardly electrify the text.

Beyond the loss of resonance, an untranslated allusion or quotation may become unintelligible or downright misleading. Imagine a reader coming upon the following sentence (Bloom has just left the Burton restaurant in disgust and thinks, with vivid illustrations, of a communal kitchen for all Dublin):

Le Père O'Flynn leur donnerait des ailes. (F 167)

Padre O'Flynn li farebbe correre tutti. (I 231)

El padre O'Flynn haría liebres de todos ellos. (SP 205)

O padre O'Flynn diria cobras e lagartos dêles. (P 193)

Pater O'Flynn würde sie alle auf den Schwung bringen. (Go 194)

Fader O'Flynn skulla skrämma dem alla. (SW 178)

A clerical person, not met with before, is thought capable of doing something (and not, it seems, the same thing) to an unspecified group of people. The readers of the above translations will be hard put to find out who *they (leur, li, sie, dem)* are; and there is no trace of *them* in the sentences immediately preceding. Not all translations succeed too well in catching the meaning of Joyce's sentence: "Father O'Flynn would make hares of them all" (170). It would take an unusually intuitive reader to relate Father O'Flynn back to the phrases with which the translators come to terms with "don't talk of your provosts and provost of Trinity":

> sans parler des professeurs et Principal de Trinity. (F 167)

> non parliamo di provosti e di quello di Trinity. (I 231)

> fragt kein Mensch danach, ob einer Probst oder Direktor des Trinity. (Go 194)

The German version, without any plural, does not even have an antecedent for *sie alle.* Now the English-speaking reader, too, may not know the song that links the idea of such potential communicants of the common feast as the Provost of Trinity (whose house Bloom has just passed a few minutes ago) to Father O'Flynn:

> Talk of your Provost and Fellows of Trinity
> Far renowned for Greek and Latinity
> Gad and the divils and all at Divinity,
>   Father O'Flynn would make hares of them all.[18]

But he will at least suspect the presence of something more than plain prose, and it is fairly obvious that Father O'Flynn is not just one of Bloom's acquaintances. If the reader is inquisitive enough he may find the relevant song. The most inquisitive spirit would do the reader of the translations little good. Father O'Flynn, a strange and unaccountable character, remains unintegrated, and so are the lines that translate the song fragments (but not *as* song fragments). The German version *fragt kein Mensch danach . . .* is on a completely wrong track, hinting at some philosophical bent in Bloom's thought. In some translations *would make hares of them all* is interpreted to mean *would put them to fright.* The Spanish translation, remaining literal, works in some possible cannibalistic overtones (this is the Lestrygonians chapter), but *haria liebres* may be something quite different from *make hares.* There is no tension between the original meaning of the song (which could not possibly be evoked in any translation) and the new deflected one that Bloom gives the lines.

Most of the translators obviously did not know the song about Father O'Flynn. But even if they did, could they somehow indicate that Bloom remembers a song, perhaps by formal devices like italics, quotation marks, or even a footnote? All of these outward marks go against the very grain of *Ulysses.* Some translators have found the separate publication of a companion volume with annotation the best solution.[19]

Since "Father O'Flynn would make hares of them all" cannot be adequately translated as a recognizable line from a particular song, with all its implications, a translator might be grateful to be told, by the critics, what then are the most important functions of the sentence that ought to be preserved? Not, probably, the literal meaning of the potential metamorphosis of a group of people into hares? Rather the fancy that Father O'Flynn is superior to some learned people at some sort of activity? Is the connection with the previous fragment to be made obvious, even if the reader can have no idea what the relation is? Is the main function of the sentence that it is a memory of a different sort from the surrounding ones, not from Bloom's everyday experience, but from the realm of imagination, of poetry? Should a distinctive rhythm or jingle characterize the sentence as nonprosy, the content as fictional? Or is, perhaps, the melody that may accompany the words in Bloom's mind more important than any sense? Should some sort of musical notation be provided? Or should the translator aim chiefly at the tone—one of genial and facetious admiration (if that's what it is)? Or again, do we need a reference to something edible to account for this particular association within its context? Questions of this sort may help to assess priorities in translation, but an analysis of the component functions would also contribute to our understanding of *Ulysses*.

Theoretically an entirely different background could be substituted, some allusion that would evoke associations with which Danish or French readers could replace Father O'Flynn. A transplantation of this sort would not be easy to perform, especially if the connection with Trinity College, part of Bloom's immediate experience, is to be upheld. Father O'Flynn, moreover, reappears in the Circe chapter. So none of the translators have replaced him, even if his public appearance is utterly cryptic. A legendary figure is occasionally replaced by an indigenous one, especially in the French translation, by far the freest of them all. "Sir Lout's toys" (44) became "les joujoux du Grand Pitaud" (F 47). The French translators were not too timid to bring "Ham and his descendants mustered and bred there" (171), without regard to Old Testament references, much closer to the French cuisine: "Toute la famille Cochon emmourtadée chez Madame Tartine" (F 168). Joyce may well have encouraged this procedure himself. In his own playful translation of a little poem by James Stephens into five languages, he freely introduced Boreas, Fra Vento, Ragnarok, and a German proverb as well as some puns of his own.[20] Joyce, who, for all we know, would have made hares of them (the translators) all, did not, however, give us his views about changing specific allusions in *Ulysses* that are tightly interlaced with the whole surrounding texture.

The translations could be examined, furthermore, with regard to sound, rhythm, alliteration, onomatopoetic effect, musical qualities of the prose, and, especially, matters of style. There are, for example, no real and adequate equivalents to the literary styles whose progression makes up the Oxen of the Sun chapter. And still less can the styles of individual and highly characteristic writers be parodied. The results of further comparison would bear out what we knew all along, that a translation becomes inevitably flatter, that every one of its particles is less capable of an epiphany than those of the original, that motifs and overtones have been lost in transit. But perhaps the premises themselves ought to be questioned: in the perspective adopted here the ideal translation has been assumed to be the one that could be subjected to the same sort of scrutiny that Joyce scholars devote to *Ulysses* and that it would yield the same results. These demands are utopian. Translations are not undertaken for scholars—even if scholars are no more, ultimately, than ordinary readers with better training, slightly better equipment, and more time at their disposal.

But once we acknowledge that a translation cannot, in the nature of language, be all things to all readers (as *Ulysses* seems to be), we may come to realize that we do not know what can reasonably be expected of a translation. What are its prime requirements? If principles like correctness, accuracy, internal consistency, preservation of motifs, correspondences, overtones, symbolic superstructures, tone, music, and many others are at variance, as they undoubtedly are, what are the preferences? The translator is really left to fend for himself as best he can; it is only afterwards, when we see the results, that we come and say, "Now *this* won't do." The theory and the principles of translation will probably get more scholarly attention than they have received so far, and some guiding lines that are more than the vaguest of general rules may emerge in the course of research that is being conducted now at several universities. One of the more practical problems is to make the complete resources of every language more readily available than they are now, when every translator is still dependent on his own memory and a shelf of reference books that he will find inadequate for his purposes.

Translation, too, is the art of the possible, and the perpetual squint at the original cannot do justice to its full achievement. The only facts it brings out are the deficiencies. Even a theoretically perfect imitation, rendering faithfully each shade of meaning and reassembling all the constituent parts of the original in the other language, if it were possible, might, for all we know, fall completely flat and lack all life. For all its numerous inaccuracies, the French *Ulysse* is generally considered a work of literature almost in its own right. It also contains some splendid details, like an ingenious "Yeux pochés à la blême" (F 161) for Bloom's "Poached eyes on ghost" (165), which skillfully combines *yeux* and *œufs* in its sound, alludes to the paleness of a ghost (*blême*) and is yet pertinently culinary, by suggesting *à la crème*. This is brilliant and delightful even if it still falls short of Joyce's ingenuity (which could be demonstrated). Goyert's German translation, which generally fares worst in any comparative study, at any rate received Joyce's approval as well as his praise. He is reported to have said that he preferred some of its passages to the original.[21] Both the French and the German translations have had a lasting influence on contemporary writers.

Joyce's *Ulysses* has not yet yielded up all its secrets, and most of its readers concede that it may have more surprises in store for them. Critics of the translations are far less ready to grant, with equal humility, that they may not have exhausted at a first reading all the meanings that the translators put in. Not all the subtleties of a translation are obvious at once, and our minds, quick to notice errors, may fail to perceive hidden allusions and touches that would, if we but knew, enrich their context. The translator does not normally authorize a commentator to point out *his* intentions and *his* finesses to the uninitiated. So some of his best achievement may well pass unacknowledged. Every translator will moreover arrive at a point where he realizes, with resignation, that any further exertion of time, research, and ingenuity would be a waste for all practical purposes since no reader would be patient or sensitive enough to appreciate the result. And then, of course, hardly a translator is given seven years to devote to his work and few publishers encourage extensive revision and rewriting at the galley and page proof stage.

Ulysses has been translated more than a dozen times already, and more attempts will be made.[22] As a bibliographical fact, *Ulysses* is translatable, but a more differentiated answer is needed if the possibility is called into question. The enthusiasm with which translations of *Ulysses* have been received (even where they have been gravely criticized) proves that the book has a great deal to offer in the refraction of a different and perhaps unsuitable language as well. At the same time there is ample documentation for the view that not all the qualities of *Ulysses* can be re-created in translation. That the task is not worth doing is usually said by those privileged to have access to the original anyway. For the alternative to reading *Ulysses* in translation is not, in practice, to turn to the undiminished splendor of the original, but not to read *Ulysses* at all. Even a pale reflection of the real thing is better than nothing, and certainly better than being fed with half-truths and clichés *about* the book.

The student of *Ulysses* can learn from the translator, who is a neglected expert, often a modest one, more concerned about getting on with the job at hand than talking about it and not inclined to make a display of his insights and discoveries. He is also a creator, remaining within or behind or beyond or above his handiwork. He gives us a commentary, not an authorized one, but a complete one, even if every individual gloss is incomplete (and some are wrong). We can benefit from his predicament and learn from his frustrations. They help show us just what makes *Ulysses* tick.

1969

Notes

1. Jan Parandowski, "Begegnung mit Joyce," *Die Weltwoche* (Zürich), 11 February 1949.

2. Privatdruck. (Basel: Rhein Verlag, 1927).

3. (Zürich: Rhein Verlag, 1930). In subsequent editions the only claim made was "vom Verfasser autorisierte Übersetzung."

4. (Paris: La Maison des Amis des Livres, 1929). Later editions simplify the imprint: "traduction intégrale par Auguste Morel, assisté de Stuart Gilbert, entièrement revue par Valery Larbaud et l'auteur."

5. Letter to Claud W. Sykes, 10 February 1927, *Letters of James Joyce,* ed. Richard Ellmann (New York: Viking Press, 1966), III, 153-54. Madame Maria Jolas has informed me that Joyce also asked her husband, Eugene Jolas, to help check the translation but that he did not have the time necessary for it.

6. See Breon Mitchell, "A Note on the Status of the Authorized Translation," *James Joyce Quarterly* 4, no. 3 (Spring 1967): 202-5; and Jack P. Dalton, " 'Stately, plump Buck Mulligan' in Djoytsch," *James Joyce Quarterly* 4, no. 3 (Spring 1967): 206-8.

7. Alan M. Cohn, ed., "Joyce's Notes on the End of 'Oxen of the Sun'," *James Joyce Quarterly* 4, no. 3 (Spring 1967): 198-99.

8. Samuel Beckett, "Dante . . . Bruno. Vico . . . Joyce," in *Our Exagmination Round His Factification for Incamination of Work in Progress* (London: Faber and Faber, 1936), p. 14.

9. *Ulysses* (Basel: Rhein Verlag, 1927), I, 293. The phrase was changed to "wenn sie dumpf *grübelte*" (Go 298). It is all very well to chuckle over what is actually a fairly well-known translator's trap, but in my somber studies I have now become less sure about the wrongness of the naïve error, or the correctness of the improvement. We may well question if Gerty MacDowell—insofar as the passage is a slanted transposition of her own thinking—is quite conscious and in control of the phrase as it is sandwiched in between two items of what looks like an interior scene: "as she mused by the dying embers in a brown study without the lamp" (*U* 354). The odd collocation tends to externalize the phrase in question and gives it a more spatial tone. Gerty seems to be a prey of language and its changeable applications. What should of rights connote emotional abstraction comes close to wallpaper, to decorative surrounding. Even in its historical sense, "in a brown study" seems pleonastically misapplied, coming close upon "mused." In another meaning, "apparent thought, but real vacuity" (as Brewer's classical *Dictionary of Phrase and Fable* defines the phrase), it would again be aptly characteristic but—awkwardly—not something Gerty would think of herself. Neither a somber mood nor a room done in brown would baffle a translator; but that uneasy hovering in between does. If my feel of the passage is accepted, an adequate translation ought to include that touch of wrongness, and obviously can't. Quite apart from discontextual grace benefits of "a brown study" in Nausicaa, the chapter whose Art is painting: a study is after all also "a sketched idea of a painter." Since Gerty's former friend no longer rides in front of her house on his bicycle but has been called in by his father "to study," there is more tenuous reason for Gerty's study to become gloomy. Such excessive indulgence in the chapter's "studied attitude[s]" (see *U* 355) cannot be matched by translinguistic re-creation.

What is of general and even positive import is that translators' errors magnify potentialities of the original, and are revealing. In some vital sense, Stephen's/Shakespeare's "lousy Lucy" *is* a woman, especially in the textual company she keeps, right before *"femme de trente ans"* and "first child a girl" (*U* 215). Events in Circe are also anticipated, and, conversely, Shakespeare's women actors were boys. The *appearance* too is worth translating. The educated Italian version, emphatically masculine, "quel pidocchioso di un Lucy" (I 292), is faultless but deprives the name of its feminine air and does not incite the reader to further investigation.

10. Arno Schmidt, *"Ulysses* in Deutschland, kritische Anmerkung zu einer James-Joyce-Übersetzung," *Frankfurter Allgemeine Zeitung* 26, no. 249 (October 1957).

11. See the discussion of "built of breeze" (*U* 164) in the translation issue of *James Joyce Quarterly* 4, no. 3 (Spring 1967): 176-77.

12. *A Portrait of the Artist as a Young Man* (New York: Viking Press, 1966), p. 217; *Jugendbildnis* (Zürich: Rhein Verlag, n.d.), p. 321.

13. Frank Budgen, *James Joyce and the Making of "Ulysses"* (Bloomington: Indiana University Press, 1960), p. 263.

14. "De Vertaling van *Ulysses*: Interview mit J. Vandenbergh," *Utopia* (Eindhoven) (James Joyce Issue), 6 June 1969, p. 11.

15. Stuart Gilbert, *James Joyce's "Ulysses"* (London: Faber and Faber, 1952), p. 193.

16. "De Vertaling van *Ulysses*," p. 11.

17. *Moral Essays*, Epistle I.

18. Alfred Percival Graves, "Father O'Flynn" in *Irish Minstrelsy*, ed. H. Halliday Sparling (London: Walter Scott, n.d.), p. 330.

19. Giulio de Angelis, *Guida alla lettura dell'Ulisse di J. Joyce* (Milan: Lerici Editori, 1961); John Vandenbergh, *Aantekeningen bij James Joyce's "Ulysses"* (Amsterdam: Uitgeverij De Bezige Bij, 1969).

20. *Letters of James Joyce*, vol. 1, ed. Stuart Gilbert (New York: Viking Press, 1957), pp. 317-19, and my article "Seven against *Ulysses*: Joyce in Translation," *James Joyce Quarterly* 4, no. 3 (Spring 1967): 189.

21. Daniel Brody reported that Joyce "erklärte mir persönlich, dass er die deutsche Übersetzung für die beste halte, sie sogar an manchen Stellen seinem Original vorziehe." Quoted from *Frankfurter Allgemeine*, 5 November 1957, in *James Joyce Quarterly* 4, no. 3 (Spring 1967): 205.

22. Shortly after this essay was completed, two more European translations came out (and more have appeared since): *Ulysses*, translated into Dutch by John Vandenbergh (Amsterdam: Uitgerverij De Bezige Bij, 1969) (see note 14); *Ulisses*, translated into Polish by Maciej Słomczyński (Warsaw: Państwowy Instytut Wydawniczy, 1969). The Danish translation by Mogens Boisen was heavily revised and republished in 1970: *Ulysses* (Copenhagen: Martins Forlag). These translations were widely reviewed and helped to reawaken interest in the various problems involved.

2

Transluding off the Toptic; or, The Fruitful Illusion of Translatability

Finnegans Wake, always obliging with zesty titles, offers "transluding from the Otherman or off the Toptic," something that Shaun boasts of (*FW* 419.24). James Atherton has told us that this echoes a claim James Clarence Mangan made about some of his poems, that they were "translated from the Ottoman, or from the Coptic," and Joyce, in his essay on the poet, leaves it open whether "learning or imposture lies behind such phrases" (*CW* 76). Whatever Shaun, the speaker, or Joyce, the author, had in mind, the cues assembled in the *Wake* quotation can be deflected for my purposes to my topic more readily than the discursive pedantry of criticism normally allows. Translating from any language, Ottoman, or Coptic, or Joyce's, well, English, means that something changes, becomes "other" and often—very much—off the topic. Learning and imposture, in the original or in the translation, are not always easy to disentangle. What I am going to highlight is that translating is not only a game, but that in transluding the games to be played with the text are what may well change most drastically. The optics of this essay, which is based on a talk to German-speaking translators, will be on *lector ludens,* on the playful, serious, fascinating opportunities of the text, which we, in our minds, translude into something congenial, always in our own fashion. The subject is *Ulysses,* however, and not *Finnegans Wake.* Just imagine, how would you translate "transluding from the Otherman or off the Toptic"?[1]

When Hans Wollschläger's new German translation of *Ulysses* came out in 1975 it aroused a good deal of attention and was naturally compared with

Georg Goyert's earlier one of 1927 (revised 1930). As a coordinator and consultant in the venture (together with Klaus Reichert), I had a good and sobering chance to reflect on what is and what is not translatable. The role of consultant, responsible for accuracy and "correctness," could easily have deteriorated into that of a law-and-order philologist. No one would of course underestimate a philological component in *Ulysses,* least of all the reviewers, who were also quick to remark that (what they thought to be) pedantic expertise does not in itself guarantee an adequate, spirited rendering, that in fact it may get in its way. There is an ingrained fear that whatever is "scholarly" has to be lifeless, and it often is. Wollschläger, fortunately, was enough of an autonomous stylist not to take on trust any of the processed insights of the Joyce industry as they found their way into the margins of his first draft. Many were integrated, some modified, and many rejected with regret, or with disdain. The three of us, as expected, had divergent views—and practically no time to deliberate thousands of points at issue in seminarlike conferences. It is only fair that in such matters the translator will have the decisive word.

An illuminating, though devious, way to approach any tricky passage in *Ulysses* (and they all are) is to imagine how we would program a translator, tell him what there "is" on the page. What are the meanings, functions, effects, etc. (plural throughout), and which ones deserve preference? What may be, what must be sacrificed? First we should get some clarity, "understand" a phrase or sentence, or allusion, then we should sort out priorities. Traditionally, and rightly, in prose fiction we want to preserve the sense, the reality encapsuled by the words, and in *Ulysses* external reality, a referential world outside, is blatantly conspicuous. A German or Polish or Japanese *Ulysses* should allow its reader to reconstruct, mentally, a specific, dated, and faded Dublin from its pages, with the "loose cellarflap of number seventy-five," "the hopscotch court with its forgotten pickeystone," and also "Butler's monument house." What is "Butler's monument house" (*U* 151) anyway? The house in which George Butler & sons sold their musical instruments is close to O'Connell's monument and was therefore named "monument house." This is what Dubliners and Bloom know and do not give any thought to in passing. The translator must give it considerable and mainly futile thought, and it shows. If you write "Du coin de chez Butler en face du monument" (F 148), you are descriptively accurate but sound like a guide book and not like an unreflective local citizen. Goyert's "Butlers Denkmal Hausecke" (Go 172) suggests erroneously (Goyert could hardly know Dublin) that someone called Butler had a monument named after him. The Italian version, "della casa monumento nazionale di Butler" (I 205), stresses the monument not glanced at in the text and proclaims it national. Wollschläger's unchanged "Butler's monument house corner" (Wo 151) is alien and seems to imply an institution—it is easy to cavil at all such makeshifts. So that reality, often highhandedly brushed aside in up-to-date theoretical arrogance, is in itself quite a problem. And nothing is simplified by our growing awareness of the superrealism, the verisimilitude, as something manufactured through language, an illusion. *Ulysses* is also a kaleidoscopic rearrangement of words and a contrived artifact flaunting its own contrivances. Realistic conformity, for all its increased importance, no longer deserves the uncritical preference that translation traditionally, almost automatically, has accorded it, even if its absence will always have to be deplored. So it is all a matter of compromises, a balance of priorities. These priorities can also represent critical emphases and schools of interpretation. We can glibly decree that a translator has no right to favor one attitude above all others. Yet even the best-informed choices and preferences remain subjective. There is, in particular, one subjective law at work that affects translators as well as critics: priority is given to what *we* happen to recognize. My findings, interpretations, are better than yours.

Conflicting priorities are bad enough, but, worse, each target language imposes restrictions of vocabulary, idiom, aspects, usage. There is a vague consensus of what one's own language permits—and therefore excludes. There are certain things that would fit very well but that you "cannot say." Reviewers happily censure phrases that "are not possible in German," and often they are not. The authorities invoked are Habit, Taste, and, ultimately and unchallengeably, a goddess called Sprachgefühl. But Intuitive Legislation may not realize that the equivalents in the original were also, prior to 1922, not possible in English. Every translator is conscious of how many things one's own language does not care to name or even recognize. Quite apart from cultural differences: take the terminology of the turf, of cricket, of heraldry, or anything that has grown historically and erratically (like British law or Irish toasts). Such problems of course are common to all translation and need not especially concern us here. What vexes a Joycean translator is that the signifiers themselves can no longer be neglected. Not that they ever could of course, but Joyce makes this frustratingly evident. Strictly speaking, and in particular for a Joycean context, there are no equivalents ever, neither for extreme and *ad hoc* words like "bullockbefriending" nor for simple and everyday ones like "home, ale, master" that Stephen Dedalus already considered to be different if said by an Irish or an English speaker.

What do you call them?

What in English is called "dulcimer," most dictionaries would agree, is "Hackbrett" in German. This might well do in ordinary circumstances, but not when it occurs within a cluster of Bloom's oriental images, among turbans, mosques, a scroll—and then "A girl playing one of these instruments what do you call them: dulcimers" (*U* 57). "Dulcimer" is vaguely exotic, mysterious; "Hackbrett" prosaic and solid, and it is furthermore disturbing that a butcher, too, can use it as a chopping board. We do not want to be reminded, however, of Mrs Mooney and her cleaver, but of eastern seduction, perhaps even more precisely of Coleridge's "damsel with a dulcimer." This echo might be our chance; if some German translation of "Kubla Khan" should exist, we could borrow its term from there. The only one I consulted said "Harfe," both inaccurately and unuseably, for the harp in Joyce has of course been preempted for something sentimentally Irish. (The gentle reader might pause here to consider how much time-consuming and unprofitable rummaging may be necessary in order not to come up with a word better than the dictionary provides. One should also bear in mind that no translator could ever devote as much attention to such a detail as is possible in a critical essay or a workshop.)

There is something romantic about "dulcimer," something quaint as well as vague. Who after all knows what a dulcimer is? Bloom probably does not, and he cannot offhand recall the word. His slight memory delay is more plausible for a foreign-sounding, melodious word like "dulcimer" (originally *dulce melos,* a sweet song) than for a staid "Hackbrett." In fact this German word would hardly surface in Bloom's mind in this particular daydreamy mood. Goyert picked on an incorrect term, "Ein Mädchen spielt auf einem jener wieheissensienoch Instrumente: Cembalo" (Go 68), most likely to suggest at least an appropriate aura and tone. It may be a matter of luck and vocabulary. In French *tympanon* is sufficiently quaint and removed from everyday objects to call for a mnemonic effort. The context demands something out of the ordinary, unfamiliar, and the German language does not seem to supply it. But you can never know that a word may not exist after all. Following an earlier airing of the "dulcimer/Hackbrett" dilemma, a correspondent offered the ideal solution, "Zymbal," which fulfils the musical and romantic requirements very well (we really did not remember "what do you call them?").

Maybe too much is made of a small problem. Bloom's act of memory, however, is later repeated, "whatdoyoucallthem dulcimers" (*U* 273)—or, if you want, it has become a set association in itself. That already gives the term more weight. There is also a similar delayed search for another somewhat unusual word, that delicate web, "fine like what do you call it gossamer" (*U* 374, and "what do you call it gossamer" is repeated at *U* 414). This time there is a fittingly odd word in German, "wie heisst das doch Altweibersommer" (Wo 524, "wie nennt man das doch Altweibersommer," Wo 582). One might well pause before recalling what literally means "summer of old women." The nature of this association has changed, however. In the original it was the rhythmic and phonemic similarity of "gossamer" and "dulcimer" that produced a similar verbal reflex. Yet nothing connects "Hackbrett," or "Cembalo" (or, for that matter, even "Zymbal"), with "Altweibersommer"; or "tympanons" with "fils de la Vierge" (F 57, 368); or "ribeche" with "filo di vergine" (I 81, 506). In the translations the signified objects trigger off the thoughts, with diminished probability; in the original it is the words themselves. Translations then become more thing-oriented; the language as co-author recedes. Though a musical instrument and a natural phenomenon have been preserved, the nature of the association has been transformed. Even so, there may also be incidental gains. Though a crossreferential web has been disrupted, the Italian and French versions manage to enrich the Nausicaa chapter by one more evocation of the Blessed Virgin, a gift of language.

Without End

Translations curtail choices. On Sandymount strand Stephen opens his eyes and finds the outside world still going strong: "There all the time without you: and ever shall be, world without end" (*U* 37). This is the Proteus episode, admittedly difficult. One word is repeated in our sentence, a common preposition, "without you . . . without end." Does the first one denote Stephen's absence or noninvolvement—"ohne dich" (Go 45), "senza di te" (I 55)? Or do we have one of the main themes of the chapter, the contrast between the world without you and the world within? Later on Stephen will think about "Throb always without you and the throb always within" (*U* 242). Some translators opt for this: "hors de toi" (F 39), "ausserhalb deiner" (Wo 54). Joyce can have it both ways, so effortlessly that you probably never even noticed; the translator usually cannot. A translator would also not primarily aim at a sentence in which an identical preposition occurs twice in differing circumstances, the first one common, the second one ("world without end") ritual and formulaic. So this wholly subordinate Protean performance will disappear. The translator's problem is not, anyhow, to deal with that second "without," but to use the standard rendering of the Church's "*in saecula saeculorum*": "tous les siècles des siècles," "nei secoli dei secoli." This shows up another hazard. The correct rendering of the Church's words in Italian and French cannot possibly evoke the end *of* the world and not serve as incidental negative preparation for such climaxes as the appearance of the End of the World in Circe. It is for reasons like this that the German version departed from the ecclesiastical formula and decided on a more literal "Welt ohne Ende" (Wo 54).

Interconnective losses are inevitable. We may, however, turn the tables and claim that what happens in translating parts of Proteus is part of the meaning of Proteus, in whose service Joyce enlisted—as though he could help it—the Art of Philology. Language is a matter of wayward transformations. "World without end" links back to a Greek phrase that varies *aiōn* in the New Testament. One forms, "*eis tous aiōnas tōn aiōnōn*" (as in Gal. 1:5), became "*in saecula saeculorum*" in Latin—and maybe "our aeone tone aeones" in *Finnegans Wake* (552.7). The resonant Latin went two ways in English; the

Bible renders it "for ever and ever," the doxology opted for the familiar form discussed here. In either version the original *aiōn* has been lost, and we might similarly and pointlessly complain about its disappearance.

Somehow, also, Stephen's echo of a word that is no longer there is a gratuitous invitation to look into its philological mutations. The Proteus chapter is also about the chancy development of words like *aiōn* through the ages and through the cultures. Etymologists like Skeat would tell us that it is related to Latin *aevum*, lifetime, age, one of whose adjectives, *aeviternus*, was shortened to *aeternus* and spawned "eternal" and "eternity." Another derivation (and shortening), *aetas*, came into English by way of French in the form of "age." A Germanic cognate is "aye" in the sense of "ever," and *ever* is related to it. It may be a coincidence that Stephen, on the next page, brings together three members of the family: "before the ages he willed me and now may not will me away or ever. A *lex eterna* . . ." (*U* 38).

The Greek *aiōn*, as Homer knew it, meant a lifetime or life itself. The sweet life (*glykys aiōn*) of Odysseus was ebbing away when we first meet him, and Kalypso the nymph first says he should not let it, *aiōn*, waste away (*Od.* 5.152, 160). By the time the Christians used it, it had come to mean an age, a very long period, an eternity. The word itself has survived and had a great revival in theosophy: "eons they worship" (*U* 186). Mulligan mocks: "Any object, intensely regarded, may be a gate of access to the incorruptible eon of the gods" (*U* 416. Notice that I am doing something similar, intensely regarding as my object the word *aiōn* itself). The poet George Russell has derived his pen name from it, as Stephen knows: "Mummed in names: A.E., eon" (*U* 195). Leopold Bloom does not know this and vainly gropes for the meaning: "A.E.: what does that mean? Initials perhaps. Albert Edward, Arthur Edmund, Alphonsus Eb Ed El Esquire," but somehow unwittingly stumbles upon it (justifying my circuitous course): "The ends of the world" (*U* 165). So we are back at our point of departure, a Protean world without end. The point of this excursion is not to interpret a passage, for it does not, but to illustrate that *Ulysses* also thrives on the morphological, semantic, and cultural translation of words, "whorled without aimed" (*FW* 272.4). Every word is an accident—or miracle—of etymological metamorphoses.

Weaving and Looming

True to its nature, the Proteus chapter makes it difficult to pin down phrases or words:

> To no end gathered: vainly then released, forth flowing, wending back, loom of the moon. (*U* 49–50)

Loom of the moon. Chances are that our first impression is one of hearing, or at least registering (perhaps even *seeing*), the sound effect, something a translation should aim at. The moon is given, *lune, luna, Mond* (the awkward fact that a German moon is masculine has troubled translators before), and a chiming word should match it. Even more so when we think of further dark monosyllabic echoes within the chapter, "tomb: womb: noon," or later on "doom, gloom, boom" and, of course, Bloom. But language does not come forward with suitably matching echoes. It does not even seem possible to muster a close phonemic companion for the moon in the respective languages. No one would blame the translators. But that means that the music is switched off in favor of the correct meaning.

So what is the meaning of "loom"? There seems to be agreement among the translators that it is something to weave upon. (Such agreement is not in itself persuasive proof, for translators reasonably consult their predecessors, especially those authorized versions that proudly display the author's approving benediction on the title page.) So we get "Webstuhl des Mondes" (Go 60), "Webstuhl des Monds" (Wo 71), "telai de la luna" (I 72), "telar de luna" (Sp 82), or an enlarged, glossing version: "écheveaux du métier de la lune" (F 52). Again the German is rather technical (a composite containing a chair) and clumsy, hardly fitting into Stephen's prose poem. Or, to rephrase the observation: a German reader would not get the impression that Stephen is mentally verbalizing a poetic phrase. In all translations the weaving is prominent; Penelope beckons perceptibly.

These pertinent, though not uniquely felicitous, textile readings may occlude the homonym "loom," a nautical term for an instinctive appearance, a shimmer, something looming into view. It would fit well into the image of waves, night, and moon. As it happens, both meanings are continued in the next sentence, the weaving into "a toil of waters" (if "toil" is derived from French *toile*, Lat. *tela* and *texere*), the visual glow in "a woman shining in her courts." Proteus both weaves and looms; the text is a texture, and meanings loom. A translation should, but cannot, suggest both.

What happens when no recognizable meaning looms into view, as in a tantalizing stage direction: "Bloom, in gloom, looms down" (*U* 607)? What does Bloom, looming down, actually do? He looks down, most probably, and some Circean charm (or Sirenlike assonance) has imposed "looms," as though in continuation of Corny Kelleher's cluster of a fourfold "tooraloom" (*U* 604), which will soon interfere with the words of a whole passage, engendering forms like "assuralooms" (*U* 608). How would you program a translator here? It is revealing, and perhaps reflects on changing views away from mere denotation, that earlier translations resorted to perplexed paraphrase: "In Dunkelheit steht Bloom traurig da" (Go 607), is flat and somewhat evasive; the French, more ambitious, has "Bloom ténébreux profilé baisse son regard" (F 535); nor is there any ripple of discomfort in "Bloom guarda a terra incupito" (I 783). But more recent translations try to intimate what in another essay I will call dislocution: "Bloom steht dumpf verschlummert da" (Wo 752); "Bloom soombrío contempla el suelo" (SP, Valv. II, 225).

Misleading

We cannot trust sounds or looming shapes, especially in Proteus, as said before. One such shape is a foreign *"Duces Tecum"*; it occurs within Stephen's imagined visit to Uncle Richie Goulding, whom he visualizes filing "a writ of *Duces Tecum*" (*U* 39). Clearly it is a legal term. Lawyers would know its meaning and relevance. But not automatically readers of *Ulysses*, who might be at a total loss. Even a reader whose curriculum included Latin might legitimately wonder if *Duces* is the plural of *dux*, leader (as it might well be), or an inflected form of the corresponding verb *ducere* (which it is: the legal summons enjoins that "you shall bring with you . . ."). Such a momentary grammatic indeterminacy is also what Proteus is about (and it is quite in keeping that a word like *Duces* conventionally offers rival pronunciations, the *c* being either an original *k*- sound or a palatized *tch*). This minor digression is neither necessary nor very exciting; it merely cites one more instance of translation itself being integrated into *Ulysses*. But it is odd that *dux* and *ducere* suggest what the text irritatingly refuses to provide, guidance or leadership. And as if to confirm this, in the next sentence Stephen thinks of his uncle's "misleading whistle." Proteus, *Ulysses*, Odysseus, language, sounds, glosses mislead and traduce.

At any rate there *is* a potential fleeting translation problem that can be sorted out only within the legal context. Strangely enough, later on Bloom will translate the exact Italian descendant of Latin *tecum* in a memory from *Don Giovanni*:

> *Don Giovanni, a cenar teco*
> *M'invitasti* (*U* 179)

Bloom manages fairly well, with the exception of one word: "What does *teco* mean? Tonight perhaps." A reasonable guess, based on contextual probability ("tonight" of course has other, disquieting reverberations for Bloom). Readers of foreign languages often have recourse to that kind of speculation; it is how we learn most words of a language. But Bloom is misled, just as he later will be (for all we know) when Stephen inconsiderately talks of *"dux* and *comes* conceits" (*U* 662, and see also pp.49,52) Nothing will likely lead him to the correct meaning; he is probably ignorant of the Latin words or the musical sense (nor could he possibly suspect that *dux*, leader, and *comes*, companion, might neatly describe his and Stephen's role in the Eumaeus chapter).

The intriguing, muted touch is that Bloom's slight and inconsequential *teco* mishap occurs, of all possible Dublin places, in *Duke* street. And, ironically and comfortingly, for once all the deceitful potential transmutations *can* be saved into practically any language, for *Duces Tecum*, *teco*, *dux* and Duke street will simply be taken over unchanged for the reader so minded to translude into the kind of interlockings that have been tried out here.

Incipient Intimations

At the opposite end from Protean weaving and looming we have the firm, angular Ithaca chapter. It appears precise, solidified, dehydrated, scientific, nominal. The Ithacan mode should be easier to imitate in any other language. Our example is taken from a list of Bloom's conceivable humiliations. He might have to suffer

the infantile discharge of decomposed vegetable missiles. (*U* 726)

This has become "das kindliche Werfen mit faulen pflanzlichen Geschossen" (Wo 923), "le bombardement enfantin par projectils végétaux décomposés" (F 660), "il lancio infantile di proiettili vegetali decomposti" (I 945). The stocktaking has been achieved; the French and Italian translators could translate almost word by word. Still the diction has changed, away from the predominantly scientific tendency of the original. The words in the translation are closer to the marketplace, the language of everyday feeling. The words that the original seems to avoid are right there. In fact, understanding Joyce's Ithaca diction consists in a silent, perhaps *almost* instantaneous intralingual translation. The translations into German or French, and presumably most other languages, tend to give us the plain, static, immediate result. Less of a mental process is required. The translation has already performed the work that the reader of the original has yet to do; it has already changed for us the desensualized language into one we consider more normal, or closer to our emotions. Toward the end of *Ulysses* all norms, especially linguistic ones, have been challenged. Translations easily become more normative. The difference can be illustrated by the trite fact that the German or Italian phrases are grasped at once, but not so Joyce's. It is the terminal "missiles" that give clear direction to the initial "discharge," which, at that early point, is highly indeterminate. Understanding the language of Ithaca is also more or less an accident of education. There are native speakers who would hardly be able to make sense of it at all. But even the most erudite reader will not understand at once; there seems to be a delay, however infinitesimal perhaps. The time of the deferred recognition has been taken out of the translations. A reader of "le bombardement enfantin" already knows where he is; "das kindliche Werfen" is even more instantly clear.[2] In Joyce's original phrase semantic clarity, as often in *Finnegans Wake*, is retroactive. That the reading changes becomes even more evident in the same catalogue of indignities: There must be a fair number of readers who, coming upon "the latration of illegitimate unlicensed vagabond . . ." (*U* 726) have no idea what this is all about. Many dictionaries, even sizable ones, do not list "latration." It is only after the three serried polysyllables that our supposed average readers will pick up the word "dog" and get a chance to guess that the Latinate noun may refer to either one of the animal's standard menaces, bark or bite. No such puzzlement is likely to disturb an Italian reader, where "il latrato" (I 945) leaves no room for doubt;

or in German, where you simply cannot drum up any recondite synonym for "Gebell" or "Bellen."

A non-Ithacan way of describing the difference is to claim that Joyce's phrases are funnier than their translations. The principle, however, is concealment—maybe also in part a linguistic equivalent to the disguise of Odysseus in his palace. Or we could call the principle verbal deviation. Something as simple and instantly perceptible as a dog's bark (which in real life is recognized at once) has to be translated out of a word far removed from experience.

Not that such language deviation from assumed norms has to depend on difficult words like latration. In the book's first sentence Mulligan is "bearing" a bowl—not "carrying." The solemnity of the gesture is achieved, not by a similar bookish synonym, but by some trick of phrasing like "porteur d'un bol" (F 7) or "in Händen" (Wo 7). But what about a sentence of unsurpassable simplicity—"It's she!" This is what Bloom, as Rip Van Winkle, is made to say in Circe (*U* 542). In French this must become "C'est elle!" (F 497), in German "Sie ist es! (Wo 704)—what else! What is not caught are the strange and always faintly amusing conditions in which one might say or hear "It's *she*." Translations hit the norm and miss the deviation.

Perhaps someone can articulate what it is that accounts for the perversely poetic effect of

the incipient intimations of proximate dawn (*U* 704),

and why it is largely absent from either

les indices premiers de l'aube proche (F 629)

or

die ersten Anzeichen naher Dämmerung (Go 718)   ·

or

die ersten Anzeichen der nahenden Dämmerung (Wo 893).

Again the relative insipidity of the translations owes something to their having to use "ordinary" terms for "incipient" as well as "proximate"; also to the absence of an opening alliteration. The translations make uneventful reading. No semantic tension is created by "les indices premiers" or "die ersten Anzeichen"; these are even stereotypes. Reading Ithaca can be a matter of incipient intimation followed by interpretive dawn. This, through no fault of their own, is not equally true of the versions offered by the translators.

Relationships and Gushes

Translating enforces choices, not alone lexical ones. The very quality of a perception may be involved. In Nausicaa a climactic rock bursts high in the sky, and the wording may make us wonder what exactly it is that the spectators, notably Gerty MacDowell, see, or register, or associate:

and it gushed out of it a stream of rain gold hair threads and they shed. (*U* 367)

What is that stream of rain gold hair threads? Do the first three words qualify "threads," or are there privileged couplings, of rain with gold, or hair with threads? Any one of the four nouns can engage, it seems, in strange relationships with its neighbors. There are hazards. The phrase is abristle with topoi and literary echoes. Once we single out "gold hair" or "gold threads" or "gold rain," we seem to be putting stresses. If we treat "rain gold" as a unit (particularly if in German this becomes "Goldregen"), Zeus as a shower of rain may well be overemphasized as a mythological possibility. That would metamorphose Gerty into Danae, and she might not object. Nor would she perhaps scorn the potential role of Lucrece: many of the Roman virgin's attributes (gold, ivory, alabaster, rose, etc.; Stephen noted her "bluecircled ivory globes," *U* 197) could, but need not be, gleaned from *The Rape of Lucrece*. Her "hair, like golden threads," we read in line 400, played with her breath.

Such are the temptations of special correlations. It is not simple to determine the phrase grammatically, and maybe we do not have to. We would also falsify the meaning by fixating too strictly what is no doubt *also* a string of subjective effects. We can read it as a transcript of shifting impressions. What gushes from that rocket may resemble rain—is seen as golden—makes you think of hair—looks like threads. Once we start thinking more in terms of successive associations, the indeterminate, multifaceted delights of the four nouns may become even more entrancing.

Other languages are not as conveniently loose as English is; the translators' languages allow them far less flexibility and force them to sort out, or impose, grammatical relationships. Note that, in the translations presented, the sequence of "rain (1) gold (2) hair (3) threads (4)" is hardly ever adhered to. Clearly the original order was not a dominant concern in a tricky enough task. Idiomatic compulsions must also be accountable for the considerable disparities well in evidence.

In French, "il s'en échappa en torrent une pluie (1) de cheveux (3) d'or (2) qui filaient (4) et ruisselaient . . ." (F 359), the threads have been transformed, to good effect, into a verb, "filaient," which pairs neatly with "ruisselaient." This may compensate for the assonance of "threads" with "shed," which the other renderings neglect. Romance languages cannot simply string nouns together, but have to indicate relations. A virtue has been made of this necessity in "un torrente de lluvia (1) de hebras (4) de cabello (3) de oro (2)" (SP 405), where a torrent of genitival *de*'s function like the serial arrangement of Joyce's nouns. The Italian version, similarly, threads "un fiotto di pioggia (3) di fili (4) d'oro (2)" (I 494), and inadvertently drops the hair in the process. The first German translation, by contrast, has redundant gold: "ein

Strom goldenen (2), haarfeinen (3, 4) Goldregens (2, 1)" (Go 413). One thing non-English languages do not capture is the excitement expressed by the quick yet strong monosyllables. German can try it with compounds: "ein Strom goldregnender (2, 1) Haarfäden (3, 4)" (Wo 511). Werner Gotzmann's recent exemplary German rendering of the Nausicaa chapter, meant to be a corrective to Wollschläger, "ein Strom regengoldener (1, 2) seidiger Fäden (4)," retains the original order and replaces hair with silk.[3] A Spanish version in turn leaves out the threads: "un torrente de cabellos (3) di oro (2) en lluvia (1)" (SP, Valv. I, 555).

Though the order of impressions is manifestly not kept, each translation is also, in its own choices, *more* orderly and predetermines relations for us. What none of the renderings seem to aim at is an impressionistic release from grammatical or semantic strait jackets in favor of a metamorphotic string of images. The languages would probably allow for a naive, nominal, more cinematographic, and gushy enumeration of visual transformations, something in the nature of, very simply, "ein Strom von Regen Gold Haar Fäden" (I can vouch only for the German, but could at least imagine "d'une pluie de l'or des cheveux des fils"). I am not championing such a solution as "better," but merely remarking on the lack of any attempt *away* from whichever syntactical domination. Syntactical slackening would probably have been considered incompatible with the (assumed) prevalent narrative procedure. We are slowly learning that Ulyssean narration may be less determined and more variable than we used to think, and in the long run recognition of this will also affect translations, again away from conventional norms.

On the whole, translators avoid syntactical, or tonal, turbulences, even where those have been acknowledged and language would not imperiously forbid them. Any semblance of ungrammaticality might all too easily be attributed to their defective command of language or to idiomatic lapses. But, in our example, even the most venturesome translator would have to strain very much to open his version both toward a somewhat overloaded literary flourish *and* what the text literally calls "a stream of" associations. The point would not merit so much illustrative verbiage if an important part of the meanings of *Ulysses* were not now uncovered as emerging, precisely, from its oscillation between rivaling ways of reading even its little phrases.

Thy Speech Bewrayeth Thee

There is only one original—the number of possible translations is not limited. This is true even of individual passages like a challenging sentence of which we have, so far, four rivaling German attempts. Mulligan's

—And going forth he met Butterly (*U* 17)

was first done, straightforwardly, by Georg Goyert in 1927:

(I) Und als er weiterging, traf er Butterly.[4]

That is what Buck Mulligan says, more or less verbatim. Butterly looks like a good Irish name; another person of the same name, or the same person (who would know this in the twenties?), will appear later on. *Ulysses* is full of meetings. Any subsequent wording will be faulty to the degree that it departs from Goyert's unassuming paraphrase. Goyert's translation was revised in 1930, and by then the sentence had changed. The French team had most likely been tipped off by the author. Mulligan's words are a slight variation of a biblical matrix, "Going forth, he wept bitterly" (Matt. 26:75, Douay version). The French turned this into

> Et étant sorti dehors, il rencontra Lamermant. (F 21)

Of course, you will not meet a Lamermant in the New Testament or in Dublin, but he is an appropriate near-avatar of the adverb "amèrement." The German revision followed suit:

> (II) Und als er weiterging, traf er Bütterlich. (Go 23)

Bütterlich's parents are a local Butterly and Luther's "weinte *bitterlich*"; we can appreciate the onomastic success. The activities of wept and met are less easy to conflate, in German or in French. And again people named Bütterlich hardly exist in Dublin or even Germany. Readers probably remained puzzled. By the mid-seventies it seemed feasible to skip quotidian Dublin and make straight for the biblical form, with a blatant distortion:

> (III) Und er ging hinaus und weinte Buttermilch. (Wo 26)

The effect is jocular and Mulliganesque, in fact more obviously so than in the original (where the allusion had gone unnoticed for a long time). The sentence is alive and within audible distance of the Gospel. Yet there is no longer a meeting in this Book of Meetings. On the other hand only this version retains "butter" (a maybe casual and maybe sacrificial reference, see *U* 185). A reviewer took up Wollschläger's spirited and much advertised "und weinte Buttermilch," yet proposed an alternative that would both echo the words of St. Matthew and reinstate a meeting with a person, going back to the name Goyert had made up:

> (IV) Und ging hinaus und traf Bütterlich.[5]

It is open to everyone to add further remedial touches, which is one way of attesting a basic intranslatability. Once an early innocence, as exemplified in (I), is dispelled, all sorts of schisms set in. Reality or quotation? Weeping (III) or meeting (I, II, IV)? Personification of an adverb (II, IV) or a verbal transformation (III)? Should conspicuousness be a criterion—Mulligan's muted "going forth" jars far less on the reader than Wollschläger's almost surrealist "weinte Buttermilch"?

The assumption made here is, of course, that such questions matter and that the Gospel echo infuses the passage with irritant vigor. It metamorphoses. It changes an otherwise indistinct "he" (*Ulysses* is a work in which unstressed pronouns like "he" can be puzzling long before Molly's final musings) into a prominent disciple and saint, St. Peter, who was chosen to become the foundation of the Church—which is also so dominant in Joyce's Dublin. He is introduced into the book by the same process that led to his selection by Christ, accidents of language: "Thou art Peter, and upon this rock I will build. . . ." That this homonymous Peter was given the power of the keys adds theological resonance to Stephen's and the Buck's wrangle about the key to the Martello tower; and this within an epic full of keys given up or forgotten, crossed, played upon verbally and pictorially. In the Gospel Peter's repentent weeping is immediately preceded by his discovery, it was his language: "thy speech bewrayeth thee," or "thy speech doth discover thee" (Matt. 26:73, King James and Douay versions). Mulligan's somewhat stilted diction should have alerted us, as readers, that there is something below the surface. Reading *Ulysses* is learning to discover speech, dialect, phrasing, style, quotation. To deprive the translation of similar reverberations would be a serious loss, but the disregard of the Dublin surface can be equally damaging. Like the epitome that it is, "he met Butterly" participates imperfectly in two contexts: a tale of ordinary events in Ireland of 1904, on which some large cultural prototype is superimposed.

Every reader can play with the admirable compromises that translators have come up with. Inevitably translations are an essentially much more restricted happy huntingground for inquisitive minds in search of balanced interpretations. The problem is not alone how much outside reality or Bible "content" is being caught, but the enabling of that mysterious process of identification that Joyce conjugates so polytropically. "Butterly" is an early Odyssean disguise, or fake identity that we can metamorphose into a histrionic adverb (well suited, by the way, to Stephen, who is multiply characterized by bitterness).

Complacent demands that translation ought to do all this are futile. Of course transluding should—and cannot—provide toys equally transmutable, or joys equally kaleidoscopic. For reasons suggested here, and many more reasons omitted, translations are off the toptic, are less dynamic, less Protean, less gushing, less self-righting, less looming, less weaving, less misleading— also *more* misleading—, less synecdochal, less dislocutory, less everything and—perhaps most bitterly—less transluding. They should be admired, not trusted.

Having reasserted such platitudes, I should add that the live value of any translation may not reside so much in the published results, but invisibly in the endeavor of gauging, deliberating, choosing, and rejecting that went into them. Fortunately the transformative dynamisms of *Ulysses* by no means hinge merely on such minuscule passages as have been aired here. Enough of it will manifest itself in other ways. The changes missed in the Butterly vignette will be amply instituted in Circe; or the wayward narrative conduct; or the stylistic disruptions. Or even in the strange names and the attention drawn to them.

At ecstatic moments Stephen Dedalus wants to model his life on a mythological character who simulated the birds, and whom a Roman poet had refashioned in his Book of Translations. In Joyce's metamorphosis Stephen accurately renders the Greek *daidalos* as English "cunning" (and pairs it with silence and exile). "Ulysses" is a bastardization of the name of a Greek who cunningly adapted his conduct to changing occasions. The hybrid Latin form became Joyce's suggestive title, which intimates that the work so named is also a transmutation of Homer's epic—which in turn we surmise to be the outcome of previous reshapings. The specific terms for all these various changes clearly do not matter and are interchangeable. What is insinuated through all this, and in everything else, is that Joyce's works consist of translation and glorify all cognate processes. By their energies they acknowledge that translations suffuse and enable literature and cultures.

1976/1983

Notes

1. Philippe Lavergne tried it, with simplified optics and considerable streamlining: "traduit en Orthoman ou en Coptique, ou quoi que ce soit . . ." *Finnegans Wake* (Paris: Gallimard, 1982), p. 441.

2. An improved German version was offered by Werner Gotzmann, in a critical commentary on Wollschläger's translation and its supposed underlying attitudes: "das kindische Entladen verfaulter Gemüsegeschosse" (*Sprache im technischen Zeitalter* [Berlin], no. 86 [June 1983]: 136). Even so, a German reader will instantly respond to *faul* in "verfaulter" and "*Kind*" in "kindisches" (which is not only everyday, but even judgmental: *kindisch* suggests "puerile," is even less scientific than "kindlich"). No foreign word, or one sufficiently removed, seems to come to the German translator's aid.

3. Werner Gotzmann, "Neuübersetzung: James Joyce 'Ulysses,' 13. Kapitel, Gerty MacDowell/Nausikaa," *Sprache im technischen Zeitalter* (Berlin), no. 86 (June 1983): 153.

4. *Ulysses*, Privatdruck. (Basel: Rhein Verlag, 1927), I, 34.

5. Christoph Schöneich offered the solution of "quoting St. Matthew accurately," leaving out the subject, "er," so that the adept, on reading "Und ging hinaus," would *hear* "und weinte bitterlich" when reading "und traf Bütterlich." "*Sarg oder Koffer*—das ist die Frage," review, *Rheinischer Merkur*, 11 June 1976.

3

Foreign Readings

His language, so familiar and so foreign. . . .

Most of those whose native language is not English and who still want to weather Joyce's works will have asked themselves resignedly if they have a chance to cope at all: The obvious answer, in one essential sense, is No; a handicap, not to be overcome, will remain. Yet it is a "No, But. . . ." And it is the various buts that will be butted about here.

As a rule, foreign readers will deviate to that substitute for the original text that replaces each of its single items and turns the whole into quite a different arrangement of letters and sounds while pretending to retain somehow its soul or spirit. What happens in translation will therefore deserve some passing attention here. In a much larger sense, everything Joyce wrote has to do with translation, is transferential.

Joyce had to read Homer in English, but he learned Norwegian to study Ibsen, applied his poor German to read Gerhart Hauptmann, while his Italian gave him access to Giordano Bruno and Vico. Foreigners are underprivileged, but they have one advantage: they know that the language is strange and has to be looked at very closely. A few close looks will be spread out here in the following pages as examples of the sort of naive wonder that native speakers may well have lost. Anything watched from a distance, from outside, can be exotically fascinating. Joyce felt this fascination himself and made others feel it. He profited from it. He fared better, on the whole, with friends in Trieste, international refugees in Zürich, or a mixed clique in Paris than with his compatriots, say Dublin cronies or English publishers. The roll call of early perceptive foreign readers includes Italo Svevo, Stefan Zweig, Valery Larbaud, Louis Gillet, Ernst Robert Curtius, Carola Giedion-Welcker, Bernhard Fehr, Hermann Broch, *et al(ieni)* and is proportionally impressive, especially in an early stage; that is, before Americans reclaimed him for the English-speaking world.

The foreign observer is an old literary device, since the outsider notices what is taken for granted by the member of a community. Joyce has varied this theme in all his works. Leopold Bloom is by no means the only one within this tradition, nor the first one in the canon.

Joyce's earliest story, "The Sisters," features an unnamed boy who becomes something of a foreign reader within the first paragraph, as he remembers words that "sounded strangely in [his] ears" (*D* 9). Their strangeness is indeed prominent, their shape odd, their meaning unguessable: it does not emerge from the context. *Paralysis* (from Greek, a loosening beside), *gnomon* (also Greek, someone who knows), and *simony* have to be defined first.[1] It was Euclid who determined, somewhat arbitrarily, because of its shape—via *gnomon* as a term for a sundial and then a carpenter's rule—what a gnomon is.[2] This is not how words normally acquire their meanings. A pre-Euclidian Greek would have been as puzzled by its geometrical sense as any nineteenth-century schoolboy. And true to its nature, the Catechism lays down what "simony" is, an offense for which one Simon once set a bad precedent.

Part of the fascination of these three uncanny verbal beings is their primary opaqueness. (Have in mind also that one would not be sure, offhand, how to pronounce any of these words; Father Flynn, similarly, had to instruct the boy in proper Latin pronunciation.) They appeal to one's curiosity, a curiosity that has yielded rich critical rewards. In fact, a reader has a way of becoming a *gnomon* right away: "an examiner, a judge, an interpreter."[3] Joyce opens with an appropriate conjunction: geometrically, "gnomon" is defined by something missing. The knowledge of an examining reader is indeed defective, incomplete. More mysteries remain unsolved in the story than there are reliable facts.

Once we inspect foreign territory we tend to find, or construe, more than we originally suspected. In Joyce's prose, this is a characteristic experience. Simony takes us straight to the account in the *Acts of the Apostles* and to Simon, who was one among about a dozen biblical persons of that name, a very common one. The name, incidentally, is based on a Hebrew verb for "hear": Sim(e)on is one who hears or obeys. Should we therefore deduce that hearing is particularly important? Maybe not, but the story is full of strange sounds, much hearsay and rumor, and contains audible silences. Our Simon, distinguished as "Magus," had his name perpetuated because of his misdeed and became famous, perversely, by doing wrong. The story of Father Flynn, too, is worth telling because something went wrong in his life. Immediately

before Simon Magus is introduced into the biblical report, we read that
"unclean spirits . . . came out of many that were possessed . . . and many
taken with palsies and that were lame, were healed . . ." (Acts 8:7–8). Now
"unclean spirits"—*pneumata akatharta* in the original[4]—can be interlaced
with another foreign term in the story, Old Cotter's "talking of faints and
worms" (*D* 10). "Faints" in distillery terminology are "impure spirits." Such
alignment may amount to nothing more than a circuitous reconfirmation of
some spiritual debasement in Father Flynn's career, but such subterranean
short-circuiting is typical of Joyce's later work. The English "palsies" in the
passage quoted derives from *paralysis;* the original used as a participle *para-
lelymenoi,* whereas the Vulgate retains *paralytici.* So the words brought
together in the protagonist's mind by chance association are contextually
related in a source—as though a minor New Testament cluster were somehow buried within the story's opening signals, concealed by conspicuous
foreignness.

Naturally this whole reading is foreign in yet another, radical sense: a
foranus was someone who was *foras,* "outside of the doors," an outsider who
is likely to use all his wits. Like a boy, for example, who, as he cannot know
what goes on inside, "studied the lighted square of window" (*D* 9), as the
second sentence in the story puts it. Much of Joyce's meaning is, and has been
from the start, somewhat outside the doors or at least a trifle removed. A near
synonym of "foreign(er)" is based on the same spatial metaphor: *Stranger,*
French *étranger,* derives from Latin *extraneus,* external, from *extra,* outside,
without. Joyce's works are very much the saga of those without, of outsiders.
It has become customary to refer to a certain kind of outsider by a different
term stressed by Joyce: exile. The etymological image is similar: an exile sits,
or perhaps, leaps, outside.

In view of what Joyce was to do later with names, we may think it
remarkable that Simon, right after his ill-conceived offer of money for spiritual power, was rebuked by Peter himself (Acts 8:20–21), Peter on whose own
name "the whole complex and mysterious institutions of the Church" were to
be founded, as Joyce often rubbed in.[5] What makes this intriguing is that the
misguided sorcerer and new convert was told off by a namesake, for Peter
himself was also called Simon (Matt. 4:18). Father Flynn in the story seems
to have hovered between the polar opposites of Simon Peter, first pope, and
Simon Magus, an early debaser. The name Simon, at any rate, was to be
carried over into the next two of Joyce's novels.

Of course a reader *need not* ever engage in such alien philologistics. Yet
the text invites some such loosening (*lysis*) aside (*para*) of the more outstanding elements, which, as often as not, have a foreign appearance. Foreign
words or phrases ask for a special effort, for some assimilation.

In *A Portrait* Stephen Dedalus has to face strange phenomena and strange
languages. It is a discovery in itself that there *are* other languages. "*Dieu* was
the French for God and that was God's name too; and when anyone prayed to

God and said *Dieu* then God knew at once that it was a French person that was praying . . ." (*P* 16). One may be punished for not knowing the plural of the Latin noun *mare*.[6] But one's own language can be just as mysterious. "Suck," an ugly sound, like dirty water going out of a washbasin, is "a queer word," especially when applied to a "fellow" called Simon Moonan (*P* 11).

Like hardly any previous novel, *A Portrait* weaves the difficult empirical processes of learning the names of simple things and the curious ways in which grownups use words. We may overlook such an everyday quality as "nice," which clearly means something good or pleasant. Mother has "a nicer smell" than father; it is "nice and warm" to see a light. But there is more. "Rump" is "not a nice expression" (*P* 9), an unpleasant one, perhaps, but there intrudes an uneasy feeling of morality, of a superior world's rulings, which may appear capricious; this world rules that reality will divide into things and into words for them, some of which are approved and some of which are not. It is not always an obvious distinction. When a pious relative, Mrs Riordan, in angry conflict calls a snappy reply to a priest "A nice answer," surely she cannot approve? And her savage reduplication, "Very nice! Ha! Very nice!" (*P* 37), undoubtedly means that she is outraged about Mr Casey's spitting tobacco juice into the eyes of a devout Irish woman. Young Stephen, a shocked and terrified listener, realizes that words can mean their own opposite, miraculously. Not all cultures, we know, allow for this kind of rhetoric. We could discover more linguistic runs in the novel hinging on other adjectives; an instructive one is "right" in the first chapter. Only trial and error teach us to handle or understand such labels. It is part of our survival strategies to master the use of words.

Even such ordinary learning processes will become something else when they are translated into languages where it is not possible to stick to the same adjective consistently, and so outside impressions gain more weight than society's verbal tags for them. A simple listing of the eight first occurrences of "nice" on only four opening pages will bear this out. Compare

> a nicens little boy . . . a nicer smell . . . nice expression . . . Nice mother . . . a nice mother . . . not so nice . . . nice and warm . . . nice sentences,

with Ludmilla Savitzky's translation of 1924:

> un mignon petit garçon . . . plus agréable . . . une expression convenable . . . Gentille mère . . . gentille . . . moins gentille . . . bon et chaud . . . de jolies phrases,[7]

and with Dámaso Alonso's Spanish version (1926):

> un niñín may guapín . . . olía mejor . . . expresión no estaba muy bien . . . Madre querida . . . [next two not rendered] . . . agradable y reconfortante . . . frases tan bonitas,[8]

and with Cesare Pavese's Italian translation of 1933:

> un ragazzino carino . . . un odore più buono . . . una bella espressione . . . Mammina bella . . . una mamma cara . . . non più cosí cara . . . dava calore . . . belle frasi.[9]

Later readers are more aware of verbal structurings, as shown by comparing an early German translation (Georg Goyert, 1926):

> netten, kleinen Jungen . . . roch besser . . . hässliche Worte . . . Hübsche Mutter . . . hübsche Mutter . . . nicht mehr so schön . . . es tat so wohl . . . schöne Sätze[10]

against a recent one (Klaus Reichert, 1972), where consistency is given priority:

> eine sönen tleinen Tnaben . . . roch schöner . . . kein schöner Ausdruck . . . Die schöne Mutter . . . eine schöne Mutter . . . nicht so schön . . . schön und warm . . . so schöne Sätze.[11]

Needless to say, retention of the same adjective or adverb is not a criterion of quality. Even where the repetition is recognized as meaningful (a recognition that has been slow in coming), its exact reproduction, where possible, would still have to be evaluated against optimal rendering within each variant phrase.

That we learn to master words is brought out in what is probably the most condensed summation of a learning process in all fiction, the opening section of *A Portrait*. An abridgment of early impacts, it moves rapidly from words for simple things, easy to verify in the outside world—like "Moocow" (an animal identified by its sound "moo" happens to be named "cow"—a descriptive *ad hoc* composite well adapted to a child's mind), "road," or "lemon platt"—to something as unreal and recondite as "Apologise" (*P* 7–8). The syntax has moved along with it, just as fast, and with it the thinking ability from impressions to generalizations. "Apologise" is quite an achievement, not easy to grasp by any standards: it is unEnglish in sound and appearance, of four syllables and of obscure meaning, but very powerful. It stands for the alternative to some traumatic punishment that could *happen* to him because of an unintended offense. It is possible to ward off some awesome consequence by saying appropriate *words*. As it happens, all of this is even contained *in* this word, though Stephen does (and the reader need) not know this. To apologize is a procedure of doing away (*apo-*) some effect by words or speech (*logos*). Its effective and etymological potency alone would qualify the word for Stephen to linger over it and the author to put it at the end of his first movement.

That *apologia* (a speech made in one's defense, as the ancients used it) also figures in the title of an influential self-justification by a famous Jesuit convert and founder of Dublin University may add resonances later on when

John Henry Cardinal Newman is named as one of the inchoate artist's self-appointed models. *A Portrait* has been taken to be Joyce's fictionalized *Apologia pro Vita Sua* (as a young man), a partial truth. Perhaps it is more an "apologuise," in the more precise version of *Finnegans Wake* (414.16), a work that always tries to excuse itself for its own deviate existence and that, to go back to origins, manages to undo the import of its words by disturbing semantemes: *apo-logia* in this meaning too.

In a conversation much later in the novel a highly articulate Stephen Dedalus says of a Jesuit theologian, Suarez, that he "apologised" for Jesus, who "seems to have treated his mother with scant courtesy" (*P* 242). Here too the term goes beyond a vague sense of making excuses; it resurrects accurately an explanation of the apparent rudeness of Jesus Christ's remark to his mother: "Woman, what have I to do with thee?" (John 2:4). In the original, so the defense by Suarez and other commentators goes, this remark was polite and respectful, but when an Aramaic idiom has to be given in Greek or English, something may happen to its tone and its understanding. No translation is free of such alterations, and *A Portrait* indirectly acknowledges that fact. What the *Wake* calls Shem's "root language" (424.17) is at work early on, in the foreignness of a loan word like "apologise" with its unrestful implications.

What a foreign reader, teased and frustrated, tends to notice much more is that words are words, the only prime reality in literature. This makes non-natives akin to Stephen, a wary reader of all sorts of signs and signatures. It is brought home to him in a well-remembered scene that the language of the Irish is not theirs, is the Englishman's ". . . before it is mine." Stephen feels "unrest of spirit," the causes of which are partly political and historical. The natives were forced to adopt the language of the conqueror, so much so that in the end their own had to be revived artificially. Of course they also changed the language that was imposed upon them; they unwittingly kept a substratum of Gaelic patterns and evolved many idiosyncratic uses, so that English as We Speak It in Ireland (as a namesake, P. W. Joyce, called it) remains noticeably distinct: "His language, so familiar and so foreign, will always be for me an acquired speech" (*P* 189). His soul frets "in the shadow of his language."

English was always an acquired speech for Joyce, and a shadow of this is over all of his works. Any foreign reader will sympathize. But the coerced have sneaky ways. Stephen Dedalus, Shem, or Joyce (a personal union is allowed this time) go on to subvert all this, perhaps an Irishman's revenge. *His* English, that of the works to follow, will appear more and more odd to the English masters; there will be more and more foreign matter, unfamiliar liberties, outlandish features, unknown arts. All the major works, incidentally, were written while Joyce himself was a foreigner in "Trieste-Zürich-Paris," a condition that the course of the twentieth century turns more and more into a norm rather than an exception.

Ulysses, when it made its much-heralded appearance in Paris, 1922, was certainly considered chaotic and exotic and was accepted, if anything, more readily on the Continent than in Ireland or Great Britain. That Ireland had made "a sensational re-entrance into high European literature," as Valery Larbaud announced, must have sounded much more convincing to international groups in Paris or Berlin than to literati in Dublin like Shane Leslie, who replied with an outburst of invective at the book itself as well as at its foreign admirers. He emphasized "devilish drench . . . muckwritten tide . . . or vomit," but did find consolation in the fact, taken for granted, that the general reader was "in no danger of understanding" the book and might escape corruption.[12] There was clearly a linguistic basis for this reaction too. A novel written in English and dealing with Irish matters was, by and large, pronounced inaccessible by those for whom its language was not an acquired one. It was thought to be European, and the dispute over this in itself proves a blurring of national borders.

There is no reader of *Ulysses* for whom some passages are not, literally, foreign and for whom many have not remained unfamiliar for a long time. *Ulysses* is in need of glosses and many of them mere translations of alien phrases, and those published have not always been outstandingly reliable. Readers and characters often go wrong, often without noticing. *Ulysses* creates numerous situations that are akin to those of its readers. Examples could be picked almost at random.

Bloom holds forth on the beauties of the Italian language, which he does not understand, and has to be told that the speakers he overheard were "haggling over money." He reacts in two ways well known to foreigners. The first is disappointment, a sigh of resignation "at the inward reflection of there being more languages to start with than were absolutely necessary." He also recognizes the strange fascination, "the southern glamour that surrounds" Italian. This very quickly leads to Stephen's generalization that sounds, like names, are "impostures" (*U* 621–22).

Leopold Bloom's own plucky shot at the glamorous foreign tongue, *"Belladonna voglio,"* does not parse too well but reveals separate items that the reader has been conditioned to spell out in the course of the novel. "Voglio" is a verb that makes it possible for Bloom to stave off nightshades, painful emotions, behind a concern for correct pronunciation. Bloom's Italian radiates psychologically: we translate the Italian into fears and hopes. A related worry interferes with an attempt to digest an opera passage, also in Italian: *"Don Giovanni, a cenar teco/M'invitasti"* (*U* 179). One word proves intractable: "What does that *teco* mean? Tonight perhaps." This is doing reasonably well; it is how we ourselves often read, unaided, out of context: "tonight" often goes with "come to supper." But from our vantage point, we know what looms in his mind within "tonight's" expected events. We may also find that *teco* (with you) is a way of implying the old wisdom (which has been reapplied by psychoanalysis as well) that *de te fabula narratur.* Our thoughts are determined by our problems.

As a fumbling linguist, Bloom is cautious and tentative. We see him struggle with some Latin. Notice that he gives two variants of *"Corpus,"* one semantic, one derivative: "Body. Corpse" (*U* 80). His rendering of *"In paradisum,"* though not the most taxing endeavor, is circumspect: "Said he was going to paradise or is in paradise" (*U* 104); the characteristic "or," allowing for possibilities, is in itself superior to some impressive scholarly glosses of Latin phrases in print.[13] Bloom copes with foreign elements as best he can. A priest's word at the funeral service he registers as *"Domine-namine"* (*U* 103). This indicates insufficient attention; Bloom is looking rather than listening. If the mental echo were a "correct" form like *"(in) nomine Domini,"* we would probably just read on, unruffled; the scramble of word order, vowels, and inflections, however, may make us pause. Bloom's re-creation is neatly parallel. Perhaps the correct vocative, *"Domine,"* heard elsewhere, is included. No doubt the English "name," a cognate, interferes with *nomine.* Bloom has just been thinking: "Father Coffey. I knew his name was like coffin," and perhaps the word more or less coincided with the Latin equivalent, so that *namine* might not be faulty, but a carryover. The point is not that the extrication just given is valid, but that we are provoked into giving some account of the confusion. A few hours later, when Bloom overhears *"in nomine Dei"* as part of "The Croppy Boy," the words become, in his mind, *"in nomine Domini"* (*U* 284).[14] Latin, Bloom muses, "holds them like birdlime," and we observe that his mind sticks to certain phrases too. He conjures up a memory from Glasnevin cemetery and an earlier visit to a church: *corpusnomine,* a conflation of previous echoes. Botched foreign phrases have a way of holding us too, the readers, like birdlime, and Bloom's own composite insinuates that names/nouns have an almost physical being. Foreigners are often seduced by the body of words. "Pyrrhus, a pier" (*U* 24) we can take to be a corpusnominal association.

Molly Bloom is not alone in interpreting "polysyllables of foreign origin . . . phonetically or by false analogy" (*U* 686). Bloom misinterprets Fergus, a mythological figure from a Yeats poem, as "Ferguson . . . Some girl. Best thing could happen him" (*U* 608–9). Readers are not immune to such imaginative leaps. Let us return to Bloom in the mortuary chapel as he watches the priest and tries to assimilate some of the Latin from the sermon in between. *"Dominenamine.* Bully about the muzzle he looks. Bosses the show" (*U* 103). One might be forgiven for imagining, one moment, some Latin ox or cow (*bos*) in "Bosses," for which there is no philological foundation; and one might wonder if there is an accidental bull in "Bully." A native reader, if asked, most probably would "know" instinctively whether there is or not. What *does* Bloom have in mind? The *Oxford English Dictionary* notices that "popular etymological consciousness" tends to connect the two words.

Readers can shrug their shoulders and go on, but not so translators; they have to put something down and therefore must make decisions. Of the two authorized translations, the German one keeps close to the animal while still getting the impression of someone powerful and overbearing: "Ums Maul sieht er bullig aus." The French version is based on quite different considerations: "Un fort en gueule, ca se voit." Nothing bullish there; the characterization stresses grossness and even verbosity. A later Italian translation suggests a blustering fellow: "Ha un muso di prepotente." This triple divergence proves nothing more than potential ambivalence; associations detected in the sentence are magnified.

The "correct" solution, one might argue, is the one provided in a reference work, Eric Partridge's *Dictionary of Slang and Unconventional English,* which says: *"bully about the muzzle.* 'Too thick and large in the mouth' . . . dog-fanciers. . . ."[15] So the phrase predates Bloom and had become stereotyped. There is a certain probability that originally the dog-fanciers who coined the saying were struck by a bull-like appearance. Tossing a phrase about, we may notice here, usually leads not to more clarity but to more complexity. The results of the above probe are merely that a word may well participate in two semantic activities. "Bully" would go well with Father Coffey as a "muscular christian"; "bull-y" contributes to a cluster of animal imagery for the priest (who doubles as Cerberus in Hades): "his toad's belly . . . said the rook . . . a fluent croak . . . Bully . . . (Bosses?) . . . sheep . . . poisoned pup" (*U* 103). It occurs midway between a dog transformed by Stephen's mind in Proteus and the animal metamorphoses of Circe.

All the speculations just given as mere illustrations may appear a trifle less gratuitous when we find a passage much later that looks like—but cannot realistically be—a reshuffling of Bloom's thoughts spiced by dog Latin. In Oxen of the Sun, where avatars tend to be bovine, a long tale about Pope Hadrian's generosity to England is spun out, and in it an initial papal bull is turned into a browsing animal with features of a bullying John Bull. In the course of this homonymous festival we come across "the famous champion bull of the Romans, *Bos Bovum,* which is good bog Latin for boss of the show" (*U* 401). This appears as though the bodies of words had changed from Dublin street wear to Roman togas or priestly vestments—transformations that do occur in both Oxen and Circe. Or words here change their nationality (as Bloom's father did). In *Finnegans Wake* something like "bull, a bosbully" (*FW* 490.35) would cause little surprise and only show once more that words have turned this condition into a way of life.

Since *Ulysses* transversally encloses a cheeky permutation of "Bully: bull: boss: *bos,"* we may digress for a while to observe what happens when such a process itself has to be translated. Since the two passages are so distant and the connection tenuous, chances are that translators did not recognize it and (let us bear in mind) perhaps need not acknowledge it in their assessment of priorities. To give a better idea of what dexterity would ideally be called for to re-create a text's low-key correspondences, two more instances of "bully" are listed, one in the Library episode, where Stephen gives examples of "Women he won to him . . . bully tapsters' wives" (*U* 193). In this phrase "bully" is a character trait, and the translations consulted all agree that it qualifies "tapsters" and not their wives. In themselves versions like "des épouses de cabaretiers brutaux," "spose di rozzi tavernieri," or "prahlender Zapfkellner Weiber," would not be worth much comment. Only the second German rendering (1976) retains the adjective used by Bloom in the morning, "bulliger Zapfkellner Weiber," and it alone would catch a potential Pasiphaean echo, if there should be one (to reinforce Stephen's "queens with prize bulls," *U* 207). What all foreign renderings miss, however, is what in this chapter may not be negligible—that in older, and Shakespearean, parlance, "bully" was also a term of endearment.

A treacherous "bully" appears in Oxen of the Sun, as if to confuse the issues even more. "But they can go hang . . . for me with their bully beef" (*U* 398). The beef in question is "Kerry cows," so we have here a tricky misuse of the phrase "bully beef," in which "bully" derives from French *bouilli,* but is tied to "beef" (related to Latin *bos*). It is interesting to see which translations opt for a form of potted meat, and which ones have diminutive cattle romping about, alive and kicking: "avec leur barbaque de cambuse"; "mit ihrem verseuchten Büchsenfleisch";[16] "e i loro torelli baldanzosi," etc.

The dispersed bits of text and how they appear in several languages are tabulated on pp. 50–51 for convenient comparison. The focus is on one of Bloom's thoughts and how it seems to radiate. The sample translations are arranged vertically in chronological order.

Given the tremendous odds, the translations emerge with credit. We see more awareness of transverse links in later renderings, when the novel was better known and the importance of correspondences more recognized. But in any foreign tongue *Ulysses* becomes less interstructured. Much of the bovinity that shapes Joyce's ends does not travel too well.[17] What translation can deal with least is translation itself, like "boss-*bos,*" where an identical choreography of equivalents is excluded by a different vocabulary. We may appreciate French "latin de latrine," which imitates "bog Latin" as derived from "bog(-house)," privy, by substituting *latrine* for a more current *"latin de cuisine."* A felicity like the original phrase itself, which suitably brings dog Latin home to bogland (Ireland), can hardly be expected.

The do-it-yourself exercise attempted here is intended also to show native readers that, while they try out switchboard connections and are forced to reflect on what the text may try to say, they are behaving like foreigners in search of sense and meaning. The perspectives given here, and the way the cards have been stacked against translators, are highly unfair and amount to a falsification. The bullockbefriending collocations may be valid by being part of the novel's intricate potential, but they are only a few among many. The above approach is as instructive and as misleading as many others. The translations should therefore be appreciated by quite different criteria, such as "accuracy" (by now, it is hoped, a somewhat shaky notion), tonal effect, or idiomatic punch.

Up to a point, *Ulysses* makes stridently clear (in the original or in translation) that we are all foreigners lost in a labyrinth. The main characters feel unacclimatized at best. Marion Bloom, with an obscure Spanish-Jewish mother named Lunita Laredo, is apt to pass judgment on Dublin in view of her childhood memories in colonial Gibraltar. Bloom's lost roots go back to Hungary and a Jewishness from which he is also excluded. Stephen Dedalus sees himself dispossessed. These topics no longer need further elaboration. In day-to-day transactions it is not so much the lack of foreign languages that causes misunderstanding, but our different perspectives or expectations, the various codes existing side by side. Dialogues are often at cross purposes (Stephen and Mr Deasy; Bloom and Bantam Lyons; much of the talking in Barney Kiernan's). This becomes most poignant when Leopold Bloom and Stephen Dedalus are finally brought together (which, in our novel-reading code, should become a climax) and some talk is attempted, largely by Bloom, but little communication occurs. Some of the conversation might just as well be conducted in different languages.

Bloom in the morning carefully and resiliently translates a difficult word of Greek origin to his wife, a word he first has to extract from a Mollyesque assimilation, "Met him. . . ." He first chooses a key too high and intellectual, "transmigration," which is scoffed at ("O rocks! . . . tell us in plain words"). Then he solicitously prepares for another hard word, "reincarnation," by homely phrasing ("some people believe . . . that we go on living in another body after death") while thinking of a suitable graphic illustration (*U* 64–65). In the Eumaeus episode with roles reversed, this considerate man, usually so much aware of the grasp of his audience, is exposed to statements jerkily expressed by Mr Dedalus, poet and professor, who all along has shown supreme disregard for his listeners. So paternal Bloom misses the patristic jargon of "soul" as "a simple substance," and responds in terms of X-rays and "simple souls" (*U* 633–34). Let us try to imagine just what it might be that Bloom actually registers when he is treated to the following discourse:

> the lutenist Dowland who lived in Fetter Lane near Gerard the herbalist, who *anno ludendo hausi, Doulandus*, an instrument he was contemplating purchasing from Mr Arnold Dolmetsch . . . and Farnaby and son with their *dux* and *comes* conceits and Byrd (William), who played the virginals . . . and one Tomkins who made toys or airs and John Bull. (*U* 661–62)

their bully beef (*U* 398)	bully tapsters' wives (*U* 193)	Bully about the muzzle he looks. Bosses the show. (*U* 103)
leur barbaque de cambuse (386)	des épouses de cabaretiers brutaux (185)	Un fort en gueule, ça se voit. Le grand manitou de l'affaire. (98)
mit ihrem verseuchten Büchsenfleisch (449)	prahlender Zapfkellner Weiber (220)	Ums Maul sieht er bullig aus. Schwingt die Fuchtel. (120)
med sin oxestek (404)	frodiga vintapparkvinnor (201)	Köttig om nosen. Chef för teatern. (110)
e i loro torelli baldanzosi (539)	spose di rozzi tavernieri (262)	Ha un muso da prepotente. È il padrone del vapore. (145)
met hun vlees in blik (462)	de vrouwen van bullebakken van tappers (226)	Wat een bullebak met zo'n muil. De baas van het spul. (121)
mit ihrem Weckfleisch (559)	bulliger Zapfkellner Weiber (271)	Bullig ums Maul sieht er aus. Schmeisst die ganze Chose. (146)
con sus novillos y todo (II, 41)	mujeres de taberneros chulos (I, 325)	Tiene cara de chulo con esa jeta. Domina la función. (I, 206)

the famous champion bull of the
Romans, *Bos Bovum*, which is good
bog Latin for boss of the show.
(*U* 401)

Ulysses
(New York: Random House, 1961)

du fameux taureau champion des
Romains, *Bos Bovum*, qui signifie en
bon latin de latrine le patron de la
boîte. (395)

Ulysse (1929)
tr. Auguste Morel (Paris: Gallimard,
1948)

des berühmten Preisbullen der
Römer war, des *Bos Bovum*, was in
gutem Latrinenlatein Besitzer der
Bude bedeutet.[18] (452)

Ulysses (1927/1930)
tr. Georg Goyert (Zürich: Rhein
Verlag, 1956)

av den berömda mästertjuren i Rom,
Bos Bovum, vilket är gott kökslatin
för överstebov. (407)

Odysseus (1964)
tr. Th. Warburton (Stockholm:
Albert Bonniers Förlag, 1964)

del famoso toro campione dei ro-
mani, *Bos Bovum*, che significa in
buon *latinorum*, padrone del vapore.
(543)

Ulisse (1960)
tr. Giulio di Angelis (Milan: Arnoldo
Mondadori, 1960)

die beroemde stier der Romeinen,
Bos Bovum, wat in goed rioollatijn
betekent baas van het spul. (464)

Ulysses (1969)
tr. John Vandenbergh (Amsterdam:
De Bezige Bij, 1969)

des berühmten Preisbullen der
Römer, *Bos Bovum*, . . . was gutes
Küchenlatein ist und heisst ver-
dolmetscht Der Boss vons Janze.
(562)

Ulysses (1976)
tr. Hans Wollschläger (Frankfurt:
Suhrkamp, 1976)

del famoso toro campeón de los
romanos, *Bos Bovum*, lo que en buen
latín macarronico quiere decir el amo
del cotarro. (II, 44)

Ulises (1976)
tr. J. M. Valverde (Barcelona: Editorial Lumen, 1976)

We have it on good authority that Bloom is understandably misdirected by "John Bull." As for the rest we can only guess. Bloom is "not perfectly certain" (*U* 662); he must be shut out, "out of doors," from most of this. The Latin is beyond him (might he hear something like "lewd house"?); *dux* is likely to sound like something in English that it is not; and what is a casual listener to make of fetter, bird, or toys? In one wrong sense, "conceits" is right. The names themselves must be cryptic. "Farnaby and son" sounds like a Dublin firm and not like historical composers. As Bloom is not an expert on ancient instruments, nor a reader of Joyce's *Letters* or Richard Ellmann's biography, he has no way of knowing who Arnold Dolmetsch is.[19] It is a tantalizing touch that, when so much noncommunication is around, Joyce throws out the name of a real person whose name in German, if it were understood, would mean exactly what at this juncture is most needed between the two, an "interpreter."

When in the next chapter some interchange of speech and of ideas finally does occur between the two different temperaments, it is ironically removed from our reach by its presentation in a form of abstract, scientific, unfelt English, which is, pointedly, written, never spoken. We will mentally change this language into the sort of idiom it is meant to replace. Runs like "disintegration of obsession" (*U* 695) will normally be rendered into something else within the same language, something very painful and direct. One psychological justification for Ithaca is that it keeps emotions at a Latinate distance. The mode of Ithaca is one last variant of the many intralingual translations in *Ulysses*. The book exposes not only a wide range of languages, but also the regional, temporal, social, and hierarchical width of the English language. Joyce in particular adds historical diversification. When a librarian has been described as "bald, eared and assiduous" (*U* 190), it is odd to come upon "singular uneared wombs" (*U* 202) a few pages later. We get an almost surrealistic effect. This is continued two chapters later with similar anatomic confusion: "womb of woman eyeball" (*U* 286). But, naturally, "uneared" does not denote an absence of the organs of hearing but is an obsolete recall, through a Shakespearean echo, of an Indo-European verb for ploughing (cognate with Latin *arare*). The semantic shock will spur us on to translate it into our own time.[20]

Ulysses is probably the first consistently intratransferential fictional work. Oxen of the Sun manifests this aspect best and most irritatingly, in a historical series of literary devices and linguistic growth. Not only have morphology and syntax changed over the centuries, but also customs and mores, attitudes, conventions, epical techniques and narrative emphases—the most radical, continuous intratranslation. No wonder this chapter is still the least assimilated one, and one impossible to translate "adequately." In some critical dismissals of its idiosyncracies we may still detect a streak of that mentality that Joyce, after all, has thematized and mocked: that whatever is foreign is unnecessary or arbitrary, if not downright inferior.

The chapter modes of *Ulysses* are, in the view presented here, so many different translations, renderings in keys that could be labeled breezy, gastronomical, literary, locative, orchestral, polyphemous, daydreamy, etc., and the separate labels matter less than the idea of a conjugation of all of language's potential and all stylistic ranges. We do not need *"Introibo ad altare Dei"* as an initial pointer, or a blatant hybrid like "Deshil Holles Eamus" as a midway reminder, nor a farewell display of "Ronda . . . posadas" (*U* 782), to learn, the hard way, what Bloom has always known, that we are in certain constellations aliens and fumbling outsiders. The foreign reader simply notices this plight a trifle more tangibly.

As always, proportions change when we come to *Finnegans Wake*. There non-English readers are truly lost, especially since they rely on their eyes and their ability to spell out graphic shapes more than on their ears for hidden sounds in hidden words. The lack of childhood echoes, sayings, songs, nursery rhymes, and the like is a severe drawback. Foreigners may take some slight comfort in the fact, freely confessed, that native readers remain in the dark as well when they have to sort out so much that is unfamiliar and alien, and above all when they have to extract their own language from the circumambient verbiage. In a conglomerate like "perensempry sex of fun to help a dazzle off the othour" (*FW* 364.24), we may detect Latin words, sex, perhaps saxophone, long before the author's dazzle also reveals a homely phrase, "six of one and half a dozen of the other." At least it is indicated by ancillary works that such back-renderings are indeed necessary.[21]

Paradoxically, the *Wake* is the most forbiddingly xenophobic of all prose works, and yet at the same time it extends a catholic welcome to all foreigners by meeting them on their own territory, and very specifically. It often says so, in "wordloosed . . . in cellelleneteutoslavzendlatinsoundscript" (*FW* 219.16) addressing the Indo-European family; in other parts it speaks Japanese or Maori. It offers foreign readers snippets that perhaps only they can understand. A Swahili speaker can count ALP's children in "meanacuminamoyas" (*FW* 201.30), which somehow adds up to 111, and there is confirmation in Hebrew numerology appended: "Olaph lamm et, all that pack." An Irish reader would be struck by an ironic interjection, "-moya," which throws doubt on whatever was said before; that too is a Wakean linguistic caution. A Swiss, coming upon "mean fawthery eastend appullcelery, old laddy he high hole" (*FW* 586.27), may wonder what is being told about apples and celery in the eastend, but may recognize at some moment that the whole also transliterates a familiar dialect song, "Min Fatter ist en Appezäller," which simply says that "my father is from (the canton of) Appenzell." To detect something familiar in an exotic guise is a basic pleasure and an incentive. A little bit of rummaging may turn up the appropriateness of the name leading back to Latin *"abbatis cella,"* the cell of the abbot (and *abbas* of course means father). The historical abbot in question was Irish, St. Gall, who was sent east to convert the heathen. Actually there is not just one canton called Appenzell, but two:

the father's cell split up during some wars over religion, and a Wakean family configuration is here echoed in Swiss history and geography. Both Appenzells, looking almost fetally entwined on the map, are moreover wholly surrounded by the canton of St. Gall, like "wrestless in the womb" (*FW* 143.21)—all of which merely exemplifies *Finnegans Wake's* outstanding obligingness. A perfect provincial miniature has been integrated, which serves well to demonstrate to a purely Swiss audience some of the overall themes and dynamics. The next line will nationalize a standard figure of the *Wake* with more local color: "Seekersenn" (*FW* 586.28) contains a name, Senn, which is very common (especially in the cantons mentioned), and also a noun that immediately evokes images of cows, cheese, and butter (*Senn* is an alpine cowherd). This connects with a Swiss German incarnation of Shaun ("Haensli") and Shem ("Koebi") within the Burris-Caseous entanglement (*FW* 163.5). The song that triggered off all these associations continues, as every Swiss would know, with the Appenzell father eating cheese. From all of this, meanwhile, the non-Swiss reader is largely excluded but will at least instantly click into tune when "old laddy he high hole" is recognized as the yodeling refrain.

Of course the distinction between native and foreign has by now become very questionable and idle. Dublin is a good city, and Ireland a much-afflicted country, to bear this out. *Finnegans Wake* unravels and reentangles colonial sedimentation through language. When native and invader crosstalk in French, donsk, scowegian, or anglease, and excheck a few strong verbs (*FW* 16.4–5), discrimination between settler and intruder, inhabitant and conqueror, seller or buyer, guest or enemy, is instantly rendered futile. A later reenactment of a similar encounter, this time garbled by Muta and Juva, is similarly confused and polyglot (*FW* 609–10). Certainty becomes a matter of betting: "Tempt to wom Outsider!" (*FW* 610.18). Everyone—Firbolg, Milesian, Celt, Viking, Norman, Sassenach, or Jew—was once an outsider. "Paybads floriners moved in hugheknots" (*FW* 541.14) refers to a specific historical occasion, but it seems to generalize that foreigners, often refugees, have difficulties with their currencies and may be a nuisance or poor risks. It is again interesting that the Huguenots, a dispersed minority, got their name from a word meaning confederates (by oath, German *Eid-genoss*). Contrary to this implication, they were disbanded and persecuted, but then found new homes and, on the whole, adapted very well and were beneficial to their new communities. Words can have similar divaricating careers.

Finnegans Wake, with its hugheknots in polyglot, is solipsistic in speaking only to itself about itself. It is aristocratic in addressing small erudite elites, even though no single expertise gets any of them very far. *Finnegans Wake* is uniquely democratic and as global as UNESCO in accepting all of us and turning all of us into foreign readers, evoking that typical mixture of frustration and fascination. So that, though we still do not understand, we simply cannot let go.

1981

Notes

1. One would have a rough idea of what all other words mean within that first paragraph simply from the company they keep. Even if one did not know the meaning of "maleficent" (*D* 9), it could be approximately determined by its surroundings.
2. The phrasing "the Euclid" shows that this name has come to stand for a subject, or a book.
3. Meanings given by Liddell and Scott's *Greek-English Lexicon*. Further derivations used in this essay are of course (see *SH* 26, 30) from Walter W. Skeat, *An Etymological Dictionary of the English Language* (Oxford: Clarendon Press, 1879–82).
4. The Greek *pneuma* (for "air," but also "ghost," "spirit") is later replaced by a disease in Eliza's uneducated phrase "one of them new-fangled carriages that makes no noise . . . them with the rheumatic wheels" (*D* 17). Verbal undercurrents of this kind were pointed out in my "He Was Too Scrupulous Always: Joyce's 'The Sisters,' " *James Joyce Quarterly* 2, no. 2 (Winter 1965): 66–72.
5. "[C]ertain institutions of the Church which I had always regarded as the simplest acts" (*D* 13). *Acts!* Later on Joyce was to use such words as clues or hidden pointers for his sources. Here it *could* be aptly coincidental.
6. Oddly enough, the plural form implied by absence, *"maria,"* looks very much like the name of the Virgin in Latin.
7. *Dedalus,* trans. Ludmilla Savitzky, 15th ed. (Paris: Gallimard, n.d.), pp. 17–20.
8. *El artista adolescente,* trans. Alfonso Donado [Dámaso Alonso] (Madrid: Editorial Biblioteca Nueva, 1963), pp. 27–30.
9. *Dedalus,* trans. Cesare Pavese (Milan: Adelphi Edizioni, 1976), pp. 3–6.
10. *Jugendbildnis,* trans. Georg Goyert (Zürich: Rhein Verlag, 1926), pp. 8–13.
11. *Ein Porträt des Künstlers als junger Mann,* trans. Klaus Reichert (Frankfurt: Suhrkamp, 1972), pp. 7–10. The form "sönen" represents childish mispronunciation.
12. *"Ulysses,"* review by Domini Canis (Shane Leslie), *Dublin Review* 171 (Sept. 1922): 112–19, reprinted in *James Joyce: The Critical Heritage,* ed. Robert H. Deming (London: Routledge and Kegan Paul, 1970), I, 200–203.
13. Don Gifford and Robert J. Seidman, *Notes for Joyce: An Annotation of James Joyce's "Ulysses"* (New York: Dutton, 1974), gloss *"Terribilia meditans"* (*U* 45) as "Terrible to mediate" (p. 42). It is not the misprint ("mediate" for "meditate") that is objectionable, but the syntactic ignorance, which may be passed on.
14. Zack Bowen, who also notices that *"nomine Domini . . . doesn't fit the tune,"* has a different view and attributes the "error" clearly to Joyce. See his *Musical Allusions in the Works of James Joyce* (Albany: State University of New York Press, 1974), p. 197.
15. In all fairness it has to be said that *A "Ulysses" Phrasebook* by Helen H. Macaré (Portola Valley, Calif.: Woodside Prior, 1981), the sort of book that explains the foreign parts of *Ulysses,* here offers a gloss that is acceptable and helpful: "beefy about the jaw" (p. 26). The *Phrasebook* is otherwise incredibly unreliable.

16. Translations, too, may bully each other. The German version of 1927 avoided the issue with a flat "mit all ihrem Fleisch" (Zürich: Rhein Verlag, II, 396). This was revised in 1930 and in many subsequent printings to "können sie mit ihrem Ochsenlouis die Blattern dazu kriegen . . ." (1930, II, 28). Here "Louis" catches the meaning of a "protector of a prostitute" or "bully." A connection was probably established with "two shawls and a bully on guard" (U 314); the German for this was "mit zwei Fosen und ein Louis passt auf . . ." (p. 353)—a *possible* link. In a later "Sonderausgabe" (special edition) in one volume ("Copyright 1956," according to its imprint), a different, third version appears. The publishers accepted suggestions received in letters, with or (probably) without Georg Goyert's consent. In this case the French rendering, "leur barbaque de cambuse," most likely served as a guideline and correction, and in the process what is merely bad meat in French (and perhaps from another animal: one etymology of "barbaque" is a Rumanian word for "mutton"), is amplified to "infected"—"verseucht," a word that seems to have been induced by "Seuche," for "plague" (U 398).

17. Remember that it is a current theme in *A Portrait*, where Stephen gets the appellation "*Bous Stephanoumenos*" (P 168, U 210, 415). *Bous* is the Greek equivalent of Latin *bos;* Homer uses the plural "*boes*" for the oxen, or rather the kine, of Helios. Antiquity often brought gods and oxen, or bulls, together; the animals were sacrificed, there was taurine worship (as on Crete), and there is the proverbial contrast, "*Quod licet Jovi, non licet bovi.*" Consider also echoes like "Thou shalt not *muzzle* the mouth of an ox . . ." (Deut. 25:4), to which St. Paul adds a question: "Does God care for oxen?" (1 Cor. 9:9; the Vulgate uses a form of *bos*). We know that Helios, for one, did care about his cattle and that Odysseus was to suffer for it. Even Stephen's often quoted "*dio boia*, hangman god," which is doubtless all in all in all of us . . ." (U 213), is rooted in this theme. The Italian *boia* for "hangman" goes back to a Greek adjective *boeios* (straps were once made from the hides of the animals). Homer mentions several such oxhides; one "*boeiê*" is described as "newly flayed" (*Odyssey* 22. 363–64). We find exactly this in a Cyclopian translation, "garment of recently flayed oxhide" (U 296). It is the Citizen mock-epically exalted, and this famous bully (and compare our quote at U 401 with "Bullyfamous" in FW 229.15) has a hangman mentality. Joyce's early warning, "Don't play the giddy ox with me" (U 7) is justified.

18. The German version of 1927 was "*Bos Bovum*, welches je für ihn in seiner Stellung ein vorzüglicher Name war" (II, 402); this is very vague and inexact. Its revised form again follows the French.

19. *Letters* I, 54; Richard Ellmann, *James Joyce* (New York: Oxford University Press, 1959), pp. 159–61.

20. Once more *this* step does not translate. In exact Italian, "singoli venti non arati" (p. 274), there is no disturbance nor any historical adjustment; the French version, "touchant les pucelages récalcitrants" (p. 198), is a free paraphrase.

21. Roland McHugh, *Annotations to "Finnegans Wake"* (London: Routledge and Kegan Paul, 1980), p. 364; Dounia Bunis Christiani, *Scandinavian Elements of "Finnegans Wake"* (Evanston: Northwestern University Press, 1965), p. 180, et passim.

II.

On *Reading*: Dynamics of Corrective Unrest

4

Dynamics of
Corrective Unrest

One of the effects Joyce's works can have on us is to make us see the obvious. Another is to create the impression that Joyce often *does* with words—not just *says*—what we may have always known, but which now we experience as acted out, as though the words were to perform what, normally, is merely being talked about. And it is upon this that the focus will be narrowed here, on a tradition that is essentially humanist, perhaps nothing more than a rehearsal of the old Socratic position of elementary ignorance. Joyce found new modes to express the trite insight that truth is elusive, that the best our minds can do is to grope for it and to improve on the groping.

To devise verbal equivalents for the mind's groping is one of Joyce's better-known achievements. He did not smooth over the fact that most of our thinking is hit or miss; and he reminds us that language, especially when it becomes public, inevitably tends to falsify the provisional nature of our perception and of our understanding. He perfected devices to counteract the pretense of certainty that is inherent in many of our statements. What will interest us here is the Joycean variation of the old theme that *"errare humanum est."* That *errare* can be mental as well as physical, and that to err also means to wander, is an oddly fitting Odyssean touch, which Joyce also exploits. And we may note here initially that the verb "err" is also built right into the first word of *Finnegans Wake,* "riverrun," where indeed it belongs.

We err, we stray, we are mistaken, we see as through a glass, darkly, we are locked into our own little cognitive systems, we project ourselves into the realities we set out to understand. But we are also equipped with the faculty to adjust our views, to learn, to compare, and even to improve. Such common-places in Joyce are not just stated and described, but thematized and vividly integrated. To demonstrate this, mainly with a few inductive examples, will be the subject of this essay.

It is a characteristic of Joyce's representational prose that almost any passage would do to illustrate a principle, but there are some phrases that seem to serve the purpose exceptionally well. So let me turn to *Ulysses,* a novel—if novel it is—that acknowledges itself in an epic tradition that it changes at the same time, and a novel early readers had admittedly great difficulties just coming to grips with. Some basic distinctions seemed impos-sible to arrive at. So the book appeared outrageous, iconoclastic, chaotic, and formless. It was pronounced unreadable. Though we no longer support it, we can easily sympathize with this latter claim. In fact the notion of "reading" literature is no longer quite what it was before *Ulysses;* it has become a much more self-conscious skill. Liberties were being taken with language, and we can imagine without strain how an earlier reader, premodernist, perhaps an editor, or let's suppose an old-fashioned schoolmaster, might have reacted to some of the phrasings. My example is not a blatant flouting of conventions, but a low-key oddity that occurs at the beginning of the Hades chapter, when Leopold Bloom, as the last and least member of a small social group, enters the funeral carriage and sits down "in the vacant place." With perceptible nervousness he fiddles with the door of a less than perfect vehicle. The sentence that Joyce wrote originally is accurate and harmless: "He pulled the door to after him and slammed it twice till it shut tight." But then he changed just one word, replacing "twice" by an adjective that is there already; and now we are faced with something we might consider a trifle askew, something that a traditional stylist might well have considered objectionable, or sloppy: "He pulled the door to after him and slammed it tight till it shut tight" (*U* 87). The repetition causes some awkwardness—which we latter-day readers can now of course interpret as a stylistic equivalent to the air of social constraint that is being indicated without any overt reference. The two tight's may actually make us aware of a silence that is both decorous, with the occasion, and uncomfortable, and we get a sense of the intrusion of an unwanted fourth member of the party. It is typical of Bloom that he fills the uneasy silence with some active bustle, here a struggle with a resistant door mechanism. Stylistic elegance would have refined a feeling of embarrassment out of existence.

It is the serial use of the same adjective, *tight,* that is queer and slightly discomposing. So we are called up to account for the irregularity. An element of time has become more noticeable. Once we have taken in the whole sentence, that first "he slammed it tight" turns out, by hindsight, to have meant its opposite, that is to say "not tight"; for a further effort was neces-sary. In the first attempt there was only an appearance of a tightly shut door, and only the second adjective denotes the improved result. So the identical word has two meanings, which we might call appearance and fact. The first one is a failed effort, the second one a success. Or we might reinterpret the whole sentence as one containing some narrative shift, first a perspective close to Bloom's own impression, the second one more like an objective statement. My rather laborious endeavor to articulate something we think we sense directly merely illustrates our habitual clumsiness in spelling out discursively what Joyce renders in brief phrases of irritating, diversified appropriateness. That my descriptive phrases are in need of further qualification is part of what I am trying to convey.

If "diversified appropriateness" sounds like an exaggeration for the mere repetition of the same adjective, we may, for a test, observe what happens to Joyce's phrase when it has to be rendered into a different language. I invite the audience to speculate, for an inward moment, how that phrase—assuming that all the tensions I have drawn attention to are a vital part of the meaning— *could* be adequately turned into Spanish. The two existent translations I have consulted offer the following. One is by J. Salas Subirat:[1]

> Tiró de la puerta detrás de él y la volvió a golpear fuerte hasta que se cerró bien. (121)

The other one, more recent, is by J. M. Valverde:[2]

> Tiró de la portezuela tras de sí y dando con ella un portazo la cerró bien apretada. (I, 183)

As far as I can make out the repetition is not retained, nor does there seem to be the same stylistic discomfort.

What we do get, clearly, is a sense of someone who persists, who improves on an initial fumble. We get a minor close-up of that Odyssean perseverance that characterizes Bloom. It is a trait Joyce singles out in his introduction earlier of the new character Leopold Bloom in chapter four. This happens at a moment when the novel itself does something similar, when it changes its gears and settles for another approach as its material. After three highly idiosyncratic chapters, in tune with the mental processes of Stephen Dedalus, we now find the clock set back to the beginning, the locality changed and similar as well as different experience treated in a different key, more down to earth, in a more ordinary way. And this is our first information about what Leopold Bloom, whose indirect thoughts open the new chapter, is actually doing:

> Kidneys were in his mind as he moved about the kitchen softly, righting her breakfast things on the humpy tray. (*U* 55)

We may well wonder what exactly Bloom's activity is, tucked away as it is into a mere subordinate clause. The verb Joyce uses, "to right," is not often used like this, nonmetaphorically. Again, the broader range of this verb is appreciated much more in comparison with translated versions, and I think it is with a slight sense of dissatisfaction at a narrower semantic spectrum. There seems to be much more involuntary precision in the Spanish phrasings,

> . . . disponiendo las cosas del desayuno de ella (Subirat, 87)

and

> . . . preparándole a ella las cosas del desayuno . . . (Valverde, I, 139)

(and the same seems to be true in all the translations that I have been able to look at). We register the loss of some general notion of righting, of arranging some breakfast things in such a manner that it can be accepted as "right," as the text will soon indicate: "Another slice of bread and butter: three, four: right. She didn't like her plate full. Right." There is a goal-orientation in "righting," as the original has it, which appears to be absent from "disponiendo" or "preparándole." We will learn very soon in the chapter that "her," the person whose judgment seems to be decisive, will be Bloom's wife Molly, upstairs in her bed, and we will also learn, if we care to find out, that the required spatial disposition of cup and saucer and toast on the tray will not figure among her outspoken concerns. So perhaps Bloom's initial endeavor may be an entire waste. What we do appreciate is the endeavor, a typical one. From the very start, Bloom is moving about and righting. This is an eminently human activity, and a necessary one. We will find Leopold Bloom at it all the time. He may not be successful, but he keeps trying. Whether it is a matter of explaining a foreign word to his wife, or making a point in a barroom debate, or coaxing a new companion, or securing an advertisement, Bloom is not easily balked and will persevere, often with a change in tactics. He is resilient and ready to adapt his approach. He has all kinds of plans for civic improvements, an ambition that finds its grotesque apotheosis, as it well deserves, in the phantasmagoric surges of the Circe chapter. In all of this Bloom is also true to his role of Odysseus, that arch-righter who excels in adjustive skills, who is never at a loss, a man of many devices.

So the activity of "righting"—and I will insist that it is an act, a process— is inconspicuously heralded at the beginning of Calypso, but it is not of course anything novel in the canon. It has always been an essential feature in the earliest *Dubliners* stories. It also found a strategic and grandiloquent expression in Joyce's famous letter to the publisher Grant Richards: that his intention was ". . . to write a chapter of the moral history" of his country (5 May 1906; *Letters* II, 134). Many of the stories concern themselves at least with the possibility of some amendment, often only with a futile attempt toward it. "Grace," for example, is about the "righting" of the ways of Thomas Kernan, victim of an accident due to alcoholic overindulgence. A rescue mission is being staged by solicitous friends who try to maneuver him toward a better life. The conclusive sermon by a Jesuit priest drives home the point, in the terminology of men of business:

—Well, I have looked into my accounts. I find this wrong and this wrong. But, with God's grace, I will rectify this and this. I will set right my accounts. (*D* 174)

It remains doubtful, and in fact improbable, whether Mr Kernan will mend his ways and set right his accounts; and it is up to us as readers even to question whether the particular solution attempted would be an improvement. The rectifying process includes the reading itself, and we are at least given some options to dissent from the views expressed within the story. So we might notice an implied contrast between a priest belaboring the need for setting right one's accounts and the satisfaction uttered by Martin Cunningham in the story that the order to which the same priest belongs, "the Jesuit Order was never once reformed" (*D* 164). Such crossreferential hints can help us re-form our opinions; they function as correctives against simplification.

"The Sisters," the first story in the collection, sets a precedent, as it were, by negation. Something, clearly, has gone wrong in Father Flynn's life, and it remains intriguing that we never quite discover what exactly it was. It becomes our task to rearrange scraps of not very reliable information into some coherent account. There is little chance that we would ever agree on one particular, "right," interpretation—answers have so far been looked for in psychology, medicine, theology, and elsewhere. In "The Dead" we watch the main character, Gabriel Conroy, in repeated attempts to rectify one uneasy situation after another, until one he never suspected throws him entirely off balance. At some stages he imagines he can improve on the situations by a change of his wording, or his tone, but the last disillusionment calls for a more profound readjustment. And again we, as readers, are correspondingly enabled to improve on our own previous assessment. On a second reading we can rearrange little incidents or trivial statements like "we're in for a night of it," or "Snow is general all over Ireland," in the light of contexts we had not discovered before. Under our eyes the story changes in its implications and in its reach. The addition of "The Dead" to the whole collection also gives it a different dimension.

Since *A Portrait Of the Artist as a Young Man* is about growing up, it entails a good deal of righting and survival adjustment. It may take the dominant form of learning, of absorbing knowledge at school or, by trial and error, of mastering various essential skills, or else of amending one's life according to Christian ideals, or again of groping one's way toward some chosen vocation. The *Portrait* is a novel of redirection.

Much of its first chapter is devoted to distinguishing such basic notions as "right" and "wrong," which is at best a hazardous experience. That first chapter alone contains thirty instances of that tricky adjective, "right." Being asked whether he kisses his mother before going to bed, Stephen Dedalus answers "I do" and is instantly mocked. His emended reply, "I don't," provokes exactly the same unpleasant result and makes him wonder "What was the right answer to the question" and, second, "was it right to kiss his mother or wrong to kiss his mother?" (*P* 14). Of course the coupling of such fundamental questions with, of all things, kissing one's mother adds a host of psychological complexities, and even without those the notion of what is right proves extremely involved. The climactic Christmas dinner scene hinges largely also on the question of who is right, Parnell and his followers, or the priests who contributed to his downfall. Grownups, who ought to know, differ violently over the justice of spitting into a pious woman's eyes; the issue seems to be connected with one's affiliations or one's position, and, oddly enough, in some languages "right" can also denote one of two possible sides in space. In a third instance of the moral or judiciary sense of "right," Stephen—in consequence of someone's vague transgression that agitates the whole school—is wrongly punished by a cruel and undiscriminating teacher. But he musters courage and appeals to the highest authority of the institution, Father Conmee, who promises to set matters right, and the chapter ends on a note of triumph (which will later be qualified). It is appropriate that the priest who will redress such wrongs carries the official title of "the Rector," and few of us probably notice that this word occurs very frequently within the first chapter, in fact no fewer than thirty-eight times.

What is a fairly new feature of the novel is that its reader, *lector,* is enlisted to become also its interpretative *rector,* someone to sift and evaluate, and not just to accept, the views put forth in the book. We are given ample opportunity to assess situations critically and in the light of further development. The esthetic views propounded by Stephen Dedalus toward the end have been taken to be applicable to—or else in ironic contrast to—the novel within which they occur. This esthetic theory is in itself a rearrangement, and subjective improvement, of the views of Aristotle, St. Thomas Aquinas, Lessing, and others. It states that "Art . . . is the human disposition of sensible or intelligible matter for an esthetic end" as a basic premise (*P* 208). "Disposition" means a pleasing arrangement or order; in literature it also means the right words in the right order; and we suddenly find ourselves not very far from a kitchen in Eccles street no. 7, where Leopold Bloom occupies himself with a judicious disposition of breakfast implements for a domestic end. In quintessential triviality Bloom is striving for an everyday correspondence to Stephen's former lofty, artistic aims.

And at this stage what may originally have sounded like a disturbing coincidence may appear to be not quite so accidental after all. When we only *hear* that initial Bloom sentence, "he moved about the kitchen softly, *righting* . . ." we may momentarily be led astray, and we will have to reject the homonymous (graphic) "writing" in the light of syntactic guidance that will immediately follow. But writing, say using a pen, as it happens, is a matter of arranging, adjusting words and of getting them in a right order, and often a matter of careful revising. We know for a fact—and we can verify it by inspecting more than sixty bulky volumes of facsimiles of Joyce's revisions— that Joyce himself moved about a lot writing and rewriting, rectifying and adding according to principles that themselves were being adapted. Joyce also altered his ground plans, or his schemas. A glance at thousands of pages is live evidence of graphic writing coinciding with corrective righting. The novel *Ulysses* was moreover considered a contemporary adaptation of a Greek epic, a modern adjustment. And the Greek epic was thought to be, according to the thesis of a French scholar that Joyce found expedient, a Greek righting of Phoenician nautical know-how, a cultural transformation to which Joyce could then all the more readily add his own revisions.

Righting is offered here as a convenient, compact, synecdochal illustration of a process that characterizes *Ulysses*. Or, to be more exact, it conflates various closely interrelated processes that are difficult to keep apart. At least four different aspects need to be singled out:

1. A character trait of persons within the book, notably Leopold Bloom, who is motivated by an urge to set matters right and equipped with a sober awareness that he himself may not be, but who is willing to rethink, rephrase, reattempt. His thinking is distinguished by alternatives and new starts. On women's menstruation, for example:

> Something in the air. That's the moon. But then why don't all women menstruate at the same time with same moon, I mean? Depends on the time they were born, I suppose. Or all start scratch and then get out of step. (*U* 368)

Bloom rarely deludes himself that he has reached a final solution. His skeptical "but then" and cautious "I suppose" remain typical and contribute to his being less than a resolute agent, or fierce avenger.

2. Righting suggests and echoes Joyce's own artistic procedures, a series of revisions, retouchings, improvements—a development also from the comparatively simple prose of *Dubliners* to the polyglot, heterographic complexity of *Finnegans Wake*. Quite parenthetically, "Joyce moved about . . . writing" might be the shortest biographical condensation.

3. Righting also affects, or ought to affect, the reader/critic; and

4. The book itself tends toward ameliorative diversity. *Ulysses,* as an event in words, seems to try to right itself through more words, as though it wanted to undo the damage of all previous presentations. The novel begins by setting off the views and talents of a lively Buck Mulligan against those of a somewhat morose and distanced Stephen Dedalus; and each of the three opening chapters also intensifies the impact of private thought and subjective refraction. But then, in the second book, a new character takes over and the book takes on a new character too, with alternative ways of processing experience. And before we are quite used to the shift, the novel begins to move

away more and more stridently from the early illusion of *reality* to a sense that literary realism, like all other devices, *is* an *illusion* and a conscious artifice. So the book increasingly, but fluctuatingly, reveals its existence as a literary artifact, and it sets out to change the modes of its own being. It tackles its tasks with highly different narrative programs, some of which are frankly conventional, others entirely new or extravagant. Since no single perspective is privileged, but all have their unique accomplishments as well as decided drawbacks, Joyce allows each of them to correct the others.

In this sense *Ulysses* is a series of radical rectifications, of alternative dispositions for varying esthetic ends. The change of techniques and styles, so often commented on, also has a remedial function. It is as though the novel itself develops a Bloomian type of consciousness of its own stratified inadequacies and counteracts or compensates whatever it is that it has been attempting so far.

In some instances a later passage literally corrects a preceding one. The last pages of the Oxen of the Sun chapter are a challenge to us. We habitually construe them as a jumble of verbiage spoken by the characters who are present. And we consider it part of our job to discern which speaker is saying which particular sentence in which role and with what kind of mannerisms. In the next chapter, Circe, it is precisely this that the author has settled for us in neat typographical order: the speaker, whether an actual person or not, is capitalized; in a parenthesis, in what has all the appearance of a stage direction, gestures, costume, and behavioristic information are set off in italics; and speech is clearly marked as such. From one point of view, this is a definite improvement by inversion; but we will soon discover that consistent application of this mode has its own shortcomings. And again it is up to the readers to correct a possible first impression that the divisions introduced are simply stage conventions, and as we go through a chapter characterized by external uniformity, we are tempted to apply categories that become more and more comprehensive and take us further away from personal, psychological, or even subconscious perspectives.

At this point already it has proved wholly impossible to keep apart the novel's corrective urges from the remedial burden thrown on the reader. The Joycean reader inevitably becomes a critic in the word's most original significance: one who sifts, discerns, judges, qualifies, makes distinctions. The difference is merely that Joyce lets us ignore less easily that we are required to do mental repair work. At one time we had to learn how to process the techniques labeled "stream of consciousness," which was often a matter of completing sentences that were psychological rather than grammatical. Such a learning or conditioning goes on with each new chapter. (It is revealing that Joyce sometimes lost a devoted reader and friend when he devised a new chapter of *Ulysses* for periodical publication.) In general we have succeeded least of all with Oxen of the Sun, that progressive string of historical narrative stances, each one of which projects the semblance of some period point of view, though none of the periods evoked could possibly have conducted its storytelling in that specific way. One result is that possibilities that would otherwise not have been accessible at the end of the nineteenth century can now be tapped. At the same time we are forcibly provoked to intervene and to wonder what may actually take place, or what words are being spoken. At every turn we are faced with incongruities and anachronisms that work against passive complacency. Part of the irritation this chapter causes may be due to our discomfort at the need to re-form, with little overt guidance, what is so obliquely presented, and to reform it beyond a simplistic translation into a twentieth-century rendering of what is supposedly actually going on.

The novel's self-redressive instinct is astir throughout. What in the Eumaeus chapter has often been taken for inert clumsiness and mere stereotype can also be experienced as an acute awareness of the narrative's own failures, which then are continually being compensated by additions and qualifications. The result is not of course apt concision (since nothing uttered can be cancelled), but an additive concatenation of rephrasings, demurs, falterings, new starts, or outright contradictions. In part this is also Bloom's fumbling alertness. The chapter is lengthened also because, on principle, no statement can ever become final, though attention may turn elsewhere. Take a short passage in which Bloom recounts his retort to the Citizen:

> So I, without deviating from plain facts in the least, told him his God, I mean Christ, was a jew too, and all his family, like me, though in reality I'm not. (*U* 643)

There is something self-contradictory in that sentence, for it contains precisely what Bloom says his retort did not, that is, deviations, and so does the whole chapter. Bloom throws in qualifications, either for the sake of clarity or else in healthy reaction against exaggerated claims. In his account "God" is instantly modified to "I mean Christ," and all kinds of trinitarian intricacies are conjured up at once. We also know that originally Bloom did not refer to Christ "and all his family" but "to his father" and then, in self-correction, to "his uncle" (*U* 342), so that we here observe Bloom at a retrospective improvement of his own former wording. But Bloom also realizes that his declared status as a Jew is not quite accurate by narrower definitions, and he adds a disclaimer, "though in reality I'm not." So his bias toward instant rectification is obvious, and it is all the more odd to see that this last phrase has been taken as final evidence of Bloom's not being Jewish, as though such complex problems of racial or religious or cultural identity could be settled simply because every line of thought is dropped at one particular point. What the Eumaeus chapter does is infuse skeptical caution about what a phrase like "in reality" could ever achieve, or it makes us wonder which of the several realities suggested should deserve priority.

When Bloom, very soon afterwards, offers the platitude that "It is hard to lay down any hard and fast rules as to right and wrong but room for improvement all round there certainly is," he also hits on the chapter's tendency and one of the novel's intellectual misgivings. There is indeed "room for improvement all round."

Eumaeus also redresses the subjective restriction of the opening parts of the novel by making ample allowance for digressions and editorial comment. The same holds true for Ithaca, whose format does not seem to preclude the insertion of any kind of heterogeneous matter—this in emphatic contrast to the entirely subjective last chapter. Ithaca presents itself as an opportune chance for apparently scientific verification, a penultimate righting in often quantifiable terms. Again it takes some discernment to uncover the chapter's factual reliability as partly spurious. The answers, it frequently turns out, simply generate more implied questions. The apparent terminal reassurance proves to become, in all probability, the most urgent appeal to the reader's corrective ingenuity. For one, the abstract, Latinate terminology entails the need for its translation into the kind of everyday, often emotional, language that is so carefully kept at a distance, as well as the need for human evaluation.

We may find an air of precision and neat differentiation:

> What proposal did Bloom, diambulist, father of Milly, somnambulist, make to Stephen, noctambulist? (*U* 695)

A minuscule system is set forth in which the three characters are categorized according to their walking habits, at a moment when none of them does any walking. The emphasis on ambulatory practices *may* (this is already a possible, but not necessary deduction) be induced by a consideration that the invitation to spend the night in Bloom's house, if accepted, would relieve Stephen of the need for further nocturnal wandering. The neologism "diambulist," incidentally, being the first term in a triadic splurge, is an example of semantic rectification in delayed recognition: what on a sporadic guess might still be a common prefix (Latin *di-*) rights itself into an abbreviated form of Latin *dies,* day, in Saussurean opposition to "noctambulist." But it is the succeeding "noct" that explains a preceding cryptic *"di."*

The threefold classification is prominent but, on closer inspection, somewhat deceptive. We may remember that Bloom has associated his daughter with sleepwalking (*U* 692). We have also witnessed Stephen Dedalus doing a fair amount of night-walking, and Bloom's Odyssean wanderings on that particular June day are a main subject of the book. The nomenclatural distribution works up to a point, without, however, achieving very much that we did not know already. In fact, the verbal overexpenditure alone is likely to incite us to investigate the conspicuous claims made by the labels. Most dictionaries would tell us that "noctambulist" is often used as a synonym for, and not a distinction from, "somnambulist," which observation merely proves that the apparent precision is less than perfect. Then we also know that Milly is not really a somnambulist; the term expresses more a fear that Bloom projects on his daughter than an actuality—this, at any rate, according to the evidence of an earlier passage (*U* 692). But above all we have little reason to assume that Stephen should be more of a nightwalker than Bloom; on the night in question, at any rate, they did their nightwalking together (and the previous chapter refers to both of them as "noctambules" (*U* 621). Or should perhaps Stephen as a noctambulist remind us tangentially of his own words, spoken earlier, that the "corpse of John Shakespeare does not walk the night" (*U* 207), echoing of course the lines of the ghost in the play *Hamlet* (1.5.10), which in turn have been echoed by Bloom during the day, a trifle inaccurately (*"Hamlet, I am thy father's spirit/Doomed for a certain time to walk the earth,"* *U* 152)? If so, that emphatic "noctambulist" would give a paternal twist to filial Stephen. Or maybe, more simply, we are invited to note how Stephen, like the ghost of Hamlet *père,* will disappear into the night? In any case, the striking word leads less to a closure than to new interpretative assignments. Moreover, we have been specifically informed, a few pages earlier, of Bloom's "nocturnal perambulations in the past" (*U* 667). And the obvious fact that Bloom habitually walks by day is surely one of the habits least likely to mark him off from his fellow Dubliners or, for that matter, from Stephen.

Such probings are just meant to show that the first-glance impression of some scientific distinction among the terms that immediately stick out in one sentence does not hold up too well to scrutiny. What exactly it achieves is still a matter of interpretative amendment. How we will still arrive at some plausible realignment of ambulatory practices is left to our own perspicuity, and does not automatically emerge from tags themselves in the manner that they seem to suggest. The point made here is simply that some mental arrangement is called for.

Ulysses is probably the first consistently autocorrective work of literature—and the intercorrections depend in part on the time of the reading. It is at some stage in our reading that we can put earlier pieces together and, for example, account for the strange behavior of Bantam Lyons at Bloom's remark that he was going to throw away his newspaper. But the more we absorb the more skeptical we can also become about what, so far, we thought we knew for certain. It is a late development in Joyce criticism that we began to wonder about things that were taken for granted, like the actual military rank of Brian Tweedy, or about Bloom's request for breakfast the next morning. The novel contains much potentiality for new doubt. Above all the novel tends to undermine our premature confidence in all kinds of norms.

Finnegans Wake defies even more norms, makes it difficult for us to trust in any of them or any of the verbal appearances. It amplifies most Ulyssean features and is even more rigorously autocorrective. It too offers serial pluralities of tentative, concealed, often contradictory accounts, refusing even to distinguish among facts, fictions, rumors, myths, fears, and the like, but it goes far beyond successive qualification. *Finnegans Wake* inclines toward instant repair, toward simultaneous retraction, as often as not within one word. Its compressed, fractured language can be seen, from the point of view stressed here, as an attempt to rectify the errors of assertive simplification at once, or to improve on one mistake by interlacing another. Alternative readings are not so much lined up in succession as integrated in the microstructure. The pretense of a simplistic truth is no longer upheld, but yields to a choice of rival improbabilities.

In such a perspective a name, or what poses as a name, as for instance "Moyhammlet" (*FW* 418.17), dissolves into an effort to articulate "Mohammed" with the simultaneous signal that Hamlet might be a more appropriate identity. Note that neither name is orthographically present. Perhaps all we can say is that, of all the nominal persons that the odd conglomerate of letters does *not* mean, Mohammed and Hamlet are the least incorrect guesses: They also hold each other in check. We might fasten on to the Irish word "moy"—which *is* physically present and means a plane (it also happens to be the name of a river)—and the common English word "hamlet"; they serve as an emendatory warning that the graphic shape may not after all, or not exclusively, refer to any human males, but to topography. What we do get are less individual or even geographic identities than a dynamic tension of specific crossinterrogations.

We are often faced with encapsuled opposites, as in

. . . scruting foreback into the fargoneahead (*FW* 426.22)

—where we seem to be looking "fore-back" in either direction and also find "head" contrasted to "back" in further spatial contrast. The phrase is also temporal: "fargoneahead" points to the future, what lies ahead, but "far gone" could be the past as well; and this meaning is reinforced by the German "Vergangenheit" as another corrective touch. We are unlikely to grasp the temporal dichotomy at one quick glance, but usually arrive at the redressive balance only in antithetical progression.

Or, to change the terminology (which is a device we might learn from Joyce's own procedures), reading *Finnegans Wake* in effect consists in our cooperative repair work. "Moyhammlet" we touch up to "Mohammed" in superior spelling. For better or worse, we handle a passage like

Loab at cod then herrin (*FW* 587.2)

either with puzzlement or else as though it were, on the one hand, a faulty rendering of a German hymn, the exact wording of which it is then up to us to restore, in this case *"Lobet Gott, den Herrn"* (Praise God, the Lord). But we may also treat it as a failure to articulate something about "loaves and fishes," and once this becomes our semantic aim, we take the liberty of improving "Loab" to *loaf* (with perhaps some philological help from the German cognate *"Laib"*) and we supply a "g" to "herrin" to have another fish alongside of "cod." Fish, of course, also links back to God by way of a historical acronym ("ICHTHYS"), which can be taken to be circuitous confirmation or else a trinitarian confusion. At some stage we may also notice that a male divine lord is being played off—potentially—against a female German *Herrin,* lady or mistress. And we can amend the whole phrase, as I have done, to an instituted praise or an irreverent codding. The fact that everyone in the audience would probably find some other reading at hand only adds to the point that I am belaboring.

In practice the readers of the *Wake* slip into the roles of pedantic schoolmasters who emend the text's deficiencies of the most self-righting verbal artifact in existence. We mentally put things right, but of course no longer toward one correct solution. We are correctors, whether we dig up hidden allusions, or set up word lists, or simply paraphrase. In *Finnegans Wake* the distinction between graphic writing and corrective righting has become futile, and the general homonymous sweep includes without strain the meanings of "rite" (as in "ritual") as well as "wright" (as in "playwright"), a cognate of "work" or "en-ergy." Examples proliferate: "selfrighting the balance," "the rite words by the rote order," "righting his name," "the wright side," "he could wright any pippap passage" (*FW* 167.33, 422.33, 597.11, 301.7). In such a way *Finnegans Wake* can also suggest, coincidentally, what the author has been doing to it, and what we in our despair are trying when we are wrighting its texture, or when we grope along its mysteries in orthographic correction or in ritual cooperation.

Finnegans Wake thrives on a principle of instant verification or, as we might term it with equal inaccuracy, of instant falsification. We have only to ask ourselves what a "wrong" interpretation of any *Wake* passage could mean and how one would go about demonstrating it, to realize some basic difference from other works of literature. Even acknowledging that not all our remedial associations are equally pertinent, or helpful, or valuable, we would be hard put to define "right" or "wrong" interpretations. Joyce's last works teach us to modify our notions as to what interpretation might be, and turns our attention toward the idea of a continuous adjustive endeavour that involves us, as it did Bloom in his kitchen, in a good deal of alert moving about. What we cannot afford at all is static inflexibility (even though you find a lot of it in Joycean criticism).

So that early close-up of Bloom's trite and not signally successful activity helps us to focus on—and find provisional terms for—a restless Joycean strain that works against premature interpretation. It is all the more surprising then that we still watch Joyce scholars strive for correct terminal solutions or ultimate formulas.

"Righting" or "The Dynamics of Corrective Unrest" is not meant to be such a formula, but merely a convenient angle of observation. It indicates not an aim, but multiple intercorrective acts, or Work perpetually in Progress.

1982

Postcorrective Note

The imminent Critical and Synòptic Edition of *Ulysses* as prepared by Hans Walter Gabler will probably not accept the wording that prompted my observations on p. 60, ". . . slammed it *tight* till it shut tight," but substitute the earlier version in autograph, "slammed it *twice* till it shut tight." The editorial principle is that any deviation from Joyce's own hand is to be rejected, unless there is cogent evidence against it. This means that my tentative constructions built around the odd doubling of *tight* may be based on a transmission error (a copyist's anticipation of a subsequent word). They would then be defensible only, if at all, as an erroneous application of a potentially valid Joycean dynamism. What does seem to confirm the dynamism itself—though not my example—is that the error must have persistently escaped the author's corrective supervision for more than three years, ever since an inattentive typist misread a phrase (presumably in 1918). So we face an instructive instance of failed, or delayed, rectification. The need for astute righting no doubt collectively obtains for officious close readings (like mine) and for textual scholarship—as well as for the judicious discrimination among the textual variants that the new, much more reliable, edition of *Ulysses* will now dangle before us.

Stay us wherefore in our search for tighteousness. (*FW* 5.18)

1984

Notes

1. *Ulises*, trans. J. Salas Subirat (Buenos Aires: Santiago Rueda, 1959), 3rd ed. First published in 1945.
2. *Ulises*, vols. I and II, trans. José Maria Valverde (Barcelona: Editorial Lumen, 1976).

5

The Challenge:
"ignotas animum"

It is strange that a quaint device that Joyce used once, and only once—the selection of an epigraph—should have gone unnoticed all this time. The following remarks propose that *"Et ignotas animum dimittit in artes,"* coming right before *A Portrait* itself, is important enough to be subjected to some minute epigraphic hieroglyphing (with deference to *U* 689).

The motto, to be sure, has been glossed—but not noticed. What commentators generally offer is the summary metamorphosis into myth and hasty symbolism, for which, naturally, there is excellent reason. But glossing over is not reading, the reading of a phrase in such a privileged pre-position, a phrase that itself exemplifies the auspicious hazards and retrospective comforts of the act of reading.

Joyce sets out in a foreign language. But he does not stipulate that his audience know Latin, aware, no doubt, that, as conditions change, even fewer readers would have benefited from a classical education. The first platitudinous observation is, tritely, that the opening already divides the readers into two broad groups: at the one end of the spectrum the (rare) erudite scholar who immediately recognizes the quotation and puts it into its proper context, at the other extreme the reader for whom it is a complete blank. Many of us will figure somewhere halfway, able, at least, to spell out some message by holding on to the familiar roots. In any case, we are Janus-faced with a common enough situation: according to our background, the line changes its meaning, and rather radically, from zero to a rich bundle of associations. This is *part of* the meaning of the sentence. Imagine, in a similar instance, the opening scene of *Ulysses,* how it would appear to a Dubliner of 1900, or even a reluctant accomplice like Oliver Gogarty himself—and how essentially different it must strike a non-Irish student today.

Commentaries are designed to provide welcome remedies. They tend to dispel ignorance with concise strokes, and with the attendant danger of wholesale skipping. To approach Joyce we may all need notes, at some stage. Notes (by the way, the exact opposite of *"ignotas"*) unfortunately have to parcel out instant information that, when in print, can be taken for relevant truth. By their nature, notes are goal- and object-oriented, not toward the inquisitive endeavor (it is their aim to short-cut this). In our comprehensive wisdom we may underrate the motive force of ignorance (of the Socratic kind). If Odysseus had set out from Troy with a copy of *The Mediterranean on Five Drachmas a Day* he would have saved himself enormous trouble, but the *Odyssey* would have become a much more tedious epic or, more likely, none at all.[1] Commentators also like to think that a final, clinching gloss supersedes all the previous trials and errors, when the best glosses, actually, can hardly be anything else.

In our case the best-intended notes go straight to the story of Daedalus and dismiss the words themselves in some synoptic translation. Quantitatively, the epigraph has been translated, many times over,[2] but the inherent quest is hardly translatable: any rendering into one of our modern European languages necessarily interferes with the word order, and this happens to a sentence introducing a novel that embodies the problematic triumphs of order. Translations stress the result and neglect the process; they make choices for us and prevent us from making them for ourselves (e.g., what is *"artes"*?). Reading (Lat. *legere,* to gather, choose) has to do with se-lec-tion.[3]

Notice how *"Et ignotas animum dimittit in artes"* does not name or state any subject. Glosses rectify this quickly by presenting the Greek inventor and treating us to highlights of his career. This is the way in which we have to transform much of what Joyce wrote down; we supply the implicit background. If we do it here, the cue is taken not from the words quoted but from the subsequent reference line that Joyce also offers, but afterwards ("Ovid, *Metamorphoses,* VIII, 188"). All that the predicate itself, without the appended bibliography, reveals is that the plot is about some one person, in the singular. Looking for antecedents, we might pick the most likely two that are present in the volume: a) the artist mentioned in the title (especially because of the conspicuous tautology), b) the artist-author whose name has also preceded. It is no secret that these two readings do in fact apply. The point here is merely that the search for identity, so prevalent in the happy Joycean huntinggrounds, has set in already as a grammatical fact and is by no means over. For another possible candidate (adding up, with the referential Daedalus, to a startling grand total of four) might also be the only other person inevitably present at this juncture, the reader, who is indeed caught up in doing just what the sentence proclaims. The same application is useful for another intriguing first exposure, the name and title "Ulysses."[4]

The sentence will now be examined in slow motion.

It gets underway in a typically modernist fashion: *"Et . . ."* This indicates continuity, that something has gone before; it presupposes a context yet to be discovered. The Daedalus story would tell us that it is a tight spot for the hero. The reader, who does not yet know this, is in a corresponding predicament.

And the first content word reinforces this: *"ignotas,"* our prime impression of the world, something unknown. And even more puzzling, we do not know *what* is unknown. The most expert Latin speaker would have to wait for direction: the adjective will come to be attached to something feminine, plural, and accusative, and so it has to be suspended in the mind. In the beginning there is ignorance, which may give way to knowledge (i-*gno*-tus is cognate with "know," "recognize," "cunning," "gnosis," "gnomon," etc.[5]).

No clarification comes with the next item: *"animum"* could mean a number of things (originally related to "breath," it was a metaphor for the spiritual faculties, mind, but also soul, memory, character, courage, pride, will, desire, etc.). Grammatically it is another, but unrelated, accusative. If, for some reason, the poet were to interrupt his declamation at this point, the audience would be at a total loss. No syntactical pattern is emerging. Imagine in how many combinations the first three words could conceivably be developed. The constellation, *ignotas animum,* pre-presents the quintessential frustration of the Joycean reader. Our speculative and emotional faculties (*"animus"*) are confronted with something unknown and as yet wholly uncoordinated, with the implied hope that the near future may, somehow, sort things out.

The verb, when it comes at last, promises orientation: *"dimittit"* can be construed with the preceding noun (though, according to the practices of Latin poets, one would do well not to stake all one's money on it, for there is no telling what is yet to follow): *dimittere animum* yields a metaphor: to send forth, to send out the questioning mind on a mission, to dispatch it—in different directions, all over the place (*di-*): for the goal has not been localized as yet.[6] The nineteenth-century concern with the historical growth of language has sharpened the view for the original images contained in composite verbs. It is here that translations will easily simplify the process by anticipating the perfective attainment at the cost of the inchoative groping.[7] Interestingly enough, Ovid uses a similar image in an almost parallel phrase for a near parallel situation; Narcissus, when stupefied by the ubiquitous voice of the nymph Echo, glances around in all directions: *atque aciem partes dimittit in omnes.*[8] The Daedalus phrase sounds like an echo of this earlier one, the repetitive technique itself reminds us of *A Portrait.*

The procedure of *dimittere* entails a high percentage of abortive rummaging and false starts; the novel will be full of it. In fact the perfective fallacy may have led to so much discussion as to whether Stephen Dedalus ever deserves our official certificate as an acknowledged artist. Joyce's characters do a lot of tentative conjecturing. To let the inquisitive mind roam around has become the desperate and often random human strategy that has gone by many names at disjointed times: speculation, stream-of-consciousness, the Joyce industry, are just some of them.

The little function word *"in"* adds nothing but the all-important direction (if it had come right at the beginning it would have facilitated our syntactical navigation a lot). But it is not until *"in artes"* that the mind can be arrested and the disposition of the now intelligible matter be perceived—from behind. *"Ignotas"* finds its retarded anchorage, the pieces fit together, the arrangement becomes clear. This is not a surprise for the circumspect interpreter of classical texts. The nature of Latin poetry makes it possible for a sentence to perform, verbally, what it says, the meaning comes about by just the mental search and postponed rearrangement that is also its theme. This is the kind of sentence—call it, say, expressive form—that Joyce liked to make up. In words not his own, but by his own judicious selection, he has warned his readers, given them a trial run. For only with the last element do the parts become adjusted and do we recognize that the sentence is that which it is. "Its soul, its whatness, leaps to us from the vestment of its appearance. The soul [*"animus"* also means soul] of the commonest object, the structure of which is so adjusted, seems to us radiant." (*SH* 213)[9]

The structure Joyce pilfered telescopes quest and achievement as well as a whole cultural and technological aftermath. Especially if *artes* is rightfully associated with invention, civilization, and the Artist in his Joycean exfoliations. Translations focus on that; they can hardly avoid rendering *artes* as "arts,"[10] thereby limiting themselves to the successful terminal stage. *Ars*, more modestly, had originally to do with fitting things together; it came to mean skill, dexterity, craft, cunning, craftsmanship, strategy, ways and means, even deceit, handicraft, science, and—finally—Art. Indo-European etymologists traced it to a root "ar-," to fit, to join.

Such elementary skills are necessary for survival, not alone for Daedalus or Robinson Crusoe. Odysseus begins the adventures as they are related to us in his epic by workmanlike fitting and joining as he puts together the raft. With an axe "well-fitted" (*armenon*) he felled trees and "joined together" (*hērmosen*) the timber, "making it fast with fastenings" (*harmoniēsin arassen*), then also "fitted" (*ararōn*) planks and used a yard-arm that was "fitted" (*armenon*)—all these derivations of (*h*)*ar*/(*h*)*er*- forms are clustered within twenty lines (*Od.* 5:234–53). Odysseus is introduced as a cunning artificer or technician "skilled in carpentry" (*tektosynaōn*), who knows how to "join" pieces "well" (*eu* . . . *technēsato*) or who steers his rudder "skilfully" (*technēentōs; Od.* 5:250, 259, 270), an arch-*"tektōn."* Odysseus and

Daedalus are fellow craftsmen. The way in which Leopold Bloom sets out on his day, applying all the known arts of arranging and adjustment (of breakfast things or door mechanisms), is viewed from a slightly different perspective elsewhere in this volume. More exactly, however, Bloom "fitted the teapot on the tray"; and "fitted the book roughly into his inner pocket" (*U* 63, 65). An appropriate pastime for him would be "house carpentry" (*U* 715). He seems to have caused a row once, Molly remembers: "he began it not me when he said about Our Lord being a carpenter at last he made me cry" (*U* 742). The book's cross-referential algebra, or the superimposed French triangles, seems to liken him to "Joseph the Joiner" (*U* 19, 391). The New Testament calls the father of Jesus *"tektōn"* (Matt. 13:55).

Ancient Daedalus excelled in all of this. He fitted things together, stones for a labyrinth, feathers for wings. Writers join words—some, like Ovid or Joyce, in exile with elaborate cunning. The readers, in their turn, try to fit the pieces together in their own agile minds. Stephen Daedalus calls the quality of *"consonantia,"* taken over from Thomas Aquinas, the apprehension of something "complex, multiple, divisible, separable, made up of its parts . . . ," by a Greek term meaning an (esthetic) joining, "harmony," "harmonious" (*P* 212–3).

Clearly the art of fitting disparate words together, by unhurried storage and retrospective arrangement, must have declined since Augustan times when the offspring languages began to dispense with their flexible endings and sentences had to comply to narrower syntactical rules. So, for all his extravagant modernity, Joyce also turned back to reinstitute an ancient technique to spell out meanings by sending the mind forward and backward. Ovid (who might have been surprised) has been enlisted to predict arts of joining that even Joyce, when he composed *A Portrait,* did not yet know. The quotation encapsules dynamic principles that were present only *in potentia,* and it exacts skills that we are still learning. It sets out with our common starting point, ignorance, and it suggests how, for lack of any better method, we might cope with it. The emphasis is not so much on the achievement, *artes* (allowing it here to mean the accomplished arts), for that remains doubtful always, but on the process. The prerequisites are not so much erudition, though that helps quite a bit, but curiosity joined to versatility. Homer called that quality, early in the game, *"polytropos."*[11] Unprecedented demands are made on the reader's agility. The one thing the reader must not be is the exact opposite of *ars:* inert (Skeat: "dull, inactive . . . L. *inert,* stem of *iners,* unskilful, inactive.—L. *in-,* not; and *ars,* art, skill . . .").

As though knowingly, Ovid had put this negation of *ars* into his opening lines. Everything arose out of Chaos, a raw, shapeless mass, or else a weight—*"pondus iners"* (*Metamorphoses* 1:7): the weight is idle, or sluggish (compare : "the artist forging anew . . . out of the sluggish matter . . . a new soaring impalpable imperishable being,"[12] *P* 169), but also something unfashioned, not yet joined or arranged by an artificer. The disposition of sensible matter has not yet taken place. It is up to a god in the poem to order the elements, and it is up to the poet to re-create such processes verbally. And it is the reader's turn to assemble the constituent parts into some meaningful arrangement.

The dyschronicity of the Latin sentence has a Joycean ring too. It seems to bring together two distinct phases as one—the initial prolonged endeavor, and the final destination: these are superimposed or, perhaps better, "entwined" (as *FW* has it at 259.7). Or, to rephrase it, the word *"ignotas,"* when mentally transferred to the end in the process of reading, will come to stand for *"notas"*, its opposite (for the *artes* have now been discovered). Metamorphoses of time are built into the sentence. Or—once more—the Ovidian micro-model illustrates the complementary facets of written language: a temporal dimension on one's first experiencing it in a process; and then, once recognized as a whole, a spatial perspective, a structure whose properties can be studied. Remember our first perplexed struggle through *Ulysses* as against the later tranquil contemplation of its symmetries and structural devices or one of its schemas.

The events related conjure up a crucial moment in the past when the mind is projecting into the future, a favorite moment, too, of Joyce, who closes *Ulysses* with a memory of a past (or even two) when Molly envisages and plans the near future (volitional and otherwise): "I will." The first page of *Finnegans Wake* reiterates a period in the past when imminent events have not yet happened again: "passencore. . . . not yet."[13]

As predicted in its motto, *A Portrait* will evoke the gropings of a developing mind at crucial stages, often in almost paraphrases of the original pattern: "his mind had been pursuing its intangible phantoms . . . ; his mind wound itself in and out of the curious questions . . . ; his mind had struggled to find . . . ; his mind, . . . wearied of its search, . . . turned . . . to" (*P* 83, 106, 154, 176, etc.). Very early a defective joining is arrived at that is as yet unknown: *O, the geen wothe botheth"* (*P* 7).[14] A considerably more mature mind is later watched casting around for rhymes and words and images for the intricately fitted villanelle. "His mind was waking slowly to a tremulous morning knowledge" (*P* 217) is yet another variation in the thematic enactment of the epigraph.

Exploration into obscure areas is not always successful. In the beginning Stephen does a lot of wondering about things not known, called "strange" or "queer." "Suck was a queer word" (12), and investigation leads, somewhat aimlessly, to a lavatory in the Wicklow hotel. "Tower of Ivory," as cryptic as anything could be, can somehow be related to Eileen's white and cold hands. "By thinking of things you could understand them" (*P* 43). About the transgression of the older students one can only speculate. In the course of Joyce's development there will be more and more conjecture and less ready-made certainty.

At Stephen's climactic awareness of the portent of his own name, classical echoes conveniently cluster. The artist, in his new-found vocation, proceeds at once to transform the first real being available, the girl in the water, into a literary composition and even into the kind of event that is dealt with in the *Metamorphoses:* "one whom magic had changed into the likeness of a strange and beautiful seabird" (*P* 171).

It all began, really, long before *A Portrait.* In "The Sisters," a story full of guesses and empty of certainties (and with a delayed identity), the boy puzzled his "head to extract meaning from . . . unfinished sentences" (*D* 11.19). The first words spoken aloud in the whole opus, "—No, I wouldn't say he was exactly . . ." (*D* 9.19) seem to have a prophetic ring, too. As Joyce went along, he had to devise new tools to simulate the mind's groping for meaning. A chapter in *Ulysses* like Proteus seems devoted to that. Eumaeus draws out another indefatigable struggle, for example: "in a quandary as he couldn't tell exactly what construction to put on belongs to" (*U* 645; note how this might describe someone grappling with a Latin text). Whether informed or not, Leopold Bloom is forever curious and wants to find out. With dimittent zeal he persists. The unknown may be something forgotten ("Black conducts, reflects [refracts, is it?], the heat"—*U* 57), or something never quite grasped: "Parallax. I never exactly understood . . . Par it's Greek: parallel, parallax" (*U* 154). Parallax, come to think of it, is an instance of sending the observant mind in two, or more, different positions and having it compare notes.

Ignorance and knowledge, error and truth, jumble incongruously in Ithaca. It is fitting that Bloom should proceed "energetically from the unknown to the known through the incertitude of the void" (*U* 697). The shuttling to and fro between these two poles is meditated in different places; "there being no known method from the known to the unknown" is part of Bloom's "logical conclusion, having weighted the matter and allowing for possible error" (*U* 701).

The artifact of *Ulysses* is made up of parts fitted together, sometimes, as in Wandering Rocks, conspicuously so. There was good reason why, as the first of all modern works of literature, *Ulysses* should have been dismantled and alphabetically rearranged for handy reference, in Hanley's *Word Index.* The index helps us when we do not, as ideally we should, recall dispersed phrases from memory. But even an ideal memory does not always see us through. It takes patience as well. Out of Bantam Lyon's unintelligible "I'll risk it" at the end of Lotus Eaters (*U* 86), even the most perspicacious reader can make no sense, and fairly little out of "Potato I have" (*U* 57). Such items, like *"ignotas,"* have to be kept in mind till further orders. That one central symbolic connection (by "throwing together") should be built around variations of "throw away," reveals something about the method of com-position: nothing should ever be wasted in Joyce's ecological universe. A late paragraph in Ithaca recalls and assembles the various scattered elements in an exemplary nucleus of "previous intimations" and delayed "coincidences." That Bloom and the reader had been tantalized by "the language of prediction" (*U* 675–76) we learn as an *after*thought.

The best correspondence to dangling *"ignotas"* are the fragments in the overture of Sirens, which demonstrates the artefactuality of composition. "Full tup. Full throb" (*U* 256.27) has to be suspended until a cluster of motifs on p. 274 suggests a context.

The hierarchitexture of *Finnegans Wake* celescalates the *artes* even further. A pragmatic list of clues to characterize it—inadequately—could be gleaned from Skeat's entry of the Indogermanic root:

> *AR*, to fit. Skt. *ar-as*, spoke of a wheel; GK. *har-menos*, fitted, *ar-thron*, joint; *ar-mos*, joint, shoulder; L. *ar-mus, ar-tus*, a limb; *ar-ma*, arms, *ar-s*, art; Goth. *ar-ms*, an arm. Ex. *harmony; arms, art, article; arm*(I).[15]

A detailed application of the above terminology would be tedious, but it would highlight some of the tectonic aspects of the *Wake* and hint at its "arthroposophia" (*FW* 394.19). In its frequent moments of partial self-revelation, *Finnegans Wake* confesses itself as "doublejoynted . . . injoynted and unlatched . . . hubuljoynted" (*FW* 27.2, 244.29, 310.31, etc.). It is "the book of Doublends Jined" (*FW* 20.15). It is made up of "parts unknown" (*FW* 380.23). Its ends are riveted by the *article* "the," its ultimate joint. It articulates contradictions.

And it insults its readers with the obscure, the unfamiliar, reveals their ignorance and inertia, provokes them into the most desparate clutching at tenuous solutions; "the endknown" (*FW* 91.28), *inter alia*, exemplifies and names the process leading to eventual recognition. The reader has to resort to an unknown degree of artful and animated dimitting—all over the library shelves and into recondite areas, a hitherandthithering bustle that affords considerable amusement to innocent bystanders. The more *ignotum* a piece looks, the more hit or miss the procedure is likely to become. Daedalus too, one presumes in self-defense, must have tried out a few preposterous ideas before he could take off.

Perplexity is integrated into the *Wake*, the tentative interpretations of cryptic documents one of its themes. Shem's riddle triggers a series of farflung guesses and one delayed correct, but not very helpful, solution. Much of chapter 4 consists of scientific investigation. The list of the names of ALP's mamafesta opens with the invocation of (also) HCE as Roman Emperor Augustus (or Greek Sebastos) "The Augusta Augustissimost for Old Seabeastius' Salvation" (*FW* 104.6). This is what the *Metamorphoses* culminate in, the glorification of Augustus along with Jupiter, who share heaven and earth between them. Having ended his poem with *"Pater est et rector uterque"* (both appellations fit HCE as well; see "rector" at *FW* 126.10), Ovid then goes on to praise the emperor even more in his *Invocatio*.

Ovid's epigraphic shorthand formula for the mystery novel (body in the library—detective applying his wits—extensive investigation—tidy revelatory realignment of parts) or scientific procedure (problem—hypothesis and experimentation—theory) is borne out elaborately in Joyce's three prose works that followed, but, paradoxically, it is also invalidated by the lack of ultimate resolution. New *ignotas* are planted all along the way to instigate new searches.

Mysteries not revealing themselves before the end belong to the oldest tricks of literature. In *Finnegans Wake* the mystification is immanent in the microstructure. Understanding trails behind. Recognition comes to pass (D.V.) in the course of time, not on the spot. This commonplace affects the minutiae. At our first go-off, "riverrun" is disquieting but becomes a bit less so once we have negotiated the first sentence, and it gains momentum when we reach the final "a long the"—and somewhere along the journey we can also pick up overtones like "reverend." The process is what the word says, and does, a running. Which is what rivers do, or time does.

Finnegans Wake, as Latin and Greek could, postpones clarification. Different from classical usage, the *Wake's* syntax generally adheres to the familiar patterns. Sentences reveal their drift, on the whole, right away, but their lexicologistics often depend on hindsight, on retro-semantification. The seasoned reader may instantly apprehend the two components of "The playgue . . ." (*FW* 378.20). But when we stumble into "The finnecies of poetry . . .", we may well have to grope around for "Finn?," "fin?," "fancies?," "phantasies" (American pronunciation?), of "finesses?" . . . etc. The continuation of the phrase " . . . wed music" (*FW* 377.16) can *then* suggest meanings like "fiancee" or "fiançailles." In this case there was also prospective conditioning. Signals like "hornemoonium" and "Mumblesome Wadding Murch" prepare the way. But, again, "Mumblesome" is retransformed into the composer's name not before the following two words have been adjusted.

No one, on first looking into "how the bouckaleens shout their roscan generally" (*FW* 42.11), can recognize the shape that this dominant motif will later take, just as it is wholly impossible to identify a still totally unknown HCE from the initial vestment "Howth Castle and Environs" (and a newcomer who is told that this "is" H. C. Earwicker has a right to be outraged). Later, perhaps, the elements may fuse in the mind of the reader, the pieces can be re-membered, re-assembled, and re-ordered. It is toward the end that "we have fused now orther" (*FW* 593.10).

No metamorphosis can occur in "raising hell" before we have reached some point of ". . . while the sin was shining" (*FW* 385.10), when, miraculously, hell can turn into hay.[16] Notice how "comming nown from the asphalt" seems to acquire even more redundant solidity when the phrase moves on to ". . . to the concrete" (*FW* 481.10), but that the sequence also allows the first part to click into its opposite and to give the whole sentence also a figurative and a grammatical twist.[17] Hesitant disclosure becomes a literal pass-time of the *Wake*.

The Wake consists, imaginatively, of what Ovid announced his topic to be. As Daedalus sent out his mind toward unknown goals, so Ovid's *animus* (here in the sense of will of purpose) led him to tell of shapes transformed into new, or different, bodies:

> *In nova fert animus mutatas dicere formas*
> *corpora.* (Met. 1.1–2)

Joyce's mind and intentions were similar. He too wrote about *animus* and *corpora,* and became an *artifex* who kept inventing new meanings for *"formas mutatas,"* eventually changing the words themselves.

Publius Ovidius Naso, a virtuoso of form, did not, for all we know, intend to compile reading exercises for verbal labyrinths two millennia away. Nor did Joyce, when he found a concise prologue, early along an unknown way, devise a freshman course in preparation of the vextremities of *Finnegans Wake*. The quote nevertheless is graven in the language of prediction. It so happens that Joyce reactivated some of the cognitive techniques (from *techne,* roughly the same as *ars:* skill, cunning, craftsmanship, resourcefulness, and ART) that were required to combine sense out of the apparently random disposition of Latin or Greek words. And he brought reading back to what it once may have meant according to the terms that served to denote it. *Read* meant discern or advise and is cognate with "riddle." German *lesen* and Latin *legere* denote a selective process. The Greek verb *anagignoskein* seems to evoke the chancy miracle most vividly, suggesting movement: *ana* (up, forward, or even backward, again), and cognition: *"gi-gno",* which brings us back to *"i-gno-*tas," etc.; the ending marks it as an inchoative activity.[18]

In his *Epilogus* Ovid celebrates reading in a less epistemological way. Proud of the *opus* just completed, he aspires to immortality: *"nomenque erit indelebile nostrum"*—his name will be indestructible. Stephen's vision—"He would create proudly . . . as the great artificer whose name he bore, a living thing . . . imperishable" (*P* 170) may owe something to this line, and the line may tinge Shem's malodorous ink (*FW* 185.25). The immortality will come about, Ovid continues—"if ever the predictions of poets have any truth"—by "the mouths of the people reading him":

Ore legar populi . . .
        . . . vivam
(. . . "then will I live")

A Berkleyan equation *legi = esse* might have appealed to Joyce too. That to be read is the only way to remain alive is certainly true, whatever else is not, of *Finnegans Wake* and all the written arts.

1978

Notes

1. Victor Bérard proposed that the Phoenicians had been compiling just some such volume for merchants and tourists and that it was later translated and edited by the Greeks to become the *Odyssey.*

2. Some available versions:
    "to arts unknowne he bends his wits," George Sandys, *Ovid's Metamorphosis Englished, Mythologized, and Represented in Figures,* ed. Karl K. Hulley and Stanley V. Vandersall (Lincoln: University of Nebraska Press, 1970), p. 359.
    "he sets his mind to work upon unknown arts," Ovid, *Metamorphoses,* trans. Frank Justus Miller (London: Heinemann, 1960), p. 419.
    "applying his mind to obscure arts," *A Portrait of the Artist as a Young Man,* ed. Chester G. Anderson (New York: Viking Press, 1968), p. 484 (explanatory notes).
    "And he devoted his mind to unknown arts," *A Portrait of the Artist as a Young Man,* ed J. S. Atherton (London: Heinemann, 1964), p. 239.
    "to uncouth arts he bent the force of all his wits," Golding's translation, as quoted in Harvey Peter Sucksmith, *James Joyce: A Portrait of the Artist as a Young Man* (London: Edward Arnold, 1973), p. 33.
    "[Daedalus] turned his mind to subtle craft,/An unknown art . . ."; trans. Horace Gregory (New York: Mentor Books, 1960), p. 220.

3. See, for example, the entry *legend* in Walter W. Skeat, *An Etymological Dictionary of the English Language* (Oxford: Clarendon Press, 1879–82). All the etymologies I use are of course based on Skeat.

4. Cf. Marilyn French, *The Book as World* (Cambridge, Mass.: Harvard University Press, 1976), pp. 3–22, and my "Book of Many Turns," *James Joyce Quarterly* 10, no. 1 (Fall 1972): 44, reprinted later in this volume.

5. Skeat, *Etymological Dictionary,* "GEN" (p. 753 passim).

6. The bulky *Thesaurus,* or the *Lexicon Totius Latinitatis,* emphasizes that, primarily, "dimittere est in diversas partes mittere."

7. The translations that use "apply" or "devote" suggest that the goal is already known.

8. *Metamorphoses* III, 381.

9. Stephen goes on: "The object achieves its epiphany." Ovid's sentence ends on an epiphany—"a sudden spiritual manifestation" of meaning.

10. Occasionally, however, a term like "invention" is used: "und richtend den Geist auf neue Erfindung," Ovid, *Metamorphoses,* trans. Reinhard Suchier, ed. Philipp Reclam (Leipzig, 1971), p. 206.

11. *Odyssey,* 1. I dimitted my animum over this area in "Book of Many Turns," reprinted later in this volume.

12. "anew . . . a new . . ." This emphasis on novelty, with a difference, might bring us back to the beginning of Ovid's poem, its very first words: "In nova . . ." He wants to ʰll of "new . . . bodies (*corpora*)" that forms have been changed into (*Metamorphoses* I: 1–2). Ovid, like Joyce, told old stories anew. *A Portrait* is also a transformation of a myth, of themes and techniques, in *Metamorphoses* into new shapes.

13. An extrinsic but fitting anachronism is that when Joyce copied the epigraph the unknown art (if we take it to be the technology of flight) had become sensationally well known.

14. I am following Hans Walter Gabler's emendation in *James Joyce's "Portrait,"* ed. Wilhelm Füger (Munich: Goldmann, 1972), p. 20. The conflation contains, coincidentally, the signal "botheth": "geen wothe" does suggest *both* "wild rose" and "green place"—the inarticulate Stephen is a coauthor of *Finnegans Wake*.

15. Skeat, *Etymological Dictionary*, p. 752.

16. Cf. "A Reading Exercise in *Finnegans Wake*," reprinted in the present volume.

17. Hugh Kenner supplied this example, in conversation.

18. Liddell and Scott's *Greek Lexicon* arrives at the specific sense of reading via "perceiving, knowing well, knowing again, recognize." The point made here is not that Joyce knew this Greek verb, but that the ancients realized, painfully well, the precarious nature of the skills involved.

6

A Reading Exercise in *Finnegans Wake*

Whatever innovations James Joyce has brought to literature, to remain there, to be assimilated by writers, to be studied by the critics, there is also something eminently novel, or so it seems, in the relation that his words have to ourselves as readers. Something happens to our reading habit; it will never be quite the same again, and the transformation may alert us to some reactions that are probably inherent in that mysterious way of communication, the written letters. The following remarks are an attempt to generalize from what is essentially a personal but continuous reading experience.

The first effect to notice is a slowing down of the process. *Ulysses* cannot be rushed through. A leisurely, ambling pace is much more to the purpose; we do well to pull up from time to time for pauses that are, in both senses of the term, re-creative, and we are compelled to treat ourselves to a privilege that was forbidden to Lot's wife—to satisfy our curiosity by turning back. One of the recurrent phrases in the book, about a "retrospective arrangement," seems to hint at this demand. Events and relations arrange themselves for us if we look, or turn, back, and this holds good in a much more retrospectacular way than it does in any traditional novel.

But it is *Finnegans Wake*, really, that makes us aware just how inadequate normal consecutive reading can become, starting at the top of a page and going from left to right (or, in a different culture, starting at some other end, which comes to the same thing), unreeling a linear semantic thread. This we still do with *Finnegans Wake;* a book is not to be read—literally—backward.

But the rewards of that kind of serial advancement are limited. The restrictions can be counteracted, up to a point, by reiteration, by a theoretically interminable circular progress. Joyce's conspicuous device is to make the end fold back into the beginning and to have the reader recursing, if his patience lasts, eternally along a Viconian spiral. This still amounts to traveling along one road that happens to form a closed circuit.

From the very start the discerning reader of *Finnegans Wake* is aware that he finds himself traveling on two or more roads at the same time, roads that may or may not appear to be interrelated, but somehow always manage to coalesce verbally in the one typographical line, for there cannot be anything except a single-track string of letters. There is, for a first example, a recognizable syntactical movement from beginning to end of:

> Now eats the vintner over these contents . . . (318.20)

The sense may be a trifle odd, but not really baffling. If we are familiar with the opening line of Shakespeare's *Richard III*, however, we can *hear* an entirely different semantic development: "Now is the winter of our discontent. . . ." We may not see the thematic connection of the two lines (the context would have to provide that). What matters here is that both of them can be followed independently, both are (syntactically, semantically) self-contained. We can learn to take them both in our (one) stride.

Similarly, "Bacchulus shakes a rousing guttural" (365.6) does not in itself confuse us. A clumsy phonetic effort seems to be going on ("Bachus," an overtone, may hint at the cause for the uncouthness of the speech). A reader who has worked his laborious way as far as p. 365 of the book will have little trouble to catch one more echo of what is perhaps the most frequent phrase to come across, a reference to an episode in the Crimean War (Joyce's version): "Buckley shot the Russian General." This reader will probably also see how the manifest meaning somehow tallies with the latent one; the surface version is, perhaps, an illustration that suits the context. Another variation, for instance, spreads an air of philosophical calm about it: "Berkeley showed the reason genrously" (423.32). A first-comer opening the book at random on this page would not suspect a war incident here. This is not so different from what happens to the reader of any novel. If I know the whole series of events leading up to any given episode it will mean more to me than to the casual onlooker. In *Finnegans Wake,* however, the words themselves have acquired a new, often *entirely* new, meaning to the initiated.

The most attentive of first readers could not possibly discover the same hidden draft when coming upon the earliest occurrence of the phrase: "the bouckaleens shout their roscan generally" (42.11). Here the motif is sounded vaguely, but not at all clarified, for the first time in the book. When the traveler returns to this same passage on his second lap, he will have learned about the Crimean war and the Irish soldier aiming a gun at a Russian general, he will have become conditioned to be on the lookout for a name or noun with a consonant structure like "B-k-l" followed by a verb beginning with "sh-"; his ear will be attuned to the particular rhythm of the phrase. At one's first exposure to the sentence, there is just a noise that some persons make, a noise that may be felt to be obscure or to have an Irish ring about it. If we knew Gaelic, we might have noticed that the theme of war or strife is potentially present already: "roscan" is an inflammatory speech, a rallying song or a battle hymn. But even so, the full meaning would have escaped us. The experience is roughly similar to our perusing the opening scene of a detective novel again, with the revelations of the last chapter fresh in our minds—there too we would discover little traces that might have aroused our suspicion for the first time, but somehow did not, but in any case the whole and ghastly significance could not possibly be appreciated without the knowledge that only the whole book can provide. Some of the insights can only be arrived at by hindsight. In *Finnegans Wake,* hindsight, rather "culious an epiphany" (508.11), affects the linguistic structure, phonetically as well as semantically. The words themselves have changed their character.

It is this sort of experience that has given rise to our talk about the various "levels" of the book, a handy and useful comparison. But like a corresponding one, that of a musical score, or musical performance—many voices and several instruments in parallel melodic development—it cannot be kept up consistently, since in practice we shall hardly be able to follow the various levels right to the end, or to listen to the voices consecutively, as in a musical performance we could, even allowing for intervals. All analogies for *Finnegans Wake* seem useful at times, and all break down sooner or later.

It is certain that *Finnegans Wake* is to be absorbed slowly and, like any other medicinal poison, preferably in small doses, and in tranquillity. Pauses are necessary, to ruminate and to sort out the various itineraries that have been traversed, to glance around, backward and sideways. The reader of *Finnegans Wake* often feels himself in a world full of tricky *déjà vus,* of elusive voices uttering vaguely familiar sounds that get more familiar, if not always more clear, with each successive tour, guided or unguided, through the maze. As usual, Joyce, who has a way of indicating not only what happens in the book but also what happens to his reader, hints at this in his opening chords. "Sir Tristram," we learn, "had passencore rearrived from North Armorica" (3.4). Like Tristram, the reader is a passenger who has not yet *(pas encore)* arrived on the strange shore, or else who, in his passage, or his steps *(pas),* has rearrived once more *(encore).* This we know well enough by now. This is the path that goes round and round, circular but still linear. Yet there appears to be a different direction as well, not from front to back, but in reverse order, backward, arriving at the "rear" end. There is probably a physiological side to this, but, more prominently, a geographical one. We notice that the hero coming to Ireland is arriving both from North America in the West and, like

Tristram, from North Armorica, Brittany, France, in the East. We too, the opening ambiguity implies, can travel in either direction.

This is all very well in geography and tourism, but we cannot, in actual fact, read a book backwards, from right to left. Well, sometimes we can a bit. "Cloudia Aiduolcis" (568.10) can be tackled from whichever end we prefer. There are also characters like "natsirt" (he is the Tristram, now Tristan, of the first page, whose traveling habits seem to have affected his name), or "Kram" (388.3/2), or we may find ourselves in "Nilbud" (24.1). Occasionally, *Finnegans Wake* is palindramatic or anagrammatical, and inversion abounds.

Even so, the general drift must be forward. But the text sometimes tempts us to go back, to retrace our steps, before we can advance again, and this literally, verbally. Some such movement backwards and forwards is alluded to in the first chapter: "furrowards, bagawards, like yoxen at the turnpaht" (18.32). This is the movement of the plough; it is also, in the history of writing and the alphabet being described at the same time, a feature of early inscriptions called *boustrophedon,* which Joyce obligingly translates for us, a turning of the oxen. It is also, I feel, the situation of the reader who, in ploughing through the pages, sometimes reverses his direction and at times bovinely wonders which path to take. In his characteristic way, Joyce goes beyond naming, to presenting the thing referred to. The next sentences read:

> Here say figurines billycoose arming and mounting.
> Mounting and arming bellicose figurines see here.

The path actually does turn back on itself, and we review the same sequence in exactly inverse order. What is interesting, from the point of view of communication, is that some changes have intervened in the meantime. The word "billycoose" (which admits of several readings, among them a menacing highwayman's club, *billy,* and some amatory billing and cooing), while continuing to mean, probably, beautiful things in Italian *(belle cose),* has been turned into something patently warlike. This is, of course, as we know, also the way of the world. And there appears a difference between what we "say" first and what we "see" later: hearsay gives way to closer inspection, as good a clue as any as to what we are to encounter in, and do about, *Finnegans Wake.*

The point elaborated here is that we sometimes really travel the opposite way, that, if we do not turn back, we inevitably miss a previous meaning. In its full linguistic impact this is fairly unique. The mind is stimulated by an uncustomary kind of impulse.

Assuming that in *Finnegans Wake* several meanings are often just "there" simultaneously, and even granting their occasional transparency, we, the readers, will hardly experience the two or more meanings at the same time, right from the start. At one particular moment (or never) the mind is startled and begins to apprehend luminously that more is at stake than at first met the eye. Take a few more simple phrases: "rasing hell while the sin was shining" (385.10). I submit that before we come, at the earliest, to "sin," the secondary latent meaning has no chance to resound at all: "sin" may startle us, especially if followed by "shining." Sins do not normally shine, but suns do, and the emerging sun points its rays back to the preceding words, allowing the proverbial expression "to make hay while the sun shines" to penetrate our consciousness. Only when we have come to the end of the sentence can "hell" become "hay" in a semantic ignition delay. Semantic potential is released retroactively.

What is the meaning of "So all rogues"? Not, really, anything beyond what these words denote in any dictionary (a reader, in fact, is unlikely, at this point, to trouble about overtones). If we go on, "all rogues lean," we may or may not get on to the scent. The finishing words enable the click to occur: ". . . to rhyme" (96.3) evokes "All roads lead to Rome." Toward, or after, the end of the movement a jolt of recognition metamorphoses the rogues. The jolt of recognition may never come, as when we do not know the proverb or if we fail to respond. A large part of the irritation about *Finnegans Wake* is the certainty that we shall always remain deaf and blind to a great many potentialities of the text.

Among other things, it is this (retarded) transmutation of words that justifies a reference to Shem the writer as an alchemist—"the first till last alshemist" (185.34). Change, transsubstantiation, the metamorphoses of gods, men, animals (especially insects), protean transformation affect the words as well as the reader, the contents of whose mind are also subject to change.

The neat examples quoted above are atypical exceptions, selected for their relative lucidity; the glosses are didactical simplifications. What we are generally faced with is not such a system of tidily separable semantic curves, but rather a confusing crisscross, an apparently unpatterned welter of verbal matter, sometimes primeval, seemingly unarticulated, with a strong suspicion of a random assortment of rubbish. Some lines can usually be discerned, but statements about our perceptions, those systematic relations the rational mind is not satisfied without, stand in need of almost immediate qualification. The interpretative progress is not usually linear but consists of a haphazard zigzag and transverse leaps, the wind of inspiration blowing where, and if, it listeth. The movement, a succession of associative impulses, resembles the hop, step, and jump rather than a journey along a twisted road.

A more optical analogy would be that insights gained at one place help to illuminate some other part. By a jostle of ideas, like sparks setting off a series of mutual reflection, of interradiation, the darkness will gradually disperse.

I select two sentences from a passage of medium to light opacity to give a practical demonstration. The words are taken from Jaun's Sermon. One of the two rival brothers, Shaun, here transformed into Juanesque Jaun, delivers an edifying sermon to a circle of admiring girls. Before launching out he is at pains to find his bearings in the prescribed liturgical calendar:

> I've a hopesome's choice if I chouse of all the sinkts in the colander. From the common for ignitious Purpalume to the proper of Francisco Ultramare, last of scorchers, third of snows, in terrorgammons howdydos. (432.35–433.2)

Every reader will recognize a few features and, starting from what he thinks he knows, choose his own path. Let us start somewhere. Obviously, there is an ecclesiastical flavor about the whole passage. Even the layman is likely to understand "the sinkts in the colander" as the saints in the calendar that the Church has assigned for each day of the year. But why "sinkts"? One component part seems to be "sin." Saints contrast with sinners, and some saints were sinners first, and all of them (and priests too) concern themselves with sin. Perhaps—and here the guessing begins—we should hear and see "cinct" (girded) as well. Priests, among others, are girded.

How would we test the validity of the meanings saint/sin/cinct? There is no approved way. The priestly girdle, we might venture, is the symbol for continence and chastity (we can look this up). Priests have been voluble on this particular subject; unchastity is a favorite sin. There is a traditional relation between chastity and being cinct, wearing a belt (it dates from a time when priests had much to say and when saints were still at large). Chastity, thus implied, will also be an attractive topic in Jaun's sermon to come. Readings of this digressive kind will appeal to some readers, and not to others. They are offered here—and might be kept in mind—as possibilities. William York Tindall, an American commentator, has wittily combined "colander" and "saint," by grace of extraneous punning, remarking that a "colander is, of course, as holy as a saint." He arrives at a contrast that is not so very much different from that of saintliness and sinful unchastity.

A colander, as it is, belongs to the kitchen, and this may serve as a pointer to suggest the "sink" that occupies the busy housewife. The connection between "kitchen" and "Church" is not an isolated occurrence in Joyce's works. Readers will have various examples in mind, from Mrs. Kernan in "Grace," whose "faith was bounded by her kitchen," to "the church which was the scullerymaid of christendom" in *A Portrait of the Artist as a Young Man.* And on to the last page of *Finnegans Wake,* where the kitchen sink doubles with a gesture of humble worship: "I sink I'd die down . . . only to washup" (628.11). The female of the species has for a long time been relegated to kitchen and church, and these afforded predetermined careers for many Irish girls of the kind that Jaun is addressing.

There is also an odd scintillating character about the "choice" that is so tautologically expressed. It is hopeful and double, and yet—through the proverbial "Hobson's choice," originating from a real person who used to impress *his* own choice on his customers, whatever *they* wanted—it implies that there is no choice at all. So things are not what they appear to be. And of course "chouse" is not quite the same thing as (how it may have looked at a first hasty glance) "chose" or "choose." Its meaning is to cheat, to trick, to dupe—not a saintly occupation.

Since we are now prepared for saints, though perhaps a trifle distrustful, we shall see one or two of them in the second sentence. Francis (Francisco) leaps to the eyes. Many places were named after him, not only San Francisco in California; one of them, in Mexico, is even called S. Francisco do la Mar. It (and most of them) is beyond the sea, *ultra mare.*

In the radiating atmosphere of *Finnegans Wake,* saintliness can blaze from other words than capitalized proper names, and so it is easy to make out another saint, a prominent one, in "ignitious": St. Ignatius Loyola, the founder of the Society of Jesus. He has become assimilated to the Latin word for fire, and ignition is implied as well; and the same element seems to have infused itself into "Purpalume," which might remind us of French *"allumer"* or else Spanish *"alum*brare." These languages could have some relevance, for Loyola, of Spanish origin, was wounded when the French were attacking the Spanish city of Pampeluna, in French "Pampelune"—another rough approximation of "Purpalume." So the light spreading from the name (by Joyce's change, not etymology) may serve to illuminate the surroundings further. The analogy may be apt since spreading the light is also a saintly function and one of the aims of the Jesuit order. Moreover the place where, according to the biographies, St. Ignatius began to see the light, was the Pampeluna already mentioned.

"Purpalume" contains also "purple," a color rich in significance, also within the Church, and this may alert us to another color—"ultramarine," through 'Ultramare.' The emblematic and symbolic significance of color offers itself as a tempting but tricky subject; here it is enough to note that the two holy men of whom a glimpse has been caught so far, with respective colors, purple and ultramarine blue, seem to be part of a spectrum, a variant perhaps of the rainbow, which is so ubiquitous in the book. The circle of colors might then constitute an optical parallel (light being refracted into some of its parts) corresponding to the temporal cycle of the church year, which allots a day for each saint and is made up, as Jaun indicates himself, of the *"Common* of Saints" and the *"Proper* of the Saints."

If one saint is a Jesuit of common fame it is only proper for his partner to belong to the same order. There is a Jesuit saint of nearly equal brilliance, one of the first to join the new order, and one greatly adored in Ireland: St. Francis Xavier (Francisco de Yasu y Xavier), the Apostle of the Indies. He was a great missionary, baptizing numerous souls in India and Japan, dying before achieving his great aim of carrying the torch to China. His travels well warrant the epithet "Ultramare." Like Ignatius, his temperament was fiery, and both of them were canonized in the same year, 1622. And—just to show what use Joyce can make of hagiological coincidence—Francis Xavier was born in Pampeluna.

So a Jesuitical pair emerges, one of the many variations of a pair of complementary and often contrasting characters that we always connect with Shem and Shaun. Actually, St. Ignatius and St. Francis Xavier have been paired before, in *A Portrait* (which is colored by Joyce's own Jesuit education). In the first chapter, their two portraits are described hanging in the same long narrow corridor of Clongowes Wood College. But their joint saintly presence is invoked later, in the third chapter, before Father Arnall, also a Jesuit, launches into his sermon on the torments of hell, a regular feature during the annual retreat.

If we remember the hell sermon in *A Portrait,* we have some idea as to why one of the saints should be called "last of scorchers." It may refer to his temperament, but it calls to mind the evocation of hell with the meticulous description of each single torment: the fire of hell is one of the more memorable traits. (The torment of fire, in the sermon, incidentally, is second only to hell's "awful stench," and this might, by the sort of hindsight illumination mentioned a while ago, reintroduce the meaning of "stinks" into the already overglossed "sinkts"—a gratuitous addition, to take or to leave.) The hell fire sermon in *A Portrait* is closely modeled on a standard treatise on hell, written by a Jesuit father who in turn grounds his somewhat medieval vision firmly on St. Ignatius's teachings. In the *Spiritual Exercises of St. Ignatius* we are invited "to see with the eyes of the imagination those great fires, and the souls as it were in bodies of fire." And a few lines later we are referred to the smell (First Week, The Fifth Exercise). A scorcher indeed.

A biblical innuendo may be relevant: The fourth angel in "Revelations" "poured out his vial upon the sun; and power was given unto him to scorch men with fire. And men were scorched with great heat . . ." (Rev. 16:8–9). Seen in this particular light, the passage about "terrorgammons howdydos" may be understood, at least as far as terror is concerned. Perhaps "howdydos" corresponds in marked contrast to the casual greeting with which the preacher in *A Portrait* started off his sermon. Just such a contrast is set up by the opposition of fire and snow. Christ's coming, again in "Revelations," happens to unite the same two elements: "His head and his hair were . . . as white as snow; and his eyes were as a flame of fire" (Rev. 1:14). But fire and snow are common enough in legend, literature, and elsewhere to render this specific reference dispensable. It is mentioned here as a by-product of that combinative urge that readers find hard to resist, and also as an example of the groping that is part and parcel of the whole process.

The relation between St. Ignatius and hell fire, established in an earlier book by Joyce, may appear far-fetched, and as an attempt to explain "last of scorchers" it falls short of its aim. But we are, after all, still dealing with the saints as they are listed in the calendar. St. Ignatius Loyola is commemorated on the day of his death, 31 July. It is the last day of a hot month, the last of scorchers. A "scorcher," the slang dictionary tells us, is a very hot day. It is also a "severe person" (Loyola was that, no doubt), as well as "a scathing vigorous attack": this too would fit the context, and it is also what the girl audience is going to get from Jaun, who will give them hell in his own sweet way. That we are really given a date in the calendar is confirmed by the entry on St. Francis Xavier in any missal: his death and feast day is 3 December , a wintry month: "third of snows." (A "snow" is also a sailing boat, useful for a seafaring missionary.)

The presence of the two Jesuits is established several times over. They are invoked by name and they are fixed by their co-ordinates in space and time: the place of birth and of a decisive event and a terrestrial destination are named, and they are given their proper place in the calendar. Or, to put it another way, the pair of them plays at universality, comprising the temporal cycle of the Church year (at nearly opposite poles), and spanning the earth from Spain (their origin) to the far seas in the east and the west. Since the birthplace of one and the death dates of both are implied, the circle of human life and death is added to the picture. And, as we have seen, they also embody the spectrum of colors. On a different scale, or temperature, they range from the coldness of snow to scorching heat. Temperamental opposites are indicated too, as well as moral ones: what is common (in the sense of vulgar) is set off against what is proper (implied also in "pur" of the first place name and the traditional image of snow)—perhaps even the scorching blast of communism against traditional propriety and property. This is an aspect of the customary opposition between the two rival brothers, which again finds its equivalent in a man like Ignatius, a writer turning inward and mapping out processes of the human soul with great care, writing influential, even incendiary (ignitious) books; and the other one, Francis Xavier, a man of action and conspicuous achievements, making converts by the tens of thousands.

The two saints, in short, go a long way.

The luster of their presence sheds light on a wider context too. A few lines later we come across "farrier's siesta in china dominos" (433.8): *farrear* and *siesta* are Spanish words, the first meaning to celebrate a feast; and Francis Xavier wanted to bring the Lord (Dominus) to China. Another meaning is *"in coena Dominis"* from the feast of Maundy Thursday, another prominent day in the Church calendar. And the same sentence goes on to accommodate the militant organizer of the Jesuit order and sovereign author: "from the sufferant pen of our jocosus inkerman militant." Inkerman was a battle fought by temporal powers (where the Russian general keeps being shot). The jocosus wielder of pen and ink, however, may well be Joyce himself. In *Ulysses*, Buck Mulligan says of Stephen Dedalus, as no doubt was also said of James Joyce: "You have the cursed jesuit strain in you, only it's injected the wrong way." We know that Joyce learned a great deal from his Jesuit educators and confessed himself grateful to them for teaching him "how to gather, how to order and how to present a given material."

We have begun to see some of the order and the presentation of the material.

But, for all the order that can be imposed on the passage, enough muddle remains to give room for supplementary interpretations. The correspondence, for example, between Joyce himself, or his fictional projections, and St. Ignatius does not work out too neatly—they could also be viewed as being in opposition. Jaun is not perhaps quite on the side of Francis Xavier either. So the commentator's show of rigid order needs the qualification of other observers, which is another way of saying that interpretation is not likely to stop at any given point. And there is always the possibility of error (as the Jesuit saints would be the first to agree). Some parts, moreover, have not yielded to analysis.

"Purpalume," to give an instance, has not yet been satisfactorily accounted for. It is probably Pampeluna, essential station in both saintly careers; it contains "purple" as well as "pur." In the absence of the precise, clinching gloss (which may yet come to light), a bit of fumbling in reference works is usually resorted to. "Purpalume" resembles a cluster of Greek words, composites of *pyr* (fire, usually transliterated as *pur* in English), and *palame* (palm of the hand). A verb *purpalamao* means to handle fire, a related adjective is once used to describe a flash of lightning. A saint handling fire or manipulating a celestial flash might be appropriate. A development of the same verb and an adjective *purpalames,* for a crafty, cunning person or someone given to pranks, may remind us of the charges often made against the Jesuits, or the pejorative sense that the name of the order has acquired, or else of the cunning prankish writer Joyce. Actually the verb just cited is furthermore defined to mean "cheat" by means of sly and cunning ways. This would take up the meaning of "chouse" that we encountered before and would be in tune with the whole passage. To be in tune does not, however, prove that these meanings are actually present. Could we accept these Greek lexicographical finds as relevant when we know that Joyce was no Greek scholar? (He could fumble with a dictionary, though, just as we can.) I offer all these possibilities here with a large question mark. The question is a rather fundamental one in the discussion of the exegetical methods and the limits of interpretation. More attention might be devoted perhaps to the fact that Joyce's words do have the effect of urging us on a quest for meaning; they urge us to make up analogies ourselves, by a process of inventive extrapolation.

For the question is: Do *I* make this all up? And of course I do, at least in part. Some of the foregoing exfoliation is one particular reader's imaginative weaving of the textual threads, a development of what I think is there on the page. So while, on one hand, Joyce himself is obviously involved as author, I, as the reader, on the other side of the fictional work, find myself very much entangled as well. To the writer, the poet, the maker, the reader is joined as a maker-up. And our making things up seems to be part (to retain an analogy made up from the words of our jocosus inkerman) of our mission. *Finnegans Wake* seems to send us abroad into far away fields (linguistic, historical, here hagiographical) beyond the seas, to engage us in our own spiritual exercises.

Games are a combination of orderly rules, skills, and a touch of chance. An aleatory element may not always appeal to our reason, but it would be difficult to exclude it from the unruly jostle of verbal particles in the book. There is a game in our passage too. Gammon (also called backgammon) in "terrorgammons" is a game in which the throwing of dice determines the moves. It helps to know that the activity "to gammon" also denotes humbug, deceit, and feigning. In "terror" and "gammons" we may have the playful and the serious side of our mundane existence, another implied contrast.

The game of *Finnegans Wake,* at any rate, is an ignitious one, and once we become ignitiated there is no simple way to stop the process. Joyce's words activate us. The criterion in such exegetical sports then might well be whether there is a reasonable and meaningful relation between our secondary elaboration and the original creation.

It is the intriguing half-light of the book that tempts speculation and elaboration. And even a passage as thoroughly subjected to scrutiny as the quoted one still contains rather dark patches. Ignorance is part of the game too, and it is because of ignorance that I did not have much to say on the last part of the second sentence: the basic meaning of "in terrorgammons howdy-dos" still escapes me.*

And this interrogative is a suitable one to bring this inconclusive exercise to a close. Its exemplary aim was to display, by prolonged trial and instructive error (error/gammons perhaps), a reader's position in a fairly new kind of experience, and to show, by practical demonstration, that we, as readers, are induced to depart from ordinary, linear progression in favor of what is a series of (hopesomely) illuminated leaps.

1970

---

*When I first wrote the reading exercise I was about to end it on what looked like an appropriately interrogative note: "in terrorgammons" seems to contain *"interrogamus"*—something that is always true about our relation to any part of the *Wake.* At the last moment James S. Atherton answered one of my queries by pointing out that, as everybody would know, the phrase is built around an echo from the Litany of the Saints, often sounded in Church: *"te rogamus, audi nos."* "We sinners *[peccatores],* beseech Thee, hear us" (compare "Loud, graciously hear us . . . hear the wee beseech of thees" *[FW* 258.26, 259.3] as further variations).

The intriguing, sobering thought is that all my extensive interrogations had not enabled me to hear the appeal to my ears *"audi nos."*

1983

7

Dogmad
or Dubliboused?

The text for my sermon is lifted out of the Fable of the Mookse and the Gripes in *Finnegans Wake:* "For the Mookse, a dogmad Accanite, were not amoosed and the Gripes, a dubliboused Catalick, wis pinefully obliviscent" *(FW* 158.3). Practical convenience and ignorance make it advisable to disregard the context, except to point out a strong theological flavor, and to treat the pair of adjectives merely as an essential contrast, a summary of basic attitudes.

The first term is built around the word "dogma," which stands for a kind of truth that has been settled, incontrovertibly, by some authority like the Church. Against such assurance we have "double," "duplicity," "dubiosity," or some related notion, as well as, of course, some free circulation of Dublin booze, which in turn might suggest the voicing of conflicting opinions (originally, *dogma* just meant opinion). Now "doubt" and *"dubium"* are based on duo, two, a going in two directions. Once you have a choice of two or more you get doubt or, in theology, heresy (which is the Greek word for choice). Compare also the German *zwei* and *Zweifel,* which, in the version "on his zwivvel" precedes the passage quoted above; it is balanced against "glaubering," containing "Glaube," belief *(FW* 157.12, 11). Some familiar positions within the Shaun-Shem polarity are manifesting themselves once more.

There is abundant evidence to show that dubious Gripes is closer to Joyce than doctrinaire Mookse. Or that Shem elsewhere is "of twosome twiminds" *(FW* 188.14), which is an etymological illustration of doubt. Or I could argue that "choice" is not a far cry from the name Joyce, an author who was aware of the portent of names. It is the opinion, for example, of Adaline Glasheen in the *Third Census* that phrases like "the real choice" or "hopesome's choice" (*FW* 161.15, 432.36) refer to Joyce himself. Moreover "dubli*boused*" includes *bous,* Greek for ox, the totem animal of Stephen Dedalus.[1] But to prove that the author has affinities with some of his fictional characters or particular biases can never determine the issue, especially when authority itself is in question.

However, if you set dogma against doubt, the result is doubt and the necessity of choice. Which is what the *Wake* invites us to even in the majority of its words. When "dogma" is augmented by one letter, "d" (a letter that, in a theological domain, would seem to be most potent; notice that both adjectives begin and end with that same letter), the result is not more authority but rather a subversion of the exalted meaning. A dogged sort of tenacity is stressed. The word also becomes anagrammatically blasphemous. So even into the term whose primary function seems to be to exemplify dogmatic certainty, some heresy is planted. Of course we might object that madness (as well as inebriation in "-boused") can be an alternative, nonrational way of arriving at the truth, *in vino veritas,* etc., but such Dionysian kind of *veritas* would clash with accepted dogmas.

So the fairest way to assess the duality is to say that it *is* a duality and invites choice. And that we do not know which one of the alternatives (in themselves alternatively at variance) is preferable. But if you do not know it becomes difficult to be dogmatic.

This, sadly enough, is the whole point. And not even a point that many Joyceans would disagree with—in theory. Which then leaves the question that continues to intrigue me—the question of how we, as Joycean readers, when we could benefit from such a unique education in applied skepticism, can still be as dogmatic in our own practical performances as we are. When you might even say that Joyce's later works are consistently and blatantly *also* about: How do we know when we think we know? Why are our own legislative inclinations so strong?

Joyce himself—for what that is worth—appears to have moved away from pontifical assurance. In the phase of his dedalescence he could hold forth and lay down the law, among friends, in public lectures, in writing, in no uncertain terms, about Drama, and Life, and Art. Stephen Dedalus, with his precisely worded and obviously memorized esthetic propositions, still reflects some of that phase. But we observe the author dissociating himself from Stephen. However we may apply Stephen's esthetic doctrines in *Stephen Hero* or in *A Portrait of the Artist as a Young Man,* by the time we come to *Ulysses* we are less likely to take his Shakespeare theory straight. We can watch Stephen manipulate facts and sources and may well become more interested in his own concealed motivation, or in some reverberating analogies, than in any literary truths that are conveyed. These may still be present, in some circuitous way, but they would have to be placed, as Mr. Best has it, "in the larger analysis." And the fact that at the end of his discourse Stephen admits, or pretends, not to believe his own theory, becomes part of some larger analysis.

Later in life Joyce was much more hesitant to make pronouncements on any big issues. Somehow we are not tempted to glean his Collected Wisdom on Life and Literature from any letters written, say, after 1910, but when we want to find Joyce backing some of our own pet theories, his pristine relics like *Stephen Hero* or early Notebooks offer themselves readily.

Scholars, and that includes Joyceans, naturally believe in their own theories. In the following pages I am going to suggest, naively, platitudinously, and repetitively, that we might present such theories with less show of assurance and with, at times, a bit more Socratic modesty. To claim less is sometimes more convincing. So I am going to take a few concrete instances of what seem to me unduly dogmatic positions, as good an opportunity as any to air a few prejudices.

Suspecting the answer know (FW 286.26)

At the Paris Symposium of 1975 a lively discussion turned around *Finnegans Wake*. Philippe Sollers made his point most succinctly by saying, first, that the English language is dead and second that the only thing alive within it—and he conspicuously put his hand upon the red volume in front of him—is *Finnegans Wake*. Against this Leslie Fiedler rose and pronounced *Finnegans Wake* dead, as I understood it, on grounds of the elitism of its language. Now obviously there was a strong hyperbolic and rhetorical element in these two contradictory formulas, in accordance with the occasion, and I am not sure either of the speakers was trying to be more than metaphorically emphatic. Even so we were faced with large conflicting generalities. (Philippe Sollers, moreover, confused the issue by speaking French, appropriately enough, but his statements had to be translated into—not, as you might think, some Wakean dialect—but actually into the defunct language referred to.) As it happened, the two views expressed together neatly circumscribe one of the *Wake's* main themes. The only point to be made here is perhaps that whenever we use the form "*Finnegans Wake* is . . . ," we might do well to remember that we are engaging in a metaphor.

A somewhat more blatant example of dogmatism was offered when a friend cornered me at another symposium to announce, in the kind of tired voice you would have expected of Hercules returning from one of his more demanding tasks: "I have decoded *Finnegans Wake*." And he meant that, mind you, in the strictest, secret service sense of the word. The *Wake* is now decoded, its message laid bare, we can finally dispense with the convoluted wrapping. I know that this scholar has invested a great amount of perceptive research to discover one important and perhaps persistent strain in the book.

At the same time, the notion of deciphering *Finnegans Wake,* of replacing its verbal texture by an authoritative translation, goes against the grain of our (which means most of our) experience of reading it. For that would freeze it into an immobile system. It is easy to reject this kind of attitude, but then we might well admit that most of us dabblers at the *Wake* are still haunted by some Platonic ideal to capture its quintessential core—the ideal of the Ultimate Reduction.

While one reader claims the secret of *Finnegans Wake* is to be found in *The Book of the Dead* and that everything can be traced to its Egyptian roots, a German writer, Arno Schmidt, discovered *the* secret long ago and proclaimed that, once we get rid of the mythological camouflage, *Finnegans Wake* is nothing but Joyce's malicious tirade against Stanislaus, who, as we learn, made advances to Nora in Trieste. This turns all of the *Wake* into a variegated brother battle, amplified a bit by distracting allusions, but there is, in this view, no room for even a paternal figure HCE, and the action, of course, *really* takes place in Trieste.² Now I am all in favor of a consistently Egyptian, or biographically Triestine, reading of the *Wake,* or a psychoanalytical or sectarian one—all of these can be supplementarily useful. The objection is to such delimiting formulas as "nothing but," or "fundamentally." They express some of our dearest ambitions: the intellectual imperialism of the mind makes us strive for the formula that would make us master, by categorizing and naming.

It may often be just a matter of phrasing. A good American critic said, in conversation, that the Homeric analogies in *Ulysses* are really *"just* a smokescreen" and that the operative underlying symbolism is, really, something else. We are inclined to such enlightened sweeping, and it is difficult to escape the temptation to show, casually, that all previous scholars have been barking up the wrong plumtree. In fact, without a certain amount of pointed emphasis we are probably never even listened to. The notion of a smokescreen that conceals some deeper reality can be fruitful. Still I wonder by what criteria we can dismiss smokescreens so easily and establish more valid hierarchies of relevance, and whether we might not better acknowledge that Joyce's works have their own intricate way of dealing with appearances and realities and that smokescreens might well be the only accessible reality ever.

It is perhaps the lure of the grand comprehensive gesture that prompts Suzette Henke to begin her study by telling us that *Ulysses* "preaches the 'good news' of the Logos and offers the promise of a 'new Bloomusalem in the Nova Hibernia of the future.' "³ Does the book preach and promise? The "new Bloomusalem," that hilarious, serious proclamation by Bloom in one of his non-real non-stage performances—is this what the novel promises? And if so, why and how should it promise *that* more than any of the other grave or flippant preposterosities of the Circe chapter? And what *is* preaching the gospel of "the Logos" in this context? St. John presumably knew what he meant, but any self-respecting Greek dictionary gives us at least one fully packed page about the word, and the Fathers of the Church have disputed the matter for centuries. We are on safer ground with the second statement, "Like Stephen Dedalus, Joyce was determined to use his artistic talents for the transformation of mankind." Was he? I had not even noticed that Stephen Dedalus was ever so fatuous as that and see no reason to assume that Joyce would follow suit—but this may well be a case of my own narrow-mindedness as a reader, along with a demonstrable preference for generalities over precision on the part of the writer.

Resonant certitude is not limited to general values. When we move to particulars we are likely to become less cautious. So it is quite possible to insist on the grounding of *Ulysses* on "incertitude" and "upon the void," as Marilyn French does very convincingly in her *The Book as World,* and yet to say, without signaling any incertitude, of the Sirens chapter that "the narrator's position is so extreme that the reader is forced to rebel against it."[4] Here there are certain assumptions (like the presence of a narrator and his—if it's a he—taking a position) that may be considered either doubtful and slightly misleading or just a matter of anthropomorphic tautology and therefore unassailable, but I would like to go on record that I am *not* forced to rebel against any such position, even if I were to recognize such a position as anything more than a descriptive convenience. Given Ms. French's philosophical premises of *Ulysses,* which I am happy to see reasserted, I am frankly puzzled by the very existence of a rigid sentence like "we must choose the total eradication of emotion or we must accept our ludicrousness."[5] In passing, I would like to investigate how many *meaningful* uses of the word "must," one of the strongest in the language, are possible in literary criticism; I have yet to see a statement of the form "Stephen must . . ." that would make sense.

There is plenty of scope for doubtful assurance in matters of interpretation. Since so many documents are inspected in *Ulysses* and in *Finnegans Wake* rather inconclusively, one might be more suspicious of easy solutions than we seem to be. At the Paris Symposium Jack P. Dalton gave an example of a very precise and methodical reading of the *Wake.* His area was a list of Dublin lord mayors that James S. Atherton had compiled long ago for the *Second Census.*[6] Dalton, with the evidence of Joyce's actual source, rejected the majority of Atherton's candidates and worked out the exact percentage of mistaken identifications, lord mayors, that is, who are either not named in *Finnegans Wake,* or else are verbally present, but not in their capacity as lord mayors. The case of Bartholomew Vanhomrigh was cited, who is in the book as father of Vanessa but not as a municipal dignitary. This may well be so. But, quite apart from the question of the compatibility of statistical figures with Wakean identification, it would seem permissible to see *Finnegans Wake* as a universe where a lot is made of the commonplace that a father can also be a lord mayor, just as in *Ulysses* a father can be son and husband and cuckold and an advertisement canvasser and a wandering jew and. . . . It takes great confidence to be sure who in the *Wake* is playing which particular role at any given moment. This Dalton set out to do. And he realized, as some of us have not, that part of the task is to *exclude* meaning, in order to safeguard against the total arbitrariness of Wakean glossolalia. And so we were offered what "a *real* explication of *Finnegans Wake* looks like."[7] The explication was a solid piece of documentation, a model of accuracy. I have great sympathy with Dalton's aversion to the lunatic fringe benefits of free association. We have had too much undisciplined *complication de texte;* we do need correctives. So Dalton warned us, when identifying Sir John Eccles, lord mayor of Dublin in 1710–11, in a passage, "handshakey congrandyoulikethems, ecclesency" (*FW* 535.11), immediately and categorically, against reading Eccles street into the text as well. This may be a wise precaution, but some of us were not as adamantly sure that the association of a street, so inevitable to most readers of *Ulysses,* can be rejected out of hand, on grounds of general principles. Especially since the fictitious inhabitant of number seven himself once became lord mayor of Dublin, in the Circe chapter (where also his hands are shaken and he is congratulated—*U* 479) Bloom is a lord mayor by the same psychological and literary process as is HCE. One will have to take a dogmatic stand to outlaw Bloom's or the street's perhaps tangential relevance. The principle evoked by Jack Dalton was an otherwise uncommented Law of Parsimony of Aristotelian reputation, a sort of Occam's razor. In my long-standing connection with *A Wake Newslitter* I honestly wish we had some such criterion, and the editors would be a lot happier if the contributors all complied to some rule of parsimony. At the same time, if you really want to apply a law of parsimony to literature—*Finnegans Wake* looks like an odd choice. It seems characterized by semantic abundance, referential indomitability, a strange dynamism, and a generative force not easily restricted; and all of this is made possible by precisely such facts as that a Dublin lord mayor can become a Dublin street, and that naming the one somehow implicates the other.

If it is tricky to fix the meaning of a word we can hardly expect agreement when the total nature of the *Wake* is in question. Let me, by way of illustration, compare two statements. One is by Grace Eckley, who set out to disprove the old theory that the twin sons occasionally merge their identities. This theory, we read, "which must promote an air of futility among readers, has unnecessarily diverted an entire generation from reading the novel as a novel, that is, a work adhering to certain requirements, one of which is consistency of character."[8] By all means it is well to remember that *Finnegans Wake* is *also* a novel, but its conformity to the requirements of the genre may tell us much less than its frank transcendence of such categories. And you may wonder if "consistency of character" is really an outstanding feature of the *Wake.* And then look at the view that appeared at about the same time.

There also a redirection is asked for, but the other way. Margot Norris writes: "The novelistic interpretation of *Finnegans Wake,* which has dominated *Wake* criticism for forty years, has several serious shortcomings which have made a comprehensive and integrated understanding of the work difficult."[9]

The views are neatly opposite and go, in my simplified paraphrase, something like: "For many years the *Wake* has been, wrongly, seen not as what it is when in fact it should be seen as a novel—or else not as a novel, but as a dream" (as Margot Norris has also reminded us in her book since).[10] Notice that Margot Norris is far less authoritative in her phrasing and insists merely on some disadvantages of the novelistic reading. And it is this sort of relativistic acknowledgment that is otherwise often absent. I for one am not greatly excited by a controversy whether *Finnegans Wake* "is" a novel or a dream, but I am perversely fascinated by the anachronistic survival of the formula *"FW* is X." It is the prototype of the algebra that we are lured into using against better judgment. On one side of the equation we have *Finnegans Wake,* "Shem," "ashplant," or "snow" (in "The Dead"), and on the other side we can have almost anything we champion. It is interesting to speculate on what kinds of truth can be expressed that way and what precisely we are doing when playing this game.

A Portrait, thank God, is still a novel, and simpler, and we may go back to its relatively clear outlines. The protracted, groping, slowly unfolding title seems to prefigure the learning process that goes on in the five chapters. It opens, as we know, in a manner expressive of, and suited to, the exploratory mind of a child. The simplest language is at the beginning; in fact it would be difficult to match the simplicity of the opening with examples elsewhere in the Joyce canon. And the most simple sentence of them all has the form just mentioned above, an elementary pattern of an Indo-European sentence: "He was baby tuckoo." We understand that one all right, and so does the boy, for all we know. He seems to assimilate it and take it in good faith. Which is how it has to be taken for it is totally mysterious, and nonsensical as well. For it claims that he, the boy later named Stephen, is identical with the hero of a story just heard: how *can* Stephen be baby tuckoo? Clearly he cannot be the (doubly) fictitious character that may have been created *ad hoc* by his father— and yet there is some relation between the two; they can be aligned. Our minds can bring them together, in a conceptive-creative act. Various academic departments can be enlisted to articulate the relation that has been created by language and passed off, sneakily, as something a child could grasp. Such is the nature of the truths that we make up, or the untruths that our language provokes us to phrase. And Joyce provokes us, tantalizingly early, to investigate a mystery we have come to live with a trifle too comfortably. Many of our critical systems are founded on such improbabilities as "He was baby tuckoo"; *Finnegans Wake* somehow hinges on the same sort of mystery. Joyce, after all, started the game of predicative supererogation himself.

"He" in the sentence is Stephen, to whom the story is being told. A rapport is established between the story and the person it is addressed to. The innocent statement implicates the listener and, by extension, also the reader of the novel. It is wholesome to realize that according to who "he," the listener, is the meaning of "baby tuckoo" also changes—and this too is what *Finnegans Wake* is about, and it explains some of our confusion with it.

We cannot, of course, do without the convenient shorthand formula "A is X," with that simplifying copula "is," but it might be advisable at least to register some discomfort when we use it. If we do not, our readers or listeners will provide the discomfort. As an example, the copulative history of Molly Bloom may be abbreviated. Molly Bloom has been pressed, repeatedly and sometimes with concomitant temperamental noises, into the type of mold just mentioned. Here is a partial listing.

Molly Bloom *is*   Penelope   das Fleisch, das stets bejaht
                          potted meat   Nora Barnacle
                          Ann Hathaway   unreal
                          the Holy Ghost   a dirty joke
                          an earth goddess   a slut
                          not an earth goddess a satanic mistress
                          a distinctly lower middle-class adulteress
                          a thirty-shilling whore
                          a nodal point of Joyce's masculine experience
                          etc.

What do we mean by "is"? Most of us, I take it, can give assent to most entries of the catalogue *as a series* of attempts to circumscribe Mollyness. But notice how we respond, almost automatically, as soon as any one statement is foisted upon us as though it had some unique, clinching, ultimate relevance. Most authors (including *the* author) do not make such claims, but some of them seem to. It is then that our critical energies are released in corrective protest against, say an assertion like "For all of Molly's attractive vitality, for all her fleshly charms and engaging bravado, she is at heart a thirty-shilling whore."[11] Independent of our moral views of Mrs Marion Bloom (if we are inclined to become moralistic), and independent of whether we think of thirty-shilling whores with indignation or with nostalgia—most of us would bristle against the conclusive air of the pronouncement, perhaps that divinely disdainful "at heart": this about a novel that also exposes the futility of judgments that aspire to be final.

What falsifies such sweeping characterizations is perhaps merely that, out of typographical necessity, they have to end with a period, otherwise a signal of finality. This sign is grotesquely hyperbolized at the end of Ithaca, wholly absent in the body of the Penelope chapter, and pointedly missing at the end of the *Wake*. Our critical efforts sometimes look like dogged attempts to reintroduce the periods, full stops, where Joyce significantly utilized the potency of their absence.

As an exercise in perception, *Ulysses* prepares—or rather, literally, post-disposes—us to challenge what we already thought we knew. After many years we now begin to wonder, collectively, if Molly's father was actually a major in the British Army, if Bloom really is or was a freemason, and who now, come on, moved that furniture? These are matters of fact in the most fact-obsessed novel, and in view of our factual—to say nothing of the textual—uncertainties it is even more surprising to understand the assurance with which less tangible matters are decided, the significance of Bloom's meeting with Stephen, for example. This often looks like a case of arbitrary selection and evaluation of supporting evidence. Priorities seem to be subjective. What is more important, in deciding this issue: the improbability of Stephen returning to the Blooms?—a Homeric equivalent?—an anti-Semitic song?—a celestial constellation?—large scale misunderstanding?—Epps's massproduct or communal pissing or Molly's Dantean bedroom light? Why should any of these details have more symbolic or practical importance than any of the others? For all we know, the solution might be somewhere in Bloom's second drawer or in the Dublin water supply system. I am not trying to sound ironical about a favorite and fascinating pastime. I am merely wondering how interpretative decisions come about.

Consider how much has been made of Bloom's breakfast order for next morning. Here we have, at least, some positive twist and a possible reinstitution of proper domestic roles and reassurance for readers who would feel deprived without it. But then we cannot tell if Bloom will actually get his room service. Molly may or may not oblige, the text cannot determine her resolution, for if we know one thing about Molly, it is that she changes her mind. Even supposing Bloom will be served on the morning of the 17th, does that mean it will become a habit? Obviously we cannot predict even a fraction of the future breakfast habits of the Blooms. But I would like to push the uncertainty further into the past as well and wonder if Bloom did ask for his breakfast. We have only Molly's word for it, and toward the end of the novel the jury might well have learned not to trust any one person's unsupported evidence (do not forget, from now on Dubliners will know that Stephen attended Paddy Dignam's funeral, because that is what the newspaper said, and that Bloom won money on a bet). It is true that the shock of an unusual request sets off Molly's monologue, her irritation is real enough and kinetic. But we are not told what exactly it was that Bloom wanted. She begins with "his breakfast in bed with a couple of eggs" (*U* 738) and finally escalates the order to "eggs and tea and Findon haddy and hot buttered toast" (*U* 764). Either the order got magnified in the reminiscence, or in parodistic elaboration, but it seems to contain some fictional addition. The one constant and therefore most reliable item is the two eggs. But then it is strange that Bloom would insist on what he specifically dismissed on the previous morning: "Ham and eggs, no. No good eggs with this drouth" (*U* 56).

If Bloom did give an itemized order it is also odd that the pedantic detailed account in Ithaca fails to list it. We explicitly get a scrappy list of Bloom's modifications of his version of Bloomsday, but we are not informed about any command as innovative as the breakfast regulation. We do know, however, that the chapter's narrative slant might well withhold essential facts. But if that is true, and if we have to take narrative omissions into account as well, as indeed we have to, then there is no telling what other, perhaps even more important, omissions there may be. It does not make us *more* assured about anything.

Molly's recall of Bloom's words may be her interpretation of what the cryptic text renders as "dark bed . . . roc's auk's egg" (*U* 737), in the last, least articulated answer of Ithaca. This mixture of domesticity and mythology may consist of somnolent mumblings, it may be a distortion due to the relaxation of narrative control toward the end of some final chapters, or it might express the dissolution of some consciousness in the novel.

It is just conceivable that the last chapter, which reveals some of Bloom's misconceptions (one is about the bed on which he falls asleep—as if to suggest the doubtful nature of all sub-positions), is set off by one of Molly's, perhaps out of a sense of guilt. We know she misconstrues words all the time. If people interpreted each other's sayings correctly there would be no such novel as *Ulysses*. It would not even have a Homeric precedent, for without contrived verbal misconception Odysseus would never have escaped from the cave of the Cyclops to report the story of his adventures. Perhaps also Molly is unknowingly playing the role of Penelope as the knitter and unraveler of webs.

My point is not to propound a new oval theory of the book but to show that there may be more questions than we had thought. And I am amused to think of a Ulyssean contingency where Bloom might find himself served, by a rather resentful Molly, with a breakfast he never ordered, containing eggs that he would not want.

A minor but instructive case of misapprehension concerns the two women who appear at the beginning of the Proteus chapter, *"Frauenzimmer"* (*U* 37). Stuart Gilbert called them "midwives" and this ascription has perpetuated itself to find its culmination, probably, in an *Index and Guide to the Dramatic Characters:*

MacCabe, Mrs. Florence
Midwife and widow of the late Patrick MacCabe[12]

That is the kind of information we expect from a reference work, and the chances are that it will be used and passed on. Of course we know neither profession nor name of those two women. They move into the range of

Stephen's sight and he notices that one carries an umbrella, "gamp," and the other "her midwife's bag." And from this attribute all the trouble arose. It occurs in a cluster of female associations, from "our mighty mother" to widow, bride, St. Bride, sister, nun, misbirth, Eve and navel—this tells us very little about external reality, but a lot about Stephen's obsessions. The bag is real enough, but the profession of the woman cannot be inferred with any certainty. Around the solid objects perceived, gamp and bag, Stephen creates fictitious particulars by means of a Protean technique, and he uses an imaginary obituary phrase to provide the nascent character with a name and a piece of biography—this is not Stephen recognizing some acquaintance but rather Stephen imitating Adam finding names for created things (Gen. 2:19): Proteus is full of it, and one way of seeing the chapter is as an elaborate gloss on that scene in Edenville. Much of our interest is "to see what he would call them"; and Genesis also prefigures that art of the chapter, philology: ". . . and whatsoever Adam called every living creature, that *was* the name thereof" (Gen. 2:19). Subsequently, in Aeolus, the fiction is enlarged and varied in the Parable of the Plums. There, more circumstantial detail is added and Stephen no longer calls the women midwives (if he ever did) but, with similar poetic license, "Dublin vestals" (*U* 145).

Stephen, it is true, continues to associate them with midwives, or "babemaries"—but this seems to be his problem. When the two women reappear, in Wandering Rocks, we are given what looks like the most objective view: "Two old women . . . trudged through Irishtown . . . one with a sanded umbrella, one with a midwife's bag" (*U* 242). The narrative voice sounds so unassuming and low key that it invites trust in the *"midwife's* bag"—not, of course, that a person carrying such a bag has to be a midwife, any more than a person wearing Buck Mulligan's shoes or trousers has to be Buck Mulligan. And the same voice tells us, immediately, that it is a bag "in which eleven cockles rolled." Considerations of hygiene alone would make us wish then that the lady in question is not taking professional equipment out for a walk.

It is much more likely that the narrative voice is not objectively descriptive, but just neutrally assimilative and incorporating earlier associations. As in that other bag, "the costbag of Goulding, Collis and Ward" (*U* 252), which we know is just a dead pan carryover of one of Richie Goulding's habitual jokes (*U* 88). In such a way Stephen's appellation has simply shifted to the chapter of Wandering Bags. Oddly enough, towards the end of the chapter the two women, umbrella, bag, eleven cockles and all, "halted themselves, . . . to view with wonder the lord mayor and lady mayoress without his golden chain" (*U* 254–55). This clearly should alert the reader to the hazards of hasty identification. The chain of all this links back, trickily, to the text as a strandentwining cable of doubtful identities.

The profession of two peripheral figures in the texture does not deserve so much attention as does the ubiquitous problem of how to disentangle reality, imagination, joke, fiction, transformation, and narrative refraction. In this case we witness an already fictional character, Stephen Dedalus, within the novel creating a fictional character around him. He gives one real woman an *ad hoc* profession and a name, and the name that he gives (invents, or remembers, or transfers), Florence MacCabe, seems to bear some florid relation to the name that Joyce gave to his other main fictional character (who in turn helps to bring the pseudonymous identity of M'Intosh into being). And it all started with a gamp and a bag, juxtaposed. The reciprocity is striking: "gamp," we know, derives from the fictional character, Mrs Gamp, in a novel by Dickens, and it has come now to mean an object in reality. Around an objective bag a character is created, doubly fictitious, whom we find listed later, dead serious, in a character index. Midwifery does come in: the reader is actually attending a birth—but in some obstetric transformation of which the human mind, shown in its immense fertility, or the artistic imagination, is capable.[13]

After more than half a century of *Ulysses* we, as readers, are still eminently fallible, even on the most elementary of all possible levels. We are led astray by first impressions, inattention, printed certitudes, and by what Leo Knuth has termed "reader's traps."[14] The central character of the novel is, on the whole, aware of traps and wary of his steps. Above all, he usually knows that he may be wrong. His temperament is indeed the scientific. This shows in his thoughts, words, and deeds and often in parodistic exaggeration ("the distinguished scientist Herr Professor Luitpold Blumenduft," etc.). That his knowledge is defective does not detract from an essentially humanistic quality of his mind. He proceeds like the traditional scientist; he is ready to challenge his own assumptions. His skeptical turn of mind, his awkward "on-the-other-handness," his "but thens," handicap him against more confident monotropic opponents: the result is his hesitating approach, his wrong starts, and his reversals. Even when he sounds assertive, as in the defiant thrust "Christ was a jew like me," he is less stating a truth than pointing out an absurdity.

Bloom's best advertised model, Odysseus, survived by not trusting appearances, by not accepting things at their face value, and by creating strategic surfaces and guises in emergencies. He is a protoskeptic. When the nymph Calypso comes to announce that, after many long years, he is to be sent home, which he wanted all along, he instinctively distrusts the good news. The very first words that Homer gives him in the poem are of doubt: "Goddess," he said, "it is surely not my safe conveyance but some other purpose that you have in mind when you suggest that I should cross this formidable sea, with all its difficulties, in such a craft. Even the fastest sailing ships don't make the voyage. . . ." And he insists on the strongest possible assurance that language is capable of: "so give me your solemn oath that you will not plot some new mischief against me."[15]

This skeptical attitude has been inherited by Leopold Bloom and should have been by scientists and literary critics. The overt meaning of words is not to be trusted automatically. Odysseus could still call divine assistance to his aid through the potent form of oaths, especially when addressing a demigoddess who would be obliged to believe in the validity of language that could evoke divine repercussions. There is no such corroboration in the world of *Ulysses*, where oaths, in particular, have become next to meaningless noises or fillers (expletives) to indicate emotion or emphasis.

Through this world Bloom moves cautiously as, among other things, a rational being of remarkable flexibility. He observes, deduces, double-checks, modifies; he makes generalizations and can revise them. In this role he is the traditional, not perfectly equipped, but functional agnostic scientist. This etymological contradiction in terms is suitable, for Bloom like everybody else is contradictory. Especially so in a chapter that abounds in contradictions, terminological, logical, etymological, and metaphorical—the Eumaeus chapter.

In this late episode Bloom's language seems the least suited to the occasion, the least Odyssean one possible and quite unlikely to impress his new companion. Bloom's rhetorical mismanagement infiltrates the entire chapter, which looks like an extension of his oddly restimulated mind. It is difficult to disentangle his associative forays from the chapter's distinctive features. Eumaeus hints at a way in which Bloom would talk, or write, if he had the facility of a gentleman-author; it hints at a way in which Bloom would aspire to write the novel within which he occurs.[16] Critics who can recognize bad writing when they see it have treated the chapter with condescension and often with premature characterization, usually having recourse to the most misleading term, "fatigue," to explain some of its awkwardness.

Preparatory to anything else, I would emphasize that the chapter has so far defied our attempts to describe or classify it; to do so one might have to resort to its own tortuous language or to strain some analogies. It complies best with Senn's rule of thumb—that when we think we know what a feature of *Ulysses* really is we can be sure to be partially wrong. Naturally we may turn into complacent schoolmasters and repeat that Eumaeus is just a jumble of clichés (to label something cliché is a fashionable way of indicating one's own superiority), but any honest effort to come to terms with the whatness of Eumaeus tends to involve us in a Bloomian struggle with appearances, fictions, smokescreens, and diction.

To separate fact from fiction is one of Bloom's concerns. His suspicion permeates the story. Ironically, when he forgets it and becomes unquestioningly confident ("orthodox as you are"—this to Stephen—*U* 644), he is wrong. But normally he is intrigued by the identity of the sailor or the proprietor of the coffee place. He distrusts documents. It is Bloom who turns over the postcard that does not support the sailor's adventurous claims. The newspaper report of the funeral amusingly falsifies such nonpartisan issues as the presence of the mourners, and the reader for once is privileged to understand some mechanisms of misinformation and Bloom's mediation. As informant, object, accomplice, and victim of the communicative blunders, Bloom is deeply intricated in the tissue of untruths, which one would have no reason to distrust. It is sobering to realize that when we, as scholars, want to measure the fiction of *Ulysses* against the reality of Dublin 1904, this reality will consist for us in precisely such documents as postcards, letters, newspapers, *Thom's Directory,* or memoirs—that is, previous fictions. Clive Hart has shown that *Thom's Directory* for 1904 listed the Joyces as living in two different places and is full of similar fictitious delights.[17] Such is the reliability of documents and the nature of all reports. Errors, rumors, misprints, misinterpretations, to say nothing of deliberate whitewashing or falsehoods, are transformed into biography or history. We are not far, at this stage, from *Finnegans Wake*, where it has become entirely futile to sort out reality from myth or imagination.

Homeric roles help to confuse the issues. Odysseus is impersonated mainly by others. Bloom remains largely truthful; his one prominent guise is a rhetorical one; he is reaching for the identity of a man of letters. Otherwise he is not an inventor, but a discoverer of lies, a detective by inclination. He is explicitly related to Sherlock Holmes, looking for clues, making deductions, shifting what little evidence there is. His approach is (at least where his own anxieties do not intrude) scientific; he is careful to separate "opinion" and "conjecture" from certainty, and he sprinkles his speech and thoughts with qualifications. We learn about his "skeptical bias": "he entertains the gravest possible doubts" throughout. He communicates poorly, but he carefully inspects fictions. His penchant for reconsideration has become gigantic. When he questions the veracity of the sailor's stories and remarks to Stephen that Murphy could "lie like old boots," he immediately revises that sentence in his thoughts in what is both an expression *and* a parody of a genuine intellectual perseverance in pursuit of objectivity:

> Yet still, . . . life was full of a host of things and coincidences of a terrible nature and it was quite within the bounds of possibility that it was not an entire fabrication though at first blush there was not much inherent probability in all the spoof he got off his chest being strictly accurate gospel. (*U* 635)

Could anyone try to be more fair? This is the tentative syntax and vocabulary of probability, which always has a way of lengthening the sentence. The laborious qualifications add to the longueurs as do the metaphors freely mixed. Bloom does not express himself with the concision of a Sherlock Holmes or a Bertrand Russell; he is groping along, and Eumaeus still recaptures the devious path of verbalizing kinetic thought in all its randomness. But in its nervous oscillations the style registers discomfort at the inevitable inaccuracy of its own articulation, and it proceeds to set the matter right.[18] Bloom interjects modifying phrases and various demurrers. He is alert enough to try to repair any emerging damage. It is part of the delightful incongruity of the chapter that the reiterated application of remedial logic is mismatched by the syntax. A rational order has to be hastily super- or rather post-imposed on what has already been formulated. The rational mind has lost some of its pristine sharpness but is still functioning. The qualifications are afterthoughts and have to be clumsily accommodated as the sentences unfold. The syntactical joints are strained. The tardy rectifications distend the sentences, which seem to come to a halt only by accident or by temporary dysfunction. This is the stylistic and grammatical equivalent of the wild goose chase after truth. The lack of finality is part of it: Eumaeus has its own special affinities with *Finnegans Wake* (and many syntactical similarities, as Hugh Kenner has pointed out): the passage quoted might easily be touched up to become an item of the convoluted defense of H. C. Earwicker.

Eumaeus imitates the elusive and frustrating striving of language towards validity, and it demonstrates as well the best that we, as readers, can do to articulate views on *Ulysses* or the *Wake*. It shows that every fleeting insight is a transitory phase in a process.

In stressing a cognitive effort in its maligned style, I have so far neglected its allusive luxuriance. But this too can be seen as a hazardous reaching out toward truth. Since it cannot be stated succinctly—though perhaps simulated by an infinite regress of contradictions—it may be illustrated, figuratively. So Eumaeus abounds in metaphorical and proverbial wisdom, adages, figures and images, classical stock-in-trade like "the heel of Achilles." It begins, conspicuously enough, with the phrase "in orthodox Samaritan fashion" (*U* 613), the narrative voice introducing a method used in the New Testament, the parable, a roundabout way of saying what could not otherwise be conveyed as well. A parable is literally one thing thrown alongside another. The chapter is full of it. There are ostensible gains and outrageous risks. For a point may not be grasped ("Achilles" and "tendon" leads to "tender Achilles"—*U* 640, 658, 660) and any analogy adds its quota of discordant features. The chapter, as though it had its own self-reflective consciousness, is aware of this too and counteracts it by attaching yet more figurative devices. This results not in clarification but in an accumulative clash of metaphorical or etymological implications. It is easy to see that "Samaritan fashion" needs some adjectival support like "genuine"; and "orthodox" is, at first blush, a satisfactory, resounding choice until we realize that the parable ' of the Good Samaritan was originally directed against the complacency of the orthodox, and so the whole phrase is compromised rather than corroborated. A noun like "fogeydom" is felt to be weak on its own and so is propped with "effete" (*U* 627); that conforms to a venerable stylistic pattern, but the effect is marred, as intuition or philology can tell us. For "effete" is clearly female (and related to that word) it meant "what has ceased to bring forth young," and so it is an odd bedfellow for the masculine associations of "fogey," which once meant an invalid soldier. So dormant meanings are revived and rise in semantic protest. And we in turn are alerted and may notice, for example, that for all its biological unlikeliness, a transition like the one from effeteness to fogeydom was quite common in the preceding Circe chapter, though in a totally different mode. Or we might infer that "effete" and "fogeydom" are about as well-matched as Bloom and Stephen are in this and the next chapter, which is not to establish a significant algebraical relation between the words and the persons but simply to hint at some erratic appropriateness. The forced juxtaposition makes us first sit up and look closer and then perhaps realize that the oxymoronic phrase also reflects Bloom's social fumbles, while the incompatibility of the linguistic roots reflects tensions and conflicts.[19] Perversely, then, even the idiomatic lapses of the chapter can serve to impersonate the mind's devious navigations.

Expecting the answer guess *(FW 286.27)*

We are of course uncannily close to *Finnegans Wake,* the microcosmic verbal integration of doubt. Suppose you want to express some elusive relation, but not with the pussyfooted caution of the Eumaeus mode, not in wasteful zigzag of trailing correctives and metaphorical hopscotch. You might want to try to put the qualifications not after the respective statement, but right into it. The result is something like the diction of the *Wake,* which tends toward instant contradiction. A laborious sequence of restatements is replaced by simultaneous alternatives: serial modification becomes instant conflict. The integrity of the word (with its implied pretense of a one-to-one relationship) has to be sacrificed. In the non-Euclidean grammar of dissent of the *Wake* too much is being said incompletely at the same time. The language becomes heretic (a matter of semantic choices): its heteroglyphy alone would put it in opposition to any kind of orthodoxy.

Verbal options favor suggestive possibilities more than distinct identities. If we do not want to determine whether some person is a hunchbacked pub-keeper, or an English king, or a Shakespearean character, or the actor on the stage, in a pub, on a battlefield, or from a book or a nursery rhyme, there may be no more concise way than "when Dook Hookbackcrook upsits his ass booseworthies jeer and junket but they boos him oos and baas him aas when he lukes like Hunkett Plunkett" *(FW* 127.17). Luke Plunkett was a Dublin amateur actor who so nicely botched the death scene in *Richard III* that the audience asked for a ricorso,[20] and he now obligingly contributes to a botched nonidentification in the *Wake.* There are numerous options for phrasing what is going on in the passage. Even if we suppress a suspicion that an evangelist or some later Irish politicians are coinvolved, we are hard put to determine who is, ultimately, impersonating whom. This becomes a matter of perspective or convenience. Each person is "idendifined" in terms of the others. If, in spite of that, you still want to indulge in the reductive game of deciding that, say, "St. Patrick is Shem" or "No, no, he is Shaun," that is up to you. At the end of the Anna Livia Plurabelle chapter a voice asks "but howmulty plurators made eachone in person?" (*FW* 215.25), and the question is addressed to "my trinity scholard." One implication seems to be that whoever can sort out the persons of the mysterious Holy Trinity would also qualify to unravel those of the *Wake*. And it turns out that, the more dogmatic you choose to be, the better you are prepared for the job and the more pointless it becomes.

Practically minded, I am going to illustrate the paradogmatic nature of the *Wake* by a last example. I am choosing the Eumaean approach; in rambling qualifications I will try to impose subjective sense on a relatively simple sentence, 19 out of 218,076 words arranged in a certain order. (This is to give some quantitative dimension to the probable relevance of the following speculations.) The aim is not any new interpretation, in fact the observations made will be commonplace, and the focus is on the dynamics of the uncertainty principle. Moreover, the context will be ignored and the passage treated as though it were a self-contained unit. It is taken from Jaun's sermon:

> We may come, touch and go, from atoms and ifs but were presurely destined to be odd's without ends (*FW* 455.16).

Note that the first part is tentative, careful, and the second part, after "but," much more assured, with the emphatic word "presurely," the only one that is not standard English. And it is the reference to the origin, what lies behind us, which is expressed with caution: "We may. . . ." The assurance extends to what is yet to come. Experience teaches us the other way: the past usually looks more certain than the future. In similar reversion of what might be expected, the language of the more doubtful proposition is reasonably clear, on the surface, but it is far less obvious what we are presurely destined to be—what is it to be "odd's without ends," mind you, with that disturbing apostrophe? So there are anomalies before the statement is even looked into.

Something appears to be said about a general "us," about the human condition, the origin and goal of life. One account of it, the one that emerges almost of its own, looks like a popularized scientific view. It suggests probability ("may," "odd's"), it proceeds from the observation of the (once) smallest perceivable particles, the atoms, and it is aware of the hypothetical nature of all deductions. It acknowledges the chaos of appearance and the oddity of a seemingly infinite kosmos. Human destinies may be ultimately determined by the atoms that constitute bodies, and the indeterminable movements of the atoms may resemble the couplings and separations of human beings. An element of randomness remains. The scientific mind is doing its best to impose some normative order on what it perceives.

Evidently this view is colliding with an entirely different but simultaneous exposition of the human predicament, the traditional doctrine of the Church. In this rendering there is no doubt about the origin: we descend from our first parents, Adam and Eve, whose doings also predetermined our fate. In this reading, "odd's" resolves itself into "God's," and "odd's without ends" can be anchored in the doxology: "world without end"—*in saecula saeculorum.* Salvation is somehow connected with predestination.

The two views whose outlines have become visible are in conflict, or at least they were so at some stage in history (they remind us of controversies between the Church and Science in the nineteenth century). Here they are merged almost totally. It is as though—to change the ground—the voices of Bloom (with his scientific curiosity and materialist outlook) and Stephen (whose terminology remains saturated with Catholic concepts) were blended. (Remember how Stephen's "soul . . . a simple substance," of Augustinian origin, somehow became Bloom's "simple soul"—*U* 633–34). In *Ulysses* a deceptive answer still had to follow a misunderstood question, or else the manner of the Telemachus chapter is retroactively corrected by attitudes emerging in Ithaca. *Finnegans Wake* can do away with succession: contradiction is immediate. We *can* (as I have tried) separate it into component dictions if we want to.

But actually the two views that I dissociated are not simply *there;* they had to be extracted. It takes an act of interpretation to assemble the various textual stimuli into several homogenous systems. And it takes a bit of straining too. For the two overlapping accounts of life are not only subjective options but, moreover, incomplete and defective and literally—as a matter of letters—faulty. The transformation of "odd's" into "God's" can be supported by lexicography, but even so it *is* a transformation. And, as the documents will tell us that it occurs in oaths and asseverations, it amounts to a somewhat irreverent way to prove the linguistic existence of God. The two statements are then defective in themselves and corrective of each other, as though, under the onslaught of each one, the other were cracking a bit. The meanings are there then by some ghostly presence. Eve is really absent and conditional, but "ifs" coupled with "atoms" makes her absence so obtrusive that she seems evoked. She and Adam are hidden, perhaps here in compliance with Genesis 3:8, but discernible.

Why, anyway, should we undo Joyce's handiwork and back-translate a Wakean item into what it is at such pains to evade? *Finnegans Wake* refuses to remain content with the habitual simplifications of language. Our minds, however, can only grasp simplifications. My own, in this case, were shaped by a desire to place the *Wake* within a tension between dogma and doubt, so I reduced the coexistent conflicts into one that suited my purpose. We extract what sense we can find to rearrange it according to our needs and our categories. But let us by all means know that this is what we are *doing* and not confuse it with what *Finnegans Wake* "is."

Our sentence does not just contrast science with religion, or chance with teleology. Each of the alternatives, apart from its semantic deficiencies, contains its inherent tensions. There is no unified view of the destiny of the human soul in Christianity; Roman Catholic and Protestant terms jostle each other. The religious conception adumbrated barely conceals the seeds of its own schisms. Nor, of course, is there any generally accepted view of an atomistic universe. When Joyce was writing *Finnegans Wake* the concept of the atom was undergoing a change that was not only semantic: the atom all of a sudden became the opposite of what the word said it was, it became threateningly divisible, a newly discovered microcosm of its own, with great energetic possibilities. So the opinions of science had to be modified, and in the twenties a layman was moreover told by the closest observers of the atom that no accurate statements could be made about the comings, touchings, and goings of its parts, so that causality was in danger. One way of phrasing all this is to say that in *Finnegans Wake* an emerging pattern tends to be discredited as soon as it becomes discernible. The text begins by unraveling its Penelopean texture at once.

So far, in my reading, I have still assumed that something is being said about the human condition, life and death and a possible afterlife. But a more parochial reading could see "atoms and ifs" as the name of a Dublin church, or the name of a pub (the two were historically, and locally, connected), and so a specifically Irish destiny seems to be outlined. A local priest might well aim his admonitions at those who come from, or will resort to, the adjacent pub. The algebra of the *Wake* allows an equation of any public house with Earwicker's (if it is his) tavern. Remaining in the same environment, we can release more semantic energy if we split "ifs" into its atomic parts and take it for the abbreviation of "Irish Free State" (note that "free state" would also contrast with predestination): this state was clearly characterized by a precarious origin, erratic movements and clashes and schisms. We might then speculate upon the relations between national and personal freedom in the new independent state or the dominance of the Church. All that this exercise is aiming at is to toy with the possibility to see a sentence also as a local Irish concern.

It so happens that *"if"* is also French for the yew tree, which is the letter "I" in the Irish alphabet. Such a Franco-Irish translation would provide, circuitously, the addition of "you" (yew) and "I" to "We" and a tree for Adam and Eve, a tree that has connotations of death and resurrection. So we can guess how an arboreal reading could take over. Or let me just mention a possible Egyptian interpretation if we allow "atoms" (following James S. Atherton and Adaline Glasheen) to refer also to the creation God Atem: we would get a *Book of the Dead* version of the soul's destination to supplement the Christian one.

What I have been doing is simply to start from different "ifs" and try out the hypotheses with the necessary verbal adaptations and violations. The results are interpretative guesses, odds without end, of the kind that we have all seen. If the dramatic context of the sentence were brought in, the role of the speaker Jaun and his present strategies, still more patterns would be the outcome ("odd's," for example, would fit into the prevalent racing terminology of the passage; the human race could be connected, once more, with the circularity and imprevidibility of track events.) Even the isolation of one sentence shows that *Finnegans Wake* is multicontextual. And every interpretation also activates its own doubts. Interpretations are if-propositions. And by some sort of coincidence, *if* in Old Norse means doubt. But we hardly need this philological gloss: doubt is present in the etymological potential of the English conjunction and, more importantly, it has been dynamically staged as a process.

Why should we not take the sentence as yet one more expression of the solipsistic side of the *Wake*, its one perennial concern with its own being? Maybe it is talking just about itself: for *Finnegans Wake* does come from Adam and Eve's (inverted as "Eve and Adam's" in the very first line), there are odds without end, the book is typographically without end. Its reading is touch and go; our understanding is often limited to its particles and, as demonstrated, very iffy.

And finally let me see the sentence simply as an elaboration of what the word "odd" can imply, a semantic festival launched to illustrate its meanings. Like life, *Finnegans Wake* is odd, and "odd" is defined by what it is not: not regular, not even, not fitting into preexisting categories. It accommodatingly suggests both a deficiency, a pattern to be completed, and a surplus that defies order.

So it provokes us into completing the patterns, filling the void uncertainty with some prejudiced substance. We are tempted to press the *Wake* back into the categories that it transcends. All of the meanings that I have interpolated from the nineteen words are not there: if they were, they would not have to be extracted. The meaning, perhaps, can best be seen in the extraction itself, in the constructive process. This is not new in Joyce; the narrator of "The Sisters" had already puzzled his head "to extract meaning from . . . unfinished sentences," and in reading the story we are doing something similar, making a poor best of snippets of unreliable information. In *Finnegans Wake* information is unreliable, incomplete, and defective, and reading amounts to instant repair work in the light of what we know. For better or worse, we have to change the *Wake* into what it is not.

Quantitatively *Finnegans Wake* is characterized by utter economy and extreme redundancy. As readers we have to settle for less (than, say, the exact appearance of words and phrases) and not be content with too much. We have to accept approximations, more or less adequate (Eve out of if's) and acceptable to others. For our mental constructs we have to mis-take the verbal appearance. This would not do in normal life: "if's" is not accepted for "Eve" on a legal document, and we know that some readers will neither acknowledge it nor its principle. *Finnegans Wake* conditions us to ignore such small differences and to charge them, as well, with full meaning and to fill gaps. This restorative process is chancy. Remember that Bloom once completed an unfinished sentence by supplying a wholly correct completion: "macintosh," and this led to a tangle of identity in *Ulysses*. There it looks like an exception; it has become the misrule of the *Wake*.

My main point is that our transformations *are* transformations, both necessary and doubtful. So I would simply argue for more care in the articulation of our observations. A little more reticence, perhaps, when we use formulas like "*Finnegans Wake* is . . ."; for it is not, even if it may be useful to treat it as though it were, for the moment. As long as we know what we are doing the damage is minimal. My own parallactic reading of a single sentence is in some ways valid and, inevitably, also false, false not only in the selective bias of my perspective, but in the method itself. For I took it for granted that one atomic element is a microcosmic sample of the whole. The method works, up to a point. But the supposition may be as hazardous as all other approaches, as doubtful as reducing the *Wake*'s proliferation to the same old family nexus, or seeing it predominantly (and drearily) in terms of Joyce's letters to Harriet Weaver—or in terms of the sum total of all available notebook entries.

Falsify if you but will, simplify you must—let us not forget it. It is not my impression that we, Joyceans, always do signal our limitations. We cannot say Joyce did not give us due warning.

I am by no means suggesting that we avoid taking clear stands, that we just hem and haw cautiously and not, for example, treat *Finnegans Wake* as though it were really a novel and only that. It is important that even obstinately consistent interpretations be pursued and discussed. That will sharpen our observation, add new insights. The trouble is that the academic game encourages formulations that are often closer to the Cyclopean mode than the Bloomian or Eumaean or Wakean approach. That makes us, to the irritated amusement of bystanders, as impressive and as pompous as Gabriel Conroy or professor Shaun.

The most adequate way might be to talk like *Finnegans Wake*. After all, the language of the *Wake* is an optimal, though impractical, way to say something that can hold up to investigation. Perhaps the only true thing about life is something like "We may come, touch and go. . . ." It misfits so many contexts that it cannot be entirely wrong.

In *Finnegans Wake* Joyce may have hit upon the method to express incontrovertible truth—to enact the process of controversion itself. In reading it one becomes an agent of controversion and, presurely, one would have to remain rather dogmad in order not to become dubliboused.

1975–78

Notes

A doubly biassed afterthought
This essay was originally a talk given at Princeton in 1975, then, in another version, as an address to assembled Joyceans at the James Joyce Colloquium 1976 at SUNY, Buffalo, before it was revised, with new examples, into its printed form. There was a time when I thought that new samples might become harder to find, that dogmatic or monotropic pronouncements might, under Joyce's gentle impact, gradually fade out of scholarship and that my caveats would become as obsolete as they ought to be. This, obviously, has not happened.

One response to my essay that I did not expect was that a few readers misconstrued my trite warnings against uncritical certainty as though I had implied that any reading, no matter how sloppy or crotchety or superficial, is as good as any other. On the contrary I believe that the more scrupulous and circumspect, the more *scholarly,* our research is, the more we will shy away from doctrinaire simplification.

1983

1. "Bous Stephanoumenos! Bous Stephaneforos!" (*P* 168). The *Classical Lexicon for Finnegans Wake* by Brendan O Hehir and John Dillon (Berkeley and Los Angeles: University of California Press, 1977) does not acknowledge any of the Greek and Latin words that I play with in the passage. The conclusion is that either the *Lexicon* or my remarks have to be treated with skepticism—preferably both. As it happens, the Shem-adjective ends in what is the Latin conjunction used to introduce doubt: *sed,* which may mean nothing more than that the *Wake* conditions us to invest random elements with significance that fits the pattern we want to discover.

2. Arno Schmidt, "Das Geheimnis von *Finnegans Wake,*" in *Die Zeit* (16 December 1960), and *Der Triton mit dem Sonnenschirm* (Karlsruhe: Stahlberg, 1969), passim.

3. Suzette Henke, *Joyce's Moraculous Sindbook* (Columbus: Ohio State University Press, 1978) p. 3.

4. Marilyn French, *The Book as World* (Cambridge, Mass.: Harvard University Press, 1976), p. 137.

5. Ibid., pp. 18-19.

6. Adaline Glasheen, *A Second Census of "Finnegans Wake"* (Evanston: Northwestern University Press, 1963), pp. 151-54.

7. Words that I took down, verbatim, with some surprise.

8. Grace Eckley, "Shem Is a Sham but Shaun Is a Ham, or Samuraising the Twins in *Finnegans Wake,*" *Modern Fiction Studies* 20 (Winter 1974-75): 469.

9. Margot C. Norris, "The Function of Mythic Repetition in *Finnegans Wake,*" *James Joyce Quarterly* 11, no. 4 (Summer 1974): 343.

10. Margot Norris, *The Decentered Universe of "Finnegans Wake"* (Baltimore: Johns Hopkins University Press, 1976).

11. Darcy O'Brien, *The Conscience of James Joyce* (Princeton: Princeton University Press, 1968), p. 211.

12. William P. Woodbery, Jr., *James Joyce's "Ulysses": An Index and Guide to the Dramatic Characters* (Ann Arbor: Xerox University Microfilm, 1969), p. 589. See also there: "KEARNS, ANN: A Dublin midwife" (p. 507). Things are not helped, of course, by misinformation like the annotated Proteus chapter in the *Norton Anthology of English Literature,* rev. ed. (New York: W.W. Norton, 1968) where *Frauenzimmer* is glossed as "midwives" (p. 2440).

13. I cannot help thinking here of another identity linked with a name of a handbag in a play that Joyce helped to stage in Zürich, Oscar Wilde's *The Importance of Being Earnest.* There, one bag holding a baby and one with a work of fiction in it were confused. When the maternal

relation is finally straightened out, by means of the handbag, then, and only then, toward the end of the play, Algernon Moncrieff, the friend, is called "Algy," with the identical name that Stephen has been thinking of as he watches the two *Frauenzimmer:* "like Algy, coming down to our mighty mother" (*U* 37).

It is uncannily fitting that an ingenious manipulator of identities like Tom Stoppard should pick on Henry Carr, the actor who played Algernon Moncrieff, for his mummery of fictions, biographical fictions, and local facts, in *Travesties.*

14. A.M.L. Knuth, *The Wink of the Word* (Amsterdam: Rodopi, 1976), passim. The only disadvantage of the term is the implication of erroneous and correct readings as though there were any passages where a reader could ever go blissfully untrapped.

15. *Odyssey* 5. 173–79, translated by E.V. Rieu.

16. On this aspect see Brook Thomas's study, *"Ulysses": A Book of Many Happy Returns* (Baton Rouge: Louisiana State University Press, 1982).

17. Clive Hart and Leo Knuth, *A Topographical Guide to James Joyce's "Ulysses"* (Colchester: A Wake Newslitter Press, 1975), p. 13 n.

18. The first thing we are told that Bloom is doing is moving about the kitchen, *"righting* her breakfast things on the humpy tray. . . . Right" (*U* 55; italics added).

19. I once tried to call devices that are apt to startle the reader into awareness, or sudden shifts, "metastasis" (*James Joyce Quarterly* 12, no. 4 [Summer 1975]: 380–85); the essay is reprinted later in this volume.

20. Clive Hart and Fritz Senn, eds., *A Wake Digest* (Sydney: Sydney University Press, 1968), p. 25.

III.

On *Ulysses:*
Book of Many Turns

8

Book of
Many Turns

Joyce's works can be seen, with equal validity, either as one great whole or as a series of self-contained units. Seemingly contradictory statements can make good sense: Joyce kept reshaping the same material in more complex ways— he never repeated himself. The reiteration, even permutation, of some fundamentals is striking. We can trace the terminal actuality of *Finnegans Wake* from the germinal potentiality of *Dubliners;* but conversely we are also tempted to emphasize the unique whatness of every single work. Joyce kept repeating himself in metempsychotic succession—but if we highlight the individual incarnations, each of his major works is essentially and unpredictably different from its predecessors.

In coming to terms with Joyce's particular "other world" of words, we can choose between two different sets of terminology. Taking up Joyce's own, or Stephen Dedalus's, insistent metaphors, we can see literature as a process of conception and parturition. A quasibiological vocabulary suggests itself, which serves to describe an evolution of powerful, vital drives in a teeming world of luxuriant growth. In fact, such a monstrosity as the Oxen of the Sun chapter in *Ulysses* can be read as a hymn to fertility in its theme and by its very nature—a misbirth maybe, but the offshoot of some generative (perhaps too generative) force. If we were not trying to be so erudite about this chapter, we might be impressed by its sheer animal exuberance. It seems that all of Joyce's creations came into being through some analogous biological force and were subject to many changes during their prolonged periods of gestation.

The works are not only separate, though related, but they all got out of hand in the workshop; they could not be contained within whatever original ground plan there was. They proliferated into something never imagined at the instant of conception.

Even the smallest elements in a literary universe, the letters of the alphabet, can be fertile. Long before Joyce thought of *Finnegans Wake,* he made one of the characters in his first short story reveal her ignorance with an illiterate "rheumatic wheels" (*D* 17). The life force, like everything else in the story, has gone wrong; it has been turned into decay. So, through a tiny change of two letters or one sound, an appropriate word, "rheum" (suggesting a disease: natural development gone wrong), replaces another word.[1] In Ulysses, a typographical misbirth, which disfigures the funeral report in the newspaper, is called, with good reason, "a line of bitched type" (*U* 648), bitches being proverbially and indiscriminately fertile. The simple letter "1," whether superfluous as in "that other world" (*U* 77), or missing as in "L. Boom" (*U* 648), has a pullulating force and invites speculation.

But then it is exactly such exuberant, freakish offshoots as the Oxen of the Sun chapter that can be demonstrated to be the disciplined, programmed, calculated, systematic completion of an elaborate plan by a meticulous artificer—perhaps an obsessed one. Chaos resolves itself into the painstakingly structured order of layered symmetry, of catalogues and charts, schemas, correspondences, and parallels. The jungle is also a garden. Much of our labor actually consists of exposing the manifold coordinates in the system. To some of us the existence of such a system amounts to the major justification of a work of literature. To others, Joyce has become too exclusively a cerebral constructor and callous arranger.

In *A Portrait,* the two aspects are clearly interfused. We have now been trained to see its rigid structure as a verbal and symbolic system. But to early readers sheer disorder seemed to prevail. Richard Ellmann, drawing on internal as well as biographical evidence, uses biological terms to characterize the novel as embryonic.[2]

I take my starting point from a different but related ambiguity. It is contained in the title of the novel, that oddly trailing, spiraling, threefold phrase: "A Portrait—of the Artist—as a Young Man." It looks like an attempt, pedantic and verbose, to fix the subject as accurately as possible. The incongruous effect is that the subject becomes all the more elusive. A less clumsily delimitative title might not have made us aware of the aim of portraiture to pinpoint quiddity in the way that those portraits adorning the walls of Clongowes Wood (*P* 55) preserve something unchangeable for all eternity.

The title implies, however, that there is no portrait as such, that a choice must be made. Out of a wide variety, only *one* phase or pose can be selected. So the implication is that there must be other poses or phases perhaps equally pertinent in the room of infinite possibilities. In the novel Joyce of course gives us a series of such poses and aspects, a chronological succession in which each phase extends and modifies the previous ones. Perhaps only in perpetual qualification can that quintessential quality be circumscribed that, in itself, as the title indicates, remains beyond our grasp. The specification "as a young man" is necessary to the nature of portraiture—one particular pose must be chosen. But it also challenges the representative claim of portraiture. Time interferes with the supposedly timeless art of painting.

In the title it is the unstressed but potent conjunctive particle "as" that seems to infuse the novel. This particle denotes, as the dictionary will tell us, something or someone "in the character, in the capacity" or "in the role" of something else. The *Portrait* is a sequence of such parts of character. Stephen, knowingly or unknowingly, assumes an amazing number of character roles as he grows up. Before he appears in the flesh, Stephen has already been transformed into a fairy tale character that is specifically glossed ("He was baby tuckoo" [*P* 7]). He soon learns to play some parts, often protective ones, with varying degrees of skill and success. Stephen learns to imitate and to pretend: on the second page he is already "feigning" to run. A number of roles are prescribed to him by the communities of family, school, church, and nation, and it takes some growing up to make him realize the reticular hazards involved. His reading provides a further set of models to be imitated. In the second chapter Stephen actually prepares for a stage performance in a school play, a take-off on one of his masters. He deliberately and, at times, histrionically rejects some roles, whereas he remains quite unaware of certain others. It is easier for us than it was for some earlier readers to recognize the stagey nature of some turning points in Stephen's career. Finally Stephen chooses to become an artist; that is, a creator of fictional roles. And in *Ulysses,* the same Stephen singles out, for a dazzling display of theorizing, the writer who probably created more roles than anyone else, Shakespeare (and Stephen is aware that Shakespeare also played real theatrical parts on the London stage). Stephen's artist is compared to "the God of the creation" (*P* 215), and this God is immediately epiphanized in one particular pose—"paring his fingernails."

Somehow Stephen, who enumerates with such gusto the chosen roles of his father: "a tenor, an amateur actor, a shouting politician . . . a tax gatherer, a bankrupt and at present a praiser of his own past" (*P* 241), is a chip off the old block, with a self-written scenario that is just a bit more *recherché*. A predominant role is preordained in the family name, Dedalus, which was taken, along with the motto of the novel, from an ancient book of roles and transformation scenes entitled *Metamorphoses.*

All of this is carried over into *Ulysses* and magnified there. The conjunctive potential of that word "as" permeates all of *Ulysses.* But Joyce need no longer plant it in his title. The title *Ulysses* proclaims a role, one Leopold Bloom *as* Odysseus, or Odysseus *as* modern man. And once we catch on to this new game of aliases or analogies, there is no holding back. *Ulysses* is Joyce's *Metamorphoses,* a book of roles and guises, a game of identities, of transubstantiations. It is pantomimic in the sense of imitating everything. Molly Bloom tells us that her husband is "always imitating everybody" (*U* 771). But even without Molly's corroboration it would be superfluous, after fifty years, to reiterate all the parts that all the characters play in the book.

It is sufficient, by way of recall, to mention the first appearance of a character in the novel. Joyce portrays a real Dubliner, Oliver St. John Gogarty, who was well known in Dublin and remains in Dublin memory just because he was able to carry off so many roles with impressive alacrity. In the book he immediately assumes one particular role, that of a priest, pretending to be a vicar of Christ and a follower of St. Peter. And one of Buck Mulligan's first mocking actions concerns the miraculous eucharistic metamorphosis of mundane into divine substance. He does it, profanely but tellingly, to the pretended accompaniment of slow music, as an *artiste* in the music hall sense, a conjurer. And by means of electric current, as magic trickery, cunning deceit. His subject, however, *is* transformation, and he keeps transforming himself according to whim or opportunity. A true panto-mime, he becomes, in skillful mimetic turn, a priest, a military commander, patron of an artist, friendly adviser, medical rationalist, and so on. His repertoire transcends the boundaries of sex or humanity: he can imitate Mother Grogan or become a bird or an ascending Christ. His observer, Stephen, projects yet other roles onto him, while behind or beyond or above his handiwork an increasingly conspicuous author dangles another assortment of analogies. All of this takes place within some twenty pages comprising the first chapter.

It is no wonder that Gogarty, who could successfully bring off so many roles as doctor, athlete, poet, and later on as nationalistic senator, aviator, and carouser with the British nobility (quite apart from his histrionic talent *ad hoc*), resented the perpetuation of some postadolescent roles in fictional permanence. Joyce had obviously and maliciously encroached upon his own chosen territory, and Gogarty was only paying back in kind when he revealed (to an audience of would-be Joyce idolators) the real, as he maintained, meaning of the term "artist" in Dublin parlance, reducing, in intention, Joyce's and Stephen's role to the limited one of a poseur.[3]

The simplest way of playing imitative roles is by repeating someone else's words: thus *Ulysses* opens with an explicit quotation. The first words spoken aloud, *"Introibo ad altare Dei"* (*U* 3), are not of that everyday common speech that Joyce could evoke so well; they are neither everyday English, nor even English, nor even speech. They are "intoned," in Latin, that dead tongue with which the Church until recently chose to transmit its messages. The stability of the ritual from which these words are taken contrasts of course with Mulligan's volatile flexibility and lack of principle. The

words, in any case, are imitation, resounding for the millionth time, as prologue to the book whose characters play parts, whose actions often consist in
acting, and many of whose words are quotation to an extent that the author
never even attempted to single out individual quotes by customary typographical marks. A quotation also links the present occasion with a former one; it is
a strandentwining chord back in time. So the first words uttered aloud in
Ulysses take us even beyond the Roman Catholic Mass to the Hebrew Psalms
of the Old Testament. They span several millennia.

One capsular reflection of the whole is this: that the novel, whose Latin
title suggests a Greek hero based (as Joyce believed) on Semitic tales, begins
like a play, with stage directions in the first paragraph and an opening speech
by an Irish character whose language is English and who, with a flair for
imitation, intones a sentence from the Latin Mass, which is in itself a translation of a Hebrew Psalm. The ethnological and literary multiplicity is already
present, while on the surface of it we never for a moment leave a simple,
realistic story.

Joyce, who reveals the identity of Buck Mulligan at the outset, keeps the
question of who and what he really is suspended throughout. We first witness
mimicry, mummery, and mockery; the first voice we hear is put on, and it
continues to change. It would be hard to determine exactly where Buck
Mulligan drops all of his guises and pretenses and speaks in his own voice, if
ever he does. I think that for all his imitative zeal we can feel the man's
character behind the sequence of adornments. But it is interesting to note how
much at variance all our feelings are once we try to bring them into the open.
And so, it is no wonder that critics disagree in their assessment of Buck
Mulligan; this is in keeping with mercurial Malachi cheerfully contradicting
himself while manipulating his various *personae*.

Hence *Ulysses* appears, from the start, as a reapplication of a principle
evolved in *A Portrait.* The artist is reportrayed as a slightly more disillusioned
young man with some newly acquired roles. But the foreground is dominated
by his mercurial counterpart, who condenses a whole portrait gallery of a
vaudeville *artiste as* (to pick some more items from the script) a mocker, *as*
St. Peter, *as* a sycophant, *as* Cranly, *as* a Homeric suitor, or, in the overall
view, *as* a Shakespearean clown who sets the stage.

This stage will before long be occupied by Leopold Bloom, whose verbal
and mimetic repertoire is much more limited. Mulligan's brilliance is set off
against Bloom's lackluster commonness and common sense. Bloom's opening
words could not possibly elicit the same sort of extended commentary that
Mulligan's require. But with his trite "O, there you are" (*U* 55), Bloom at
least reaches his speechless partner, the cat, and attains whatever contact is
called for. His concern for that partner is unfeigned. And the cat immediately
responds with "Mkgnao," and two variations of the same theme: "Mrkgnao!"
and "Mrkrgnao!"

These consonantal modifications are also a comment on what the cat is *not* saying. She disdains to conform to the expected, standardized lexicological "miaow" (cf. *U* 67) in favor of some individual, variable utterance. The feline phonetics also allow us to deduce that Bloom is a good listener, attentive to subtle changes. That the cat is a versatile, mercurial animal, capable of adapting to circumstances and even manipulating them, justifies its early prominence in an introductory passage as Bloom's first interlocutor.

The first book begins on top of a tower with imitative words and divine reverberations. The second book begins below ground in Bloom's kitchen, with simple words and onomatopoetic animal noises. It is intriguing to follow one reader, the Italian translator of *Ulysses,* who claims that the consonantic structure of the cat's "Mrkrgnao" utterance is a covert evocation of Mercury.[4] This would introduce either the Homeric messenger Hermes appropriate to the chapter, or else constitute an animal echo of Mulligan's mercurial role in the parallel chapter. As the novel moves on, Mulligan's brilliance can hardly be increased, while Bloom's earthy wit and less ostentatious resourcefulness have a way of growing on most readers.

But then of course Bloom is accorded a great deal of scope. Although he is remarkably awkward in acting out such roles as he might enjoy playing in real life, like Philip Beaufoy or Don Juan, he is unconsciously carrying a much greater load than all the other characters. Most roles (Mr Bloom *as* Odysseus, Christ, Moses, Wandering Jew, etc.) have been well studied. I would like to single out a far less personal role. Within the totality of the novel, Bloom is also a part of speech. In purely grammatical terms, Bloom is also an all-round man. His name is taken through all the cases of the singular: "Bloom. Of Bloom. To Bloom. Bloom" (*U* 453), and he seems to have become a grammatical case history. On occasion he resembles a noun with a relative pronoun in various inflections like "Bloowho" (*U* 258), "Bloowhoose" (*U* 259), "Bloohimwhom" (*U* 264), in passages that seem to bring out Bloom's relativity. An inflated version is "puffing Poldy, blowing Bloohoom" (*U* 434). At times perhaps Bloom appears more like a verb than a noun, the *verbum* of Latin grammar or else of the Gospel of St. John. In the course of the novel he seems conjugated in all tenses, past, present, and future; in the active and the passive voice; in all the possible moods—indicative, imperative, subjunctive, optative—not to forget participial forms like "blooming." He becomes a universal paradigm of the school book; if we can parse him, we can parse humanity. Beyond grammar, he is anagrammatically transformed into "Old Ollebo, M.P." (*U* 678). And "POLDY" is the basis for an acrostic (*U* 678).

Bloom's nominal existence is diverse too. He has been translated from Hungarian *Virag,* and he is translating himself into such fictitious roles as Henry Flower, to which Molly adds "Don Poldo de la Flora" (*U* 778), and the author such variants as "Professor Luitpold Blumenduft" (*U* 304) or

"Senhor Enrique Flor" (*U* 327). Other transformations are geometrical, a concave distortion like "Booloohoom," or a convex "Jollypoldy the rixdix doldy" (*U* 434). Typography adds an insult, "L. Boom" (*U* 647), to the catalogue. Etymology extends the range further: Skeat's *Etymological Dictionary* relates "bloom" to "blood." Leopold Bloom does not read Skeat's "by the hour," (*SH* 26), but he substitutes his own name for "Blood" in a throwaway (*U* 151), unaware of a momentary eucharistic function. No wonder there are Bloomites in the book, and that the hero is sartorially celebrated in "bloomers" and even citified into "Bloomusalem." Thus, on the merely nomenclatural level of this ominously cluttered novel, Bloom is awarded unprecedented scope as a paradigm.

We know that Joyce found in Homer's Odysseus the universal paradigm from myth that he needed. Hence, I would like to rephrase some of my remarks in the light of Homeric analogies. I have to admit first that I always thought these analogies meaningful, fruitful, and even helpful, though some of our heavy-footed glosses may not be so. The Homeric ground plan provides another link with the past; it takes us back, as Joyce always tries to do, to first beginnings. Homer's epics are, for all practical purposes, the origins of Western literature. *Ulysses* comprises all literature from its Greek roots (as well as its Hebrew roots in the Old Testament) to its latest ramifications in Yeats and a just emerging Synge. In between, English literary history is amply documented, notably in Scylla and Charybdis and Oxen of the Sun, and there are vestigial traits of Italian, French, and German literature throughout. Homer's highly finished art is a beginning for us, but it was in turn already the culmination of a long development now lost in obscurity. It is an end turned into a new beginning, which makes it all the more fitting for Joyce's purposes.

That the Homeric poems were not, originally, written down and read but passed on orally and recited with musical accompaniment, moreover, conveniently ties them to an oral tradition very much alive in Ireland. The art of storytelling was still practiced in Joyce's Dublin in those communities that had to be culturally self-sustaining.

Joyce preferred the *Odyssey* to the much more martial *Iliad,* not merely because of his pacifist inclinations or because he needed more social relationships than a war report can provide, but also because the action of the *Iliad* is subsumed in its sequel. The *Odyssey* is wider in scope: temporal, topical, and simply human.

Even though the so-called Homeric parallels, the transposition of characters and situations, have definte purposes, it is sometimes useful not to insist on the strictly parallel nature of the correspondences: the pattern is often a crisscross one, and similarities often go by contrast. Perhaps the most pervasive Homeric features in *Ulysses* are not the one-to-one relationships that Stuart Gilbert began to chart for us, but principles or motive forces—such as the Protean force of transformation in the third chapter. Homer and Joyce both had the ability to condense certain overall principles into concise verbal form. Joyce was fond of condensing themes and techniques of his whole works into his opening words (as on the first page of *Ulysses,* which I have dwelt upon in the preceding pages). I believe that Joyce realized that the opening of the *Odyssey* is similarly fashioned, and that he was aware that Homer, much more pointedly and literally than Virgil, Milton, or Pope, put the subject of his poem right in front of us. The subject is Man. The *Odyssey* begins with that word—*"Andra"*—in the objective case, the central object, and Homer keeps it suspended over the first line. It is fortunate that Joyce, who knew little classical Greek (though a Zürich friend, Paul Ruggiero, taught him some modern Greek), recorded the first line of the *Odyssey* in the original, or very close to it. Ellmann implies that it was quoted from memory (*JJ* 585). It is misquoted, of course, and we can explain Joyce's faulty accents as the result of understandable ignorance or, maybe, as a shift in emphasis. At any rate, Joyce knew by heart and was ready to scribble beside the only authentic portrait of Mr Bloom we have, the well-known line:

Andra moi énnepe, Moūsa, polýtropon, hòs mála pollà.

It happens, fortuitously, that in Greek the accusative noun can be placed before us without a definite article and with its defining adjective being cleverly withheld for a few beats. Thus, "Man" is placed before us in his most universalized form before the focus narrows to one particular individual. This obviously suits Joyce's purpose. Greek *Andra,* however, does not refer to humanity, but clearly to a male: *anēr* (the nominative) is *vir,* not *homo.* Joyce's hero differs from Homer's in being a "womanly man."[5]

Homer's first verse, which Joyce quoted, contains and stresses two forms of "much/many": *poly-* and *polla,* and lines 3 and 4, with *pollōn* and another *polla,* emphasize even further that multiplicity that characterizes the *Odyssey* and will also characterize *Ulysses.* In the Homeric text the second noun is "Troy, the holy city" (*Odyssey* I, line 2). So even here Joyce's favorite coupling of the individual and the community of the city seems anticipated. But the word that is especially emphasized in Homer's first line, skillfully introduced after a weighty pause, is the epitheton that accompanies "man"— *"polytropos."* It has occupied commentators a good deal, and W. B. Stanford, in his excellent study, *The Ulysses Theme,* devotes some pages to it.[6] Joyce could have found most of the glosses in reference books or in the standard Greek dictionaries that he was quite able to consult. Any Greek dictionary would have given him more or less the same information that Liddell and Scott provide: Literally, *polytropos* means "much turned," "of many turns." It is taken to mean that Odysseus is a man much traveled, "much wandering." But the meaning was soon extended to suggest characteristic resourcefulness—"a man capable of turning many ways," a versatile character. It acquired a pejorative use too: it came to mean "shifty" or "wily" (in this sense the adjective is applied to Hermes, i.e., Mercury). It can mean "fickle" or just "changeable," or become a vague term for "various" and "manifold."

I submit that all of these potential meanings of the one word are, literally or figuratively, transferred into *Ulysses*.[7] When Joyce described an early plan of his novel to Stanislaus in 1915, he referred to the central section as "Ulysses Wandlungen."[8] Since Stanislaus at the time was interned by Austrian authorities, the postcard had to be written in German. What Joyce probably wanted to say was "Wanderungen"—wanderings—but he was either confused by the intricacies of the German vocabulary (where the verb *wandeln* can mean both "to wander" and "to change") and hit on *Wandlungen* (which means "changes" but not "wanderings"), or he was trying to entertain his brother by a double entendre. The result, in any case, is that "Ulysses Wanderungen" happens to be an excellent summing up of the novel and also of the two main meanings of Homer's adjective, stressing the hero's travels as well as his versatility.

But to return to the Greek dictionary. Its philological lore seems to appear, in part verbatim, throughout the book. "Wily," for example, is an epithet reserved for the voluble sailor in Eumaeus, whose pseudo-Odyssean role we have known all along ("such a wily old customer" [*U* 630]). He pretends to be much traveled, and he is in fact a resourceful inventor of tales. Another adjective, "shifty," is applied by Bloom to such "crawthumpers" as one of the Carey brothers, who plotted murder and then turned on his accomplices (the negative side of Odyssean changeability): "there's something shiftylooking about them" (*U* 81). The other adjective of the dictionary, "fickle," occurs in Nausicaa. The boy whom Gerty MacDowell admires in vain seems to her a "Lighthearted deceiver and fickle like all his sex" (*U* 362). Actually Homer's hero had appeared in just such unfavorable light to some of the early unsympathetic commentators.[9] Now I am not sure how far Gerty's boy friend qualifies for an Odyssean role of tertiary importance, but he is apparently capable of doing clever turns on his bicycle, and it is a nice touch that his name is Reggie *Wylie*. Since Joyce invites us to compare Odysseus with Leopold Bloom and since Gerty compares Bloom with Reggie Wylie, this may be a peripheral instance of Joyce's reserving some Odyssean versatility for minor characters as well.

Most editions of the *Odyssey* list, in their variant readings of *polytropos,* a different adjective, "poly*krotos*." This is in fact usually the first textual note in the book. The meaning is generally given as "wily, sly, cunning" (which corresponds to "polytropos"), but originally it meant "ringing loud, resounding." Somehow this might contribute toward making L. Boom (*U* 647) a noise in the street. Stanford's interpretation of the adjective as "knocked about"[10] would also apply to Mr Bloom. But even if this philological spectrum were outside of Joyce's ken, it is worth noting that Homer's first emphasized adjective was soon changed, distorted, or parodied—the earliest anticipation perhaps of Joyce's technique of meaningfully distorted readings.

The translation of the *Odyssey* by Butcher and Lang, which Frank Budgen assured me Joyce had used and for which Phillip Herring found notebook evidence, renders the first epithet as "the man, so ready at need." I cannot help being amused, perhaps coincidentally, by Bloom's being described as "a man and ready," and rising to make for the "yard," contemplating on his way Greek goddesses yielding to Greek youths (*U* 176–77). Immediately afterward his elusiveness is commented upon. But this connection may merely be an instance of one reader's mind being polytropically affected.

Homer's Odysseus appealed to Joyce because of his universality and his encyclopaedic turns. In him the two opposites, the individual and the universe (poles that appear throughout in Joyce's works, from Stephen's geography book in *A Portrait* to Shem's riddle of the universe), are combined. I cannot help but think that Joyce was conscious of a translation of *polytropos* into Latin, which would yield *multi-versus*, the exact antithetic correspondence to *uni-versus*.

Naturally it does not matter too much whether some general principle in either the *Odyssey or Ulysses* finds one particular verbal incarnation. But Joyce had a way of expressing in representative detail what is also present in the organic whole. The preceding philological digressions are justified, perhaps, simply because Joyce was a philologist, in the etymological sense of being a lover of words and also in the sense of being a commentator of Homer. He attributed the art Philology to Proteus, the chapter devoted to change and Odyssean flexibility.

Diverging from Homer, Joyce does not start with an invocation stating his theme, but he puts the principle into action by placing the most conspicuously *polytropos* man in the novel right in front of us, Buck Mulligan, whose shifting roles can now be reinterpreted as Odyssean. Buck Mulligan does not know how much he is hellenizing Ireland (*U* 7). Fairly early he uses the Homeric type of adjective himself, both in the hackneyed original *"epi oinopa ponton"* and in parodistic variation "the scrotumtightening sea" (*U* 5). His early Greek samples, incidentally, refer to the eminently changeable elements of water ("ponton," "thalatta") or wine.

Mulligan is resourceful and skillful in dealing with any situation at hand. But he also incorporates these qualities of trickery and deceit that the detractors of Odysseus had pointed out in antiquity. Again there is the possibility that Joyce had heard of one such detractor who claimed that Homer's account was a tissue of lies. Stanford goes on to say that this critic, whose "oration is bland, persuasive and superbly argued," is hardly trying "to do more than dazzle and astonish his audience," his aim being "to gain admiration for skill in rhetorical technique."[11] There is something very Mulliganesque in all this, but what makes the connection particularly intriguing is that the name of the critic was—Dio *Chrysostomos*.

We are on safer ground by taking Bloom's word for it that Buck Mulligan is an untrustworthy but "versatile allround man, by no means confined to medicine only" (*U* 620). "Versatile" is, of course, the standard definition of *polytropos;* "allroundman" echoes Lenehan's grudging concession that Bloom is "a cultured allroundman" (*U* 235). It echoes, moreover, Joyce's conversation with Frank Budgen in Zürich about Odysseus as a complete all-round character.[12] Lenehan, as it happens, is a little Odysseus in his own small cadging way, wandering and wily and versatile (in "Two Gallants" he is described as a "leech" and is performing an Odyssey in a minor key). It is remarkable how frequently the Odyssean characters in *Ulysses* comment on each other, and often in Odyssean terms too: Lenehan comments on Bloom; Bloom on Buck Mulligan, Lenehan, Simon Dedalus, and the Sailor; Simon Dedalus on Buck Mulligan ("a doubledyed ruffian " [*U* 88]); the Sailor on Simon Dedalus (his yarn presents Dedalus as polytropos, much-traveled: "He toured the wide world" [*U* 624]); Buck Mulligan on Bloom, etc.

Our first glimpse of Buck Mulligan shows him literally and physically as a man of many turns. Within the first few pages he is choreographically living up to his polytropic nature: he faces about, bends toward Stephen, peers sideways, shows a shaven cheek over his right shoulder, hops down from his perch, mounts the parapet, and actually "turn[s] abruptly" (*U* 3–5).[13]

Polytropia in *Ulysses* then is not limited to any one feature, or level, or any one person—not even to persons. It is polytropically distributed and incarnated throughout. Animals too, like Stephen's Protean dog on the beach or the dog following Bloom into the byways of Circe, perform feats of amazing versatility. Even inanimate objects, such as Bloom's newspaper, his wandering soap, or Stephen's ashplant, are capable of transformation. One whole chapter hinges on the volatile mutability of all things, the Circe episode. It is made up of all the previous roles in the novel and a number of new ones, a gigantic transformation scene in pantomime, where old roles are continually permuted. Among its polymorphic turns are the deviate turns of the psyche, with such authorities as Krafft-Ebbing being responsible for parts of the script.

It is appropriate that Stephen comes to grief in this sequence, also because, for all the flexibility of his mind, he fails, or refuses, to be flexible enough to deal with a real situation and to evade a blunt danger. He is not trying to select a more opportune role, but rather continues a monologue that is unintelligible and must appear provoking to the soldiers, who of course are equally inflexible. The physical altercation in Circe is between characters who are rigid and might be called "monotropic." Stephen, in crucial moments, is scornful of such advice as Buck Mulligan has given him in the morning: "Humour her [his mother] till it's over" (*U* 8). Mulligan does a lot of opportunistic humoring, and Bloom is good-humoredly trying his best.

The culminations of Circe can be regarded as outgrowths of such mimetic features as are already present in the first chapter. Circe is made up almost entirely of Mulliganesque poses and projections. In the morning Buck Mulligan begins by quoting Latin from the Mass. Near midnight Stephen enters the scene by actually responding to Mulligan's opening words: *"ad deam qui laetificat juventutem meam"* (*U* 433). His version contains one small change *(deam* for *Deum),* but it is an entire perversion, a wholly new and utterly Circean turn. The first sounds heard in Circe are the call and answers of the whistles (*U* 429), which are an echo of the first page. The first words spoken aloud, "Wait, my love," are a variant of Mulligan's "Yes, my love" (*U* 429, 4). With his conjuring imitation of the transubstantiation, Mulligan has also prepared us for magic, the technique of the Circean transformations.

An interesting scene in the first chapter foreshadows many phenomena of Circe. Mulligan, who has just challenged Stephen—"Why don't you play them as I do?"—puts on some clothes with the remark that "we'll simply have to dress the character"—a dress rehearsal for the rapid costume changes in Circe. Mulligan justifies the contradictions in his words and actions with a quotation from Whitman. In Circe all contradictions are staged. The paragraph in which Buck Mulligan is dressing (*U* 16) is, incidentally, the first in the book in which we cannot be certain which words are actually spoken by Mulligan and which are part of Stephen's thoughts. The distinction between speech and thought will make little sense in the hallucinations of Circe. Thus we do not know whether "Mercurial Malachi" (*U* 17) is actually spoken by mercurial Mulligan or not, but Mercury, Hermes, the wily, roguish god, is also presiding over the Circe chapter just as he was instrumental in helping Odysseus.[14] Mercurial Malachi paves the way for the technique of Circe.

In this view, then, an extravagant convolution like Circe is a polytropical reconjugation of familiar elements met before. Joyce manipulates his material in the most suitable manner. This technique—of adapting one's approach to the situation—is in itself an Odyssean one. Like Odysseus, Joyce chooses his speech, his role, and his narrative stance carefully and ruthlessly. Every style is a role adapted for some purpose. Part of our difficulty as readers is that we are too rigidly fixed to follow the abrupt turns, the changes of the stage, so that the verbal, situational, and narrative texture is too polytropic for our customary inertia.

Odysseus, as well as his adviser, Athene, was not particularly scrupulous in the means he employed to attain a given end, and literal truth is not his overriding concern. Nor, in a way, is it Joyce's. He is not exclusively concerned with realistic verisimilitude and can depart from it entirely. The roles, the styles, the perspectives are chosen for optimal effect *ad hoc.*

Ulysses is Homerically polytropical.[15] Voices change; characters are not fixed; language is versatile and polymorphous. The reader is puzzled by new turns. Where passages, or even chapters, are monotropic, their effect is parodistic, and they strike us by their inadequacy and incongruity; in their totality they add up to the most encyclopaedic mosaic in literature.

In the Wandering Rocks chapter the many turns are those of a labyrinth, solidified into the bricks and stones of the city. Aeolus, the first of those extravagant chapters in *Ulysses* that draw attention to their form, is made up of all the traditional rhetorical figures. It is literally composed of many turns, of *tropes*—all the preformed roles available in human speech. Language is intrinsically metaphorical. Part of the dynamism of Joyce's prose arises from the contrast of figurative to literal meaning, or the ironic unfittingness of a metaphor or a cliché fixed in some no longer congruous roles. Language, the most polytropic invention of the human mind, fascinated Joyce. Skeat's *Etymological Dictionary,* a catalogue of the historical roles of words, makes us aware of morphological and semantic transformations. Joyce makes us aware, moreover, of the various roles that even the most ordinary and familiar words always play. Such a simple and seemingly unambiguous unit as "key," for example, is capable of amazing variety and change of identity. That it can refer to those domestic objects that Bloom and Stephen find themselves without, or to symbols of power (as with St. Peter), to musical notation in Sirens, to a political institution (the House of Keys), to a name (Alexander Keyes), to connotations like a keyhole in Circe, or else to a woman "properly keyed up," etc., is all very commonplace and generally unnoticed, but belongs to the polytropic potential that Joyce found in everyday language.

Fortunately for him, the English language is particularly flexible. Its powers of assimilation, its wide and varied vocabulary, but above all its lack of determining inflection, allow Joyce the scope he needed. In English the miraculous fact that "A belt was also to give a fellow a belt" (*P* 9), which puzzles a young Stephen Dedalus, is easily possible—but perhaps only in English. Native English speakers may not realize, for example, what duplicity the simple title "The Dead" contains. A foreigner, especially if he wants to render it into his own language, may well wonder whether "Dead" is singular or plural. In the course of reading the story we could easily fluctuate in our view, at times taking the word in its more general sense until at one point it seems limited to Michael Furey before it is universalized again in the last paragraph. In other words, it seems to be a title that changes with our experience. Its flexibility is possible in English—in all other languages the meaning would probably remain fixed.

Bloom can beautifully make a trite phrase—"Another gone" (*U* 74)—do double duty, neatly referring, superficially, to Dignam's demise and internally to voyeuristic frustration. Once you try to do this in another language you will find that gender and inflection present some serious obstacles. Similarly, a "goal" scored in hockey cannot play the role of the great "goal" toward which all history moves (*U* 34) outside of the English language. English must be one of the most Odyssean languages; resourceful, pliant, homophonous, versatile, it allows Joyce to assume the voice appropriate for the occasion, multiple guises, mercurial transformations. Now the virtuoso performances of cunning and punning have appeared to some critics as questionable manipulations, forms of trickery. Interestingly enough, the two contradictory evaluations of Joyce's ways happen to reflect the two views held of the character of Odysseus—the superbly agile and ingenious hero, or else the artful, deceitful trickster. Not very surprisingly, the first one to take this negative view was the Homeric Cyclops, an early victim. It may be significant that his vision was troubled from the outset and worsened in the process. In his naiveté his one-track mind trusted words and names. For Polyphemus, at any rate, the pun on the name of Odysseus was a mean trick of some consequence, and it taught him the treacherous and potent nature of words. It taught him, one presumes, to trust no man and no man's words.

Language in the *Odyssey* and in *Ulysses* can be deceptive, elusive, often unreliable. "Sounds are impostures," says Stephen (*U* 622), and he says so in a chapter particularly suited to presenting the untrustworthy nature of all communication. The neatest instance is the funeral report in the newspaper. It contains untruths of two kinds. First the conventional hyperbolic formulae that have little relation to a real emotional involvement that they pretend to express: *"The deceased gentleman was a most popular and genial personality in city life and his demise . . . came as a great shock to citizens of all classes by whom he is deeply regretted"* (*U* 647). This form of falsification is less conspicuous but more ubiquitous than such strident deviations from factual truth as the listing of mourners present like Stephen Dedalus, C. P. McCoy, L. Boom, and M'Intosh. The reader of the novel is contextually privileged; but readers of the *Evening Telegraph* would have been seriously misled. And the characters of *Ulysses* are being similarly taken in. Even the author himself at times assumes the pose of trusting speech and language naively, by pedantically transforming, in one case, a glib and bibulous and next to meaningless "God bless all here" into a prolonged scene depicting a ceremonial benediction (*U* 338–40), one example of the rigid belief in the literal meaning of powerful words. This happens in the Cyclops chapter, which shows the clash of the unifocality of view with the multivocality of language.

The reader, as against the more shortsighted of the characters involved, has enough information at hand to adjust his views. But even today it does take a reader with at least a minimum of Odyssean agility. After half a century of *Ulysses* we have learned to regard any information provided within the novel with skeptical, in fact Bloomian, reserve. On the other hand, we invest the words of the text with unusual trust. We know that "L. Boom" is, on the realistic surface of it, simply a piece of misinformation. But we tend to rely on the assumption that the distortion means something, and usually more than just one thing. A principle of obverse truth seems to pervade the novel: somehow, "Boom" is literally true and relevant; its incongruity serves intricate purposes.

And perhaps the Latin phrase from the Mass that is irreverently quoted at the beginning of Telemachus also indicates that the book is also perversely like the Mass. Not only because it deals with transubstantiations, significant changes, but also because in it, as in the liturgy, every detail—gesture, word, vestment, etc.—is meaningful, a product of a process of condensation and accretion, and generally overdetermined.

So language as a means of communication in *Ulysses* cannot be trusted and at the same time justifies unusual trust, within a hierarchy of potential contexts. An ignorant rendering of "metempsychosis" as "met him pike hoses" is plainly erroneous in one context, but it is appropriate, word for word, to the character who enunciates it and to some major themes of the novel. Bloom's innocent statement, "I was going to throw it away" (*U* 86) is met with distrust, and its unambiguous everyday meaning is disregarded. Bantam Lyons, a particularly biased person, considers it *purely* allusive and is even willing to back his trust in it as an allusion with hard cash. Reality then turns the initial error into unexpected truth, and the reader can rely on some further nonrealistic relevance. Sounds are tricky, but even their trickiness has a communicative value.

In the episode in which a false Odysseus tells obvious falsehoods, in which the novel's real Odysseus warns Stephen against trusting the novel's preparatory Odysseus, and in which Stephen declares sounds to be impostures, the language of even the tritest of clichés has an odd way of sidelighting some truths. I have had occasion to stress some similarities between Leopold Bloom and Buck Mulligan (they concerned me for the present purposes more than their patent dissimilarities). The two form an uneven pair each with Stephen in the respective chapters of Book I and Book III. Now besides some parallels already mentioned and others easy to work out, I think a few different ones are potentially contained as homonymous asides in the first sentence of the Eumaeus chapter:

> Preparatory to anything else Mr Bloom *brushed* off the greater bulk of the *shavings* and handed Stephen the hat and ashplant and *bucked* him up generally
> . . . (*U* 612–13)

I have italicized "brushed," "shaving," and "bucked" because to me they echo, unassumingly, a-semantically, and in-significantly, the first scene, in which Buck wields his brush to shave himself. A few sentences later a connection is further made with Stephen's handkerchief "having done yeoman service in the shaving line." These frail links do not contribute much to the passage, but they do bring out, once more and in a different guise, the principle of the same elements being reshuffled within the novel, and here the elements are partly phonetic. The tiny point is that those signs singled out here are not *only* impostures. They contain a measure of oblique truth. (Incidentally, the vowel sounds of "sh*a*vings," "br*u*shed," and "b*u*cked" are the same as of "St*a*tely, pl*u*mp B*u*ck.")

Or perhaps, to improve on my phrasing, these words and sounds are, literally and etymologically,[16] impostures, being imposed upon the text as an additional layer of gratuitous correspondence, ironic contrast, deviate reliability, or polytropical pertinence.

The novel's versatile and occasionally tricky resilience then can be accounted for as a quality that Homer ascribed to his hero. Joyce went on to write an even more *polytropos* novel with an entirely pantropical hero; also, among countless other things, an Irish Ulysses: "Hibernska Ulitzas" (*FW* 551.32). Because of its polytropic nature, *Ulysses* is capable of meeting us all on our own terms, or on any other terms we may think of. Strangely enough, we still tend to forget the lesson we might have learned and to fall back on monotropical statements of the form *"Ulysses* is basically this or that," and we can only do so by emphasizing one of the potentially multiple turns in our own Cyclopean fashion.

If there is any quintessential formula for *Ulysses,* I do not think it will be contained in a resounding, world-embracing YES, nor in an equally reductive nihilistic NO and rejection of our time, but in a modest, persistent, skeptical, Bloomian "Yes but."

1972

Notes

1. Fritz Senn, " 'He Was Too Scrupulous Always': Joyce's 'The Sisters,' " *James Joyce Quarterly* 2, no. 2 (Winter 1965): 70–71.

2. Richard Ellmann, *James Joyce* (New York: Oxford University Press, 1959), 306–9.

3. "In Dublin an 'artist' is a merry droll, a player of hoaxes." Oliver St. John Gogarty, "They Think They Know Joyce," *Saturday Review of Literature* 33 (18 March 1950): 70.

4. "Notice that the first time [the cat's meow] is spelled with Mk, the second time with Mrk, the third with Mrkr. . . . That's the Greek spelling of Mercury. The cat is Mercury." Sidney Alexander, quoting Giulio do Angelis, in "Bloomsday in Italy," *The Reporter* 24 (13 April 1961): 42.

5. Joyce's version, as reproduced by Ellmann in *James Joyce* (facing p. 433), is faulty and has here been replaced by the transcription of the standard Greek text.

When Joyce uses Homer's first word, it is in a compound that includes its biological opposite, "androgynous" (*U* 210). Homer's epic is no mere glorification of unbridled virility. It may surprise some readers that an excess of manliness is not considered a compliment. Odysseus's enemies, the Cyclopes and the suitors, are characterized as "overbearing, overweening, savage, bullies." The original participle "hyperēnoreontes" (Od. 2:226, 6:5, etc.) literally denotes super-manliness (hyper + anēr) and is clearly derogatory.

6. W. B. Stanford, *The Ulysses Theme: A Study in the Adaptability of a Traditional Hero*, 2nd ed. (Ann Arbor: University of Michigan Press, 1968).

7. Translations of *polytropos* are of appropriately wide variety: fated to roam, who roamed the world over, who drew his changeful course through wanderings, the Great Traveler who wandered far and wide, adventurous, resourceful, so wary and wise, steadfast, skillful and strong, famous for cleverness of schemes he devised, for wisdom's various arts renown'd, for shrewdness famed and genius versatile, sagacious, the Shifty, of craft-renown, of many devices, resourceful, versatile, who was never at a loss, of wide-ranging spirit; subtil, aux mille ruses, fameux par sa prudence, l'esprit souple, l'Inventif; ricco d'astuzie, di multiforme ingegno; vielgewandert, vielgewandt, wendig, vielverschlagen. See also note 15.

8. Reproduced in "Album Joyciano," p. 39 in Stelio Crise, *Epiphanies and Phadographs: Joyce e Trieste* (Milan: All' Insegna del Pesce D'Oro, 1967); it is also in the Frankfurt edition of Joyce: *Werke* 5, *Briefe* I, 1900–1916 (Frankfurt: Suhrkamp Verlag, 1969), p. 574. The postcard is dated 16 June 1915.

9. "The Grandson of Autolycus," in Stanford, *Ulysses Theme*, pp. 8–25 passim.

10. Ibid., pp. 260–61.

11. Ibid., p. 148.

12. Frank Budgen, *James Joyce and the Making of "Ulysses"* (1934; reprint, London: Oxford University Press, 1972), p. 15ff.

13. After this paper was read in Tulsa a member of the audience suggested that "plump," the second word in the book, also somehow means "all-round."

14. "Moly is the gift of Hermes, god of public ways. . . . Hermes is the god of signposts: i.e. he is, specially for a traveller like Ulysses, the point at which roads parallel merge and roads contrary also. He is an accident of providence" (*Letters* I, 147–48).

15. Notice how the following translations of the epithet *polytropos* (supplementing the list given in note 7) could be deflected to characterize *Ulysses:* of many changes, various-minded, ingenious, of many turns, of many ways; aux mille tours, aux mille expédients, plein d'artifices; straordinario giramonde, multiforme.

16. Relying on etymological potential is a form of circuitous trust.

9

Metastasis

The reader is invited to evaluate the following extracts as a characterization of
Joyce's achievements and perhaps aims in writing *Ulysses:*

> I consider [his] charm to lie in his intimate sympathy and compassionateness for
> the whole world, not only in its strength, but in its weakness; in the lively regard
> with which he views every thing that comes before him, taken in the concrete
> . . . . I am speaking of . . . what he had special to himself; and this specialty, I
> conceive, is the interest which he takes in all things, not so far as God has made
> them alike, but as He made them different from each other. I speak of the dis-
> criminating affectionateness with which he accepts every one for what is personal
> in him and unlike others. I speak of his versatile recognition of men, one by one,
> for the sake of that person of good, be it more or less, of a lower order or a
> higher, which has severally been lodged in them; his eager contemplation of the
> many things they do, effect, or produce . . . , even as they are corrupted or dis-
> guised by evil, so far as that evil may in imagination be disjoined from their
> proper nature, or may be regarded as a mere material disorder apart from its for-
> mal character of guilt. I speak of the kindly spirit and the genial temper with
> which he looks round at all things which this wonderful world contains; of the
> graphic fidelity with which he notes them down upon the tablets of his mind . . .
> he has not lost one fibre, he does not miss one vibration, of the complicated
> whole of human sentiment and affection. . . .
>
> Such a writer sees . . . human instruments, with their drifts and motives, their
> courses of thought, their circumstances and personal peculiarities . . . a writer

who delights to ponder human nature and human affairs, to analyse the workings of the mind, to contemplate what is subjective to it. . . .

That charm lies, as I have said, in his habit and his power of throwing himself into the minds of others, of imagining with exactness and with sympathy circumstances and scenes which were not before him, and of bringing out what he has apprehended in words as direct and vivid as the apprehension. His page is like the table of a *camera lucida,* which represents to us the living action and interaction of all that goes on around us. That . . . scrutiny . . . he practises in various ways towards all men, living and dead, high and low, those whom he admires and those whom he weeps over. He writes as one who was ever looking out with sharp but kind eyes upon the world of men and their history. . . . This is why his manner of writing is so rare and special: and why, when once a student enters into it, he will ever recognise him, wherever he meets with extracts from him.

Perhaps a trifle too optimistic and positive; not everyone would put the same emphasis on Joyce's sympathy and compassion. But the encyclopaedic inclusiveness, the all-roundness, the "versatile recognition," the care of detail, the concern with what is subjective are all there. And the definition of, it seems, "expressive form" as "bringing out what he has apprehended in words as direct and vivid as the apprehension" is remarkably concise and almost Stephenesque.

The words were written more than a century ago by a man who never knew of Joyce, but whom Joyce had read with favor, John Henry Cardinal Newman. The silverveined prose quoted above moreover relates to St. John Chrysostomos.[1]

"Chrysostomos" appears on the first page of *Ulysses* (3). The word does not refer, in its primary contexts, to the writings of Newman. But it is the first clear disruption of the book's narrative flow. It is the first metaphorical departure from the realist framework of the opening; both its foreignness and its syntax come as a surprise for the reader. It has a privileged position; some shift has indubitably taken place.

Such shifts, or sudden transitions, serve also as signals for increased complexity (equivalent, somehow, to similar odd manifestations of the psyche as described by the psychoanalytical schools):[2] they indicate that something unusual is going on. I propose to call such a disruption *metastasis,* a term borrowed from Greek with, I hope, no disturbing overtones. Derived from a verb *methistanai* (to place in another way, change), it means "change, shift, removal, transformation," in particular as used in classical rhetorics, it means a rapid transition from one point of view to another.

That is what is happening here. The narration has proceeded to a close-up view of Buck Mulligan's open mouth: "his even white teeth glistening here and there with gold points." And then—no warning—: "Chrysostomos." The most unassuming explication is that mouth and gold are simply translated into Greek, *chrysostomos,* golden-mouthed. Which amounts to a continuation of theme with a change of form, a transference (metaphor, incidentally, too, means trans-ference or trans-lation, carrying across or over). Who does the translating? Most critics take the one-word sentence to be the first transient instant of the stream of consciousness.[3] The word fills a gap, the first acoustic pause ("Silence, all"—*U* 3), while Mulligan pretends to wait for the miraculous transubstantiation (another one of the many changes in the opening scene) to take place. The perspective has moved to Stephen, to the "tablets of his mind." Stephen is internally describing Mulligan and thereby transforming him, sketching out a new role for him and unknowingly anticipating Mulligan's advice to "Hellenise" the island (*U* 7) by Hellenizing *him* first.

The adjective *chrysostomos* became, understandably enough, an epithet for an outstanding orator, so that Stephen is also commenting on Mulligan's rhetorical skill. Specifically, the most likely figure for Stephen to have in mind is St. John Chrysostomos; but there are others.[4] Bernard Benstock comments on the appropriateness of *St. John* Chrysostomos because that part of the name is contained in the full name of Stephen's adversary, Malachi Roland St. John Mulligan, as well as in his real life counterpart, Oliver St. John Gogarty.[5]

So Mulligan is given a Greek epithet, and name, just a few moments before he remarks on the absurdity of Stephen's name, "an ancient Greek." And of course the book bears in its title the Latin translation of a Greek hero's name; in fact the opening of the chapter with its Sandycove reality is already, then, a metastatic deviation from the preceding title. The odd epithet also heralds, in one quick flash, the technique that characterizes a large part of the first half of *Ulysses* and that has gone by such names as stream of consciousness, interior monologue, or *silent* monologue. There is a transference of the rhetorics employed. Paradoxically enough, at the moment when silence prevails, when words are neither spoken nor told, when the prominent mouth ceases to be phonetically active, a golden *mouth* and a renowned *orator* are invoked. Silence is proverbially golden; and a new oratorical device is signaled, a different sort of rhetoric is introduced. In the metastasis, a technique is foreshadowed that will gradually unfold a few pages later and come to a full and dazzling first climax in the Proteus chapter, metastatic chapter par excellence.

This new technique is immediately dropped, the silent monologue interrupted in turn by two shrill whistles and the accustomed voice. This shift, too, is indicated if we allow Mulligan's command "Switch off the current, will you?" (*U* 3.31) to extend beyond the realistic framework. *This* current, the stream of consciousness, will be switched on before long. In the next paragraph, however, Joyce goes out of his narrative way to work in a rare auctorial comment. Compare the situational parallel and the narrative difference between the two sentences in close succession (the *visual impression* is in roman type, the *concomitant association* in bold face):

He peered. . . , his even white teeth glistened here and there with gold points. **Chrysostomos.** (*U* 3)	He skipped. . . . The plump shadowed face and sullen oval jaw *recalled* **a prelate, patron of arts** **in the middle ages.** (*U* 3; my emphasis)

"Recalled," though not at all surprising in traditional story telling, is unique on the first page, too; rarely does the narrator ever after—except of course in the later parodistic chapters or the imitative inserts—allow himself such editorial scope as to tell us in his own words what goes on within a mind. (Verbs like "recalled," "evoked in him," or "reminded him" and similar indications of a synoptic narrator are frequent, for example, in *A Portrait.*) It is as though Joyce wanted to demonstrate to those who care to listen, with a passing light touch, what he too, in the wake of countless writers, might have done, a narrative possibility that was to be ousted by newer, more appropriate methods. "Chrysostomos"—in tacit juxtaposition—looks forward to the new techniques; the auctorial "recalled" faces backward to a technique that is being discarded and only to be resumed with different, highly conscious purposes. The author, for a long while, prefers to be conspicuous by his absence.

A metastasis signals the disquieting presence of several levels. Joyce began "The Sisters" with a triadic flourish of signals, *paralysis, gnomon,* and *simony.* Almost every critic has used these terms as points of reference and has proved their relevance in many contexts. These words were not, however, as metastatically active, since their incongruity is integrated more fully into the telling of the story. The boy-narrator reports about *his* surprise: "*paralysis.* It had always sounded strangely in my ears" (*D* 9). The reader need not be surprised. As Joyce went along, he tended more and more toward narrative reticence, juxtapositional surprises, and the metastatical involvement of the reader. Once we are alerted to "Chrysostomos," we can interpret it in different contexts: as the translation of a visual impression, as Stephen's internal comment, as the heralding of a new technique characterized often by the sacrifice of the syntactically complete sentence structure, as a reflection on *Ulysses* itself. . . . But it *might,* after all, also be the comment of some narrator. In the case of "Chrysostomos," it is appropriate that an epithet designating a distinguished orator should convey a great deal to us. Metastases allow for the possibility of contextual shifts, they signal the intersection of various planes, they provoke speculation and, inevitably, overinterpretation.

So there may be more. St. John Chrysostomos was also known as the "Doctor of the Eucharist."[6] Even on a realistic level, Buck Mulligan, who will one day become a doctor (and is so styled, *U* 418), or who is instructing

Stephen throughout, is at that moment staging a reenactment of the transubstantiation: "the genuine Christine" (*U* 3), and the silence demanded by him is to accompany the mysterious transformation. The passage contains so much translation already (the Eucharist is translated into a female name "Christine"), that one might even surmise that Mulligan is unwittingly translating the Eucharist into English: "Thanks, old chap!" (*U* 3)—*eucharistia* is a thanksgiving, and Joyce knew enough modern Greek to remember that *eucharisto* means "I thank you." In its very nature, of course, the Eucharist has something to do with translation; it is metastatic by theological definition.

It is because of the metastatic dynamism of that one word "Chrysostomos" that I offer the possibility outlined at the beginning that, on a remoter level, the greatest prose writer of the twentieth century (as Joyce would think of himself) covertly integrates a judgment made by the greatest prose writer in English of the previous century (as Joyce did think of Newman) and deflects it to his own, then still inchoate, work programmatically intimating its scope and its quidditas. If not, the coincidences would be very strange indeed. And in the Newman passage of Oxen of the Sun there is almost a description of what has happened to the word "Chrysostomos": "Yet a chance word will call them forth suddenly and they will rise up to confront him in the most various circumstances, a vision or a dream . . ." (*U* 421). The passage is about sin (which was, of course, a favorite topic of St. Chrysostomos, too), but it seems to invite a metastatic transference; in fact, it *is about* metastatic transferences.

Ironically, the word conjured up by Stephen and applied to Mulligan extends far beyond them, for neither of the two could be characterized as sympathetic or all-compassionate. The meeting with Bloom will perhaps make Stephen a man capable of more compassion and bring him closer to "the discriminating affectionateness" of which Newman speaks. Bloom, in his fumbling way, seems to approximate some of the human qualities that Newman attributes to St. Chrysostomos.

The rapid transition from teeth and gold points to a Greek name constitutes an epitome of *Ulysses* itself—it is a cultural translation of Dublin reality. The transition represents both continuity and transformation, it's the same old thing seen, and named, from a different point of view. As the book moves on, instances become more frequent and more elaborate. They are not limited to words or phrases, but become paragraphs and whole sections: the headlines in Aeolus, the translocations in Wandering Rocks, the Cyclopean insertions, the mimetic sequences in Oxen of the Sun, and, above all, the jerky progress from one chapter to the next with a complete change of tone, style, technique, perspective.[7] Finally, *Finnegans Wake* becomes a panmetastatic verbal universe.

1974

Notes

1. John Henry Newman, *The Last Years of St. Chrysostom,* in *Essays and Sketches* (New York: Longman, Green and Co., 1948), III, 216ff. The essay was published in 1859–60. The previous chapter was devoted to "The Exile."

2. Slips of the tongue, parapraxes, dream occurrences, etc. indicate conflicts and provoke a disproportionate amount of interpretation, too. Some of the Joycean shifts are exactly of that nature.

3. For example, Bernard Benstock in his essay "Telemachus" in *James Joyce's Ulysses: Critical Essays,* ed. Clive Hart and David Hayman (Berkeley and Los Angeles: University of California Press, 1974), pp. 2–3.

4. See Don Gifford with Robert J. Seidman, *Notes for Joyce: An Annotation of James Joyce's "Ulysses"* (New York: Dutton, 1974), p. 7; and Weldon Thorton, *Allusions in "Ulysses": An Annotated List* (Chapel Hill: University of North Carolina Press, 1968), p. 12. In my article "Book of Many Turns," reprinted in the present volume, I suggest that *Dio* Chrysostomos might be relevant also as an early critic of Homer.

5. Benstock, *James Joyce's "Ulysses,"* p. 3.

6. "Surnamed *Chrysostom* ('Golden Mouthed') on account of his great eloquence, and also 'the Doctor of the Eucharist' " (*The Book of Saints* [New York: Macmillan, 1947]). One of St. Chrysostom's writings was "On the Priesthood."

7. Some transitional devices and chapter-to-chapter relations are worked out in my essay "The Rhythm of *Ulysses,*" in *"Ulysses": Cinquante ans après* (Paris: Didier, 1974), pp. 33–43, reprinted later in this volume.

10

Bloom among the Orators: The Why and the Wherefore and All the Codology

Most of us take delight in the well-turned phrase. Eloquence is a virtue in many cultures, like the two that interest us here, the world of the Homeric epics and of Joyce's (but not only Joyce's) Dublin. *Ulysses*, in one of its many ways, brings the two together; the novel seems to assemble a more than average proportion of gifted speakers into its relatively narrow confines. These speakers find various pretexts to pass the time of day and night in loquacious company, and Joyce helps them in aligning a series of scenes in public houses or in publike constellations—a newspaper office, a library, a maternity hospital room, or a cabman's shelter, all of which can turn into the setting for a contest in verbal skills. *Ulysses* is full of talk and much of it may sound like talk for talk's sake. Don't let us forget that the one conspicuous narrative deviation on the first page of the novel, that metastatical word and name "Chrysostomos," re-Hellenizes "golden mouth" as a traditional figure of speech for men who had a way with words.[1]

No one is safe from the lure of the spoken word. Even as aloof a person as Stephen Dedalus is "wooed by grace of language" (140). Nor is he immune to the even greater temptation—in the Library episode—to display his own superior mastery of words and Shakespearean diction. Dubliners excel in talk and enjoy it; they are, moreover, competent judges of each other's performances. *Ulysses* contains many comments on the language of its protagonists. Even Molly Bloom, not Dublin's foremost intellectual, has been endowed with a shrewd sense for the wrong or pretentious note.

Skillful speakers, like tenors, are admired and successful. The performance itself can be more important than any information conveyed or idea presented. The glib talker, whatever his level, can usually make it through the day and at least get his drinks provided for. Lenehan is a case in point: "his adroitness and eloquence had always prevented his friends from forming any general policy against him," we learn in *Dubliners* (*D* 50) and find this comment confirmed in *Ulysses*, where he is still able to market a limited stock of witticisms, no matter how much the worse for wear, to his own best advantage. The stories in *Dubliners* highlight types who know how to turn a phrase and get on in the world, such as Gallaher in "A Little Cloud," with "his fearless accent" (*D* 70) and his memorable "sayings" (*D* 73). By 1904 he is still held out as a model for, of course, journalism. From all we know of Corley in "Two Gallants," he may not have much to say, but apparently he can say it with aplomb and it works well enough. Mrs Mooney, of "The Boarding House," is full of confidence; she has social opinion on her side and the right arguments, but also, we can assume, she will know how to reexpress them properly. Other characters remain tongue-tied and self-conscious. Thomas Malone Chandler only wishes "he could give expression to" his emotions (*D* 73), but clearly will never think up Byronic cadences; and no matter how he tries on rare occasions, he will never sound like a man of the world in a public bar. A man like Farrington, bulky and muscular, in "Counterparts" is miscast in a job that depends on copying words and sentences, and in a crisis he lacks the wit to cope with it verbally. When his tongue finds what he takes to be "a felicitous moment" (*D* 91)—and it looks like a fairly unique event—the words chosen actually precipitate his downfall and their first result is "an abject apology"; that is, the instant annulment of those words. Gabriel Conroy's superiority in "The Dead," such as it is, is also due to his command of words that suit the occasion. He can confect a speech, with allusions and quotations, and the speech is adequate (most likely he will be asked to speak again next year); his reputation is confirmed. Conversely, when he fails with words (as he thinks), he is disconcerted, afraid he may have "taken up the wrong tone." His accomplishment may be reinterpreted as "orating to vulgarians" (*D* 220), but, for all practical and public purposes, the power of words *is* an asset.

Among the hierarchies within *Dubliners* there is one that is rhetorical. This is seen best in the oratorical rivalry among the visitors of Mr Kernan, in "Grace," with the lower ranks vainly striving for attention and acknowledgment. The story appropriately begins with a defective tongue and culminates in the glib speech of a professional preacher with "resonant assurance."

Lily, the caretaker's daughter, is right: "The men that is now is only all palaver" (*D* 178). And it is largely palaver that men are judged by.

"winged speech"

The tale of the *Odyssey* can be interrupted in praise of the man who has a way with words, and this is often its hero. The preeminence of Odysseus in verbal as well as practical resourcefulness has led one classical critic—one of the few to be mentioned in *Ulysses,* and that in the chapter dealing with rhetorics—to claim that the initial epithet, *polytropos* (*Od.* 1.1), suggested the hero's ability to utilize "many tropes," that is the whole arsenal of rhetorical tricks.[2]

This semantic twist is doubtful enough, but the linguistic cunning of Odysseus needs little demonstration. It is established in his first speech, a skeptical reply to the nymph Calypso. The reply is introduced by the common formula *"epea pteroenta,"* to alert the listener to the "winged words" that will follow. After them the nymph at once comments upon what he has said and how he has said it. "Thou that hast conceived and spoken such a word" is the stilted version of Butcher and Lang for the original

hoion de ton mython epephrasthes agoreusai (*Od.* 5.183),

which is, literally, something like: "Such a *mythos* (= word, saying, tale, fable) have you thought up to say aloud (publicly)." The point is that before the painful moment of parting, the goddess takes time out to remark upon the quality of the speech and to review it as a significantly clever example. We notice, by the way, that Joyce's Dubliners too have a penchant for evaluating words and speeches.

The first spoken words of Odysseus are sandwiched between *"epea pteroenta"* and *"hoion mython,"* and even if Joyce never looked at the original, it is interesting that *epos* and *mythos,* both terms that primarily referred to the act of speaking, have come to stand for important concepts, important for Homer's art and for Western culture. *Ulysses* has helped to redefine their meaning.

Naturally the novel plaits a tag like *"epea pteroenta"* into its texture: "the winged speech of the seadivided Gael" (324). This phrase has become proverbial (Homer uses it more than a hundred times), almost the prototypical cliché, the kind of thing that Joyce tends to assimilate into his work both as one of the many literary comedowns, the timeworn and overused set pieces that have become unfit for any other than parodistic use, *and* in its (once) metaphorical aptness and precision. For "winged" sets words off from the more pedestrian duties that they normally perform. It signals occasions for them to soar above quotidian banalities.

As it happens, "winged" (or *pteroenta,* from *pteron,* feather) suggests that to parts of language can be attached what Joyce's first acknowledged patron saint in an emergency fixed onto himself. This is a procedure that, as we know, calls upon some ingenuity and has its inherent risks. The Daedalus myth, as built into *A Portrait* (where the image of a "winged form," *P* 169, is stimulated inter alia by the contemplation of the poise, balance, and rhythmic rise and fall of words, *P* 166–69, and where language itself, in accordance with myth-inspired ecstasy, begins to take off from the ground) and into *Ulysses*, implies both the success and the Icarian variant of failure. The hazardous plight of words engaged in ecstatic flight contributes much to the Joycean comedy of incongruities. There can be a rhetorical *hubris* too, an attempt by language to overreach, aim too high. For example, the speech by Dan Dawson, as reported in Aeolus, accumulates altitudes like *"serried mountain peaks"* and is in itself *"towering high on high"* (125), but there is one short step from *"overarching"* to *"overarsing"* (123).

"Most amusing expressions"

Ulysses begins on a raised platform, with a sustained showpiece and recital by the most accomplished orator and impersonator of them all, Buck Mulligan of the golden mouth and the inexhaustible (though perhaps, in the long run, slightly repetitious) repertoire. Never at a loss for the right word, he usurps many of Stephen's roles of priest and bard and also, at one turn, provides himself with wings. With "his hands at his sides like fins or wings . . . fluttering his winglike hands" (19), he proclaims his ascension in a Daedalus-cum-Christ routine while doing an Icarian caper down toward the sea. From the start he links up with the classical tradition, uses familiar Homeric tags, and invents Homeric types of epithets. He generally finds a trope for every ploy. With his rapid changes of voice and act he is indeed, as a later parody has it, "mirth-provoking," and causes "considerable amusement" (307). One would naturally invite him to one's party, as George Moore does later in the day (and the exclusion of Stephen Dedalus, with his cryptic utterances and sullen asides, is understandable too). Mulligan is a worthy successor of Mahaffy and Oscar Wilde, a voluble quoter and himself eminently quotable. There is hardly a reader who would not remember the Buck's first words, spoken aloud, and ceremoniously. At least we remember that the Latin of the Mass is mockingly misappropriated.

The extroversatile Buck heralds Ulyssean techniques and a Homeric role that is to be played in a more modest key, and much more fumblingly, by Leopold Bloom, who has inherited some of the skepticism, much of the resilience, and most of the curiosity of Odysseus, as well as a number of minor traits but not, unfortunately, the verbal ingenuity. Bloom is not a gifted speaker. In a culture that values speech at times more than truth, he is denied eloquence. This is not to disagree with Richard Ellmann[3] and others who have emphasized Bloom's gift of expression or even his poetic diction. This diction, the remarkable crispness and spontaneity of his language, his certainly more than average wit, are confined to his unspoken thoughts. When lovable, adaptable, considerate, inquisitive Bloom opens his mouth and speaks aloud (what the Greeks called *agoreusai,* as in *Od.* 5.183), he may become a bit of a bore. At least that is how he strikes most of those who know him in Dublin (and the criteria applied throughout in this essay are, of course, mainly those of Bloom's fellow Dubliners and not some absolute standard of eloquence). Bloom knows it and is known for it. (You would not invite him to your party for the epigrammatic sparkle that he might provide.)

The brisk, supple commonsense of his many inner observations ("He boomed that workaday worker tack for all it was worth," 118, is a fair sample) rarely finds voice. With most of us Bloom shares the inhibitions that make us falter and grope for the clinching expression (which may be one of the reasons why it is so easy to empathize with him). He speaks as most of us do, haltingly. In the Aeolus chapter, which paradigmatically parades most rhetorical devices of the classical heritage, he comes out with a report like: "I spoke with Mr Keyes just now. . . . And he wants it if it's not too late I told councillor Nannetti from the *Kilkenny People*" (146). There is nothing wrong with that except some confusion and perhaps a certain lack of dramatic tension. This is how we conduct some of our daily conversation, but it is hardly the stuff that would make an irate, impatient, fidgety, and, moreover, thirsty, newspaperman hold his breath even if he were interested in the trivial business transaction. Mulligan would never speak like that.

Bloom's early morning classroom lecture about metempsychosis is faultless, and didactically sound, but it manifestly does not grip the attention of his audience of one. This is typical. Try asking readers of *Ulysses* if they remember what Bloom's first spoken words are, as they remember Mulligan's. Few of them do, and for good reason, for Bloom's opening line is singularly nonmemorable, a mere response to the cat's request (and significantly, Bloom tends to re-spond, re-ply, rather than initiate talk). What Bloom says is "O, there you are" (55).

The two openings of the novel contrast pointedly. Mulligan, from an elevated position, on top of an outstanding historical fortification, puts on an act, in a solemn voice, intoning, speaking up to *"Deus,"* though frivolously. Bloom, in the most commonplace of all rooms, a kitchen, from below ground level, speaks, in the most ordinary fashion, down to an animal, but without condescension. The unspectacular words are sufficient for the rapport with the cat that is needed. Note, incidentally, that Bloom begins his day by saying "you," while Mulligan starts out with "I" *("Introibo")* (3).

And, while on the subject of first words, we may observe that Stephen is first heard saying "Tell me" (4), which happens to coincide with the first words of the first line of the *Odyssey* in many translations.

With intimates like the cat or Molly or (for all we know) Milly, Bloom is still more at ease; with an old friend like Josie Breen he may even venture a flourish like "your lord and master" (157). Toward others he is more reserved. Approaching Larry O'Rourke, he rehearses a little speech, which he then keeps for himself. He rarely tries to match the elocution of the Irishmen around him, but he admires them for their wit. Simon Dedalus is one of them: "Most amusing expressions that man finds. Hhhn: burst sidewise" (103). The Muse in general is reticent toward Bloom and does not inspire his expressions.

Surely a chapter like Circe gives evidence of Bloom's aspirations to be a great orator as well; he would enjoy swaying a large audience. In Eumaeus, with some of the inhibitions gone, his submerged eloquence finds a belated outlet but also, tragically, only a completely unresponsive audience. On the whole Bloom is aware of his limits and rarely exceeds them without provocation. Lenehan recalls an occasion when Bloom was holding forth on a favorite subject, astronomy, at some length, but it is obvious that the attention of most of his listeners was elsewhere, and Lenehan ultimately turns the event into the kind of lively story that Bloom could never bring off (233–35). Bloom is at his best as a silent observer and internal commentator. Ironically, his job connects him with the "modern art of advertising," which depends so much on the catchy phrase that Bloom can judge but not make up. The ideal "of magnetising efficacy to arrest involuntary attention, to interest, to convince, to decide" (683) remains an ideal.

Of course Bloom is not at all inarticulate, he is simply not particularly eloquent; his talk, not very exciting, is still more interesting than that of some others. Early in the day he runs into one of the least inspired speakers, Charles M'Coy, who treats him to an unwelcome, protracted report on his response to the news of Dignam's death. This textbook illustration of narrative tedium (which Bloom, as far as Fate will allow him, relieves by voyeuristic attention) may indicate the lack of interest in news that the eating of the lotus fruit caused (*Od.* 9.95), but it mainly shows that someone else is treated by Bloom as he often is by others. Marvin Magalaner long ago pointed out that M'Coy is Bloom's forerunner, an earlier version of him.[4] As M'Coy tries to wedge his way into the prestigious conversation of Cunningham & Co., he obliges, unbidden, with physiological terms of the Bloomian kind ("Mucus," "thorax," *D* 158) but remains neglected very much as Bloom will be in the same company in the funeral carriage.

The Hades chapter assesses Bloom's place in society. Attention rarely turns to him and, when it does, it is against his will. This happens when Molly's concert tour is mentioned, and again when his unorthodox remarks on death, in a different key from accepted ones, clash with the appropriate ritualized formulae (95). But he is ignored or thwarted when he wants to contribute to the conversation, when he volunteers his story about Reuben J. Dodd and son. There is, however, also good rhetorical reason for the usurpation of Bloom's tale. He gets off on a risky start by announcing, twice, how "awfully good" the story is, and only a skilled storyteller can live up to such a promise. When he settles down to the unmistakable tone that is required ("There was a girl in the case, . . . and he determined to send him to the Isle of Man out of harm's way . . ."), he is not too successful in keeping paternal and filial indentities apart, and there are interruptions for clarification until Cunningham takes the story away from him and presents a reedited, and superior, version, which he insists on carrying to its climax. Clearly Bloom's narrative talent would not qualify him to negotiate "the funny part" (94–95).

As it happens, Bloom's story is launched just about when the carriage is closest to the newspaper offices off Sackville street. In general, Bloom stays away from the uncongenial role of a storyteller. The reader knows why in this case, after the sight of Blazes Boylan, and with a moneylender looming into view, he has deviated from his usual practice.

The episode in which Bloom fares best is the visual, projectional, reflective, and almost wordless scene on the beach. As a silent, dark, mysterious stranger he can appear attractive to a girl who is hesitant to move. He realizes that talk would not have improved the encounter. "Suppose I spoke to her. What about? Bad plan . . ." (370). He briefly considers gambits but shrewdly rejects them. A man like Boylan would not have any such qualms. A few sentences he throws out are enough to show that he hits upon the right tone with ease, in front of a shop girl or a barmaid. "What's the damage?" or "Why don't you grow" (227, 265) are not great aphorisms, but impressive enough to cause a blush or a sigh.

"Impromptu" (141)

With his commonsense approach and his commonsense vocabulary, and some business to attend to, Bloom walks into the newspaper office, where a rhetorical seminar is going on. For a moment he stops the stylistic analysis in progress by asking a few questions, short but to the point, "pertinent" (124) in fact. This word characterizes him, his speech and his acts; he "holds on to" whatever is at hand. His purposeful bearing and his simple statements set him off from the grandiose mannerisms of most others. His own words are trite, factual, polite, and unexciting. Yet his exit and his reappearance are decorated by theatrical gestures and elocutionary flourishes. As long as he remains peripheral he is treated with neglect, condescension, or mild ridicule, but as soon as he has to assert himself, he becomes a nuisance.

Joyce chose the rhetorical context of the Aeolus chapter, of all the possible settings, for a close-up view of Bloom in search of a pithy retort to Menton's recent snub. He moreover gives Bloom the advantage of a moment's unruffled leisure and the benefit of hindsight. If we try to imagine how some of the more sharp-tongued Dubliners would have reacted, or remember how Odysseus was able to deal with his adversaries, we can appreciate the endearing flatfootedness of Bloom's effort:

> I could have said when he clapped on his topper. . . . [No inspiration yet; the
> sting is slow in coming. So try again:] I ought to have said something about an

old hat or something. No . . . [Try once more:] I could have said. [The sentence without a pointed *mot* is still incomplete.] Looks as good as new now. (121)

As good as new? No "topper" is forthcoming, "old hat" is about right. Cousin Bloom will never be an orator.[5] Nor, for that matter, was another figure who is featured more in this chapter than in any other one. Moses— who also at times found it hard to get his people's attention—was "not eloquent . . . but I am slow of speech and of a slow tongue" (or *"impeditioris et tardioris linguae sum,"* Exod. 4:10).[6]

To make up for a deficiency in brilliance, Bloom often has some pertinent factual information, for which, worse luck, there is not much of a market in his environment. One's reputation is based more on Aeolian luster, which, in the book, is glorified and mocked, but expansively displayed throughout. A later chapter will be devoted to the seduction (and the vacuity) of musical performances. Sirens through appropriate changes shapes words with regard to their sensuous appeal. Its overture is the most conspicuous example in the whole book of the celebration of pure aural entertainment, a matter of sound and phrasing and orchestration, an orgy of tonal rhetorics, before, secondarily, the sense can and will come through.

The music, to which Bloom listens, serves the same function to those present that talk does in Cyclops; it affords distraction. But in Barney Kiernan's pub Bloom imprudently tries to compete. Not a habitual pubcrawler, he is lured by circumstances and a specific invitation into the locality, and because of his displaced aggression the otherwise silent observer becomes unusually talkative. He behaves with oddly un-Odyssean rashness; he distinctly does not resort to "words of guile" or "deceit" (as in *Od.* 9.282), but appears naively truthful and accurate in what he says and at times unnecessarily officious and intrusive, which aggravates his already precarious situation.

"that kind of talk" (302)

Cyclops, one of the gregarious chapters, develops traits and themes from Aeolus: coming and going, rambling and interrupted dialogue, discussion and parody of newspaper mannerisms, narrative disruptions, a shared cast (Lenehan, Lambert, O'Molloy, Hynes), and the application of oratory—a reasonably comprehensive list of rhetorical forms could be gleaned from this chapter too.[7] Again we have a group of some expert talkers and a few expert critics. The Citizen excels in one kind of invective and takes the opportunity to address the public in several set speeches.[8] Even the dog Garryowen holds the stage for a spell of cynical oratory. Bloom inadvertently maneuvers himself into the position of a public speaker. He is not comfortable in the role and breaks off his proclamation of love in a somewhat abrupt manner, obviously sensing that the audience is not quite with him. The scene is set for his second speech toward the end of the chapter, with the externals of a temporary rostrum and an expectant gathering. Rhetorical repetition characterizes Bloom's parting words (342), which clearly have a kinetic effect, but again this is not the occasion for a grandiose peroration. The burst of forensic eloquence is exceptional for Bloom (it becomes the rule in Circe, but Cyclops serves in many ways as a rehearsal for the later chapter), and remains a qualified success. The reader knows what unusual provocation has led to this singular tortuous climax.

All along in the chapter, Bloom has been a multiple transgressor. It is not his own fault, nor even quite strictly true, that ethnically he does not really belong to the group. He might know, however, that to avoid being treated and treating again is not good policy (though others manage to get around this one with impunity). But beyond all that, Bloom proceeds in the wrong conversational key. He informs and instructs, or argues, or voices *his* grievances—but he does not amuse. There is a tacit code that Bloom seems (or chooses) to be unaware of. The prevalence of such codes is signaled early on in an act put on between the Citizen and Joe Hynes when they go through the ritual of the passwords of the Ribbonmen, with all the required gestures (295),' as if to establish some of the rules of the game.

There are other violators present. Bob Doran, who bears his own understandable grudge against providence, irately seizes upon the literal sense of the word "good" in relation to Dignam's death and Christ and is instantly admonished—"they didn't want that kind of talk in a respectable licensed premises" (302). There are indeed "premises" that one had better observe. Remarks about the responsibilities or the ethnic background of divinity are clearly taboo, even if other blasphemies may be cheerfully applauded. Fittingly, an earlier verbal transgression of Bloom is worked into this chapter, his "giving lip to a grazier" (315). This observance of his own personal code above the socially accepted one led to his dismissal from a job.

The tacit rules are simple enough. You keep the party going by being wittily entertaining (which may amount to finding new permutations for old jocularities), and you play straight man to the Citizen and prompt him to his histrionics (though you may laugh behind his back). But you do not seriously argue or waste everybody's good time with explanations or technicalities. To define a nation, or love, or injustice, just does not make you popular. Who cares, anyway, about mortgages, insurance, or hoose drench?—except perhaps widows or cattle, but none of those are present. The nameless narrator is irritated by Bloom as he is also once by J. J. O'Molloy when he helps out with some legal point about the laws of libel: "Who wants your opinion? Let us drink our pints in peace," as though mere factual clarification were somehow to disturb that peace (321).

Bloom is a disturbance, and part of it is due to the sense that he has little value as an entertainer. His inauguration speech is exemplary. The floor at the moment is being held by Alf Bergan, one of Dublin's wits and one thoroughly familiar with the ground rules (he may break some other ones; surely the public reading of the letters received from hangmen is hardly professional etiquette for a civil servant—but the letters *are* amusing). He offers a report on naive Denis Breen as a diversion (Breen, taunted by the verbal insult "U.p.: up," promptly tries to bring a gravely different code, the legal one, to bear upon what has been designed only "for a lark" (299). Bergan appears impatient with serious talk about capital punishment and uses (what is no doubt Bloom's phrase) "deterrent effect" to broach the much more fascinating topic of the erection of a hanged man (304). To this there are, in neat instructive juxtaposition, two responses. The one, entirely in the spirit of the game, by Joe Hynes:

—Ruling passion strong in death, . . . as someone said

is a maliciously clever shift of a well-known line to a new, amusing context. The deviant response is, naturally, Bloom's

—That can be explained by science. . . . It's only a natural phenomenon, don't you see, because on account of the . . . (304)

We, the readers, can see how Bloom does not want to have the talk turn around erection at this particular moment, but scientific explanation has a way of spoiling the fun. Accounts are the last thing wanted, and Bloom's speech is, once more, rudely thwarted, this time by the narrator, who instantly substitutes a commentary on Bloom for Bloom's verbatim lecture. And a parodistic interpolation follows right away in which Bloom's characteristic approach and his interest in medical evidence are satirized. Bloom has started on the wrong foot; he comes out "with the why and the wherefore and all the codology of the business" (304). He wants to argue and only provokes arguments *ad hominem* and quips at his expense, often with anti-Semitic overtones—"Professor Luitpold Blumenduft" (304).

"Mr Bloom with his argol bargol"

The scientist Bloom, "Mister Knowall" (315), with his useful though tedious contributions about sheep-dip, rower's heart, discipline, insurance, or persecution, is out of place, "putting in his old goo" (310–11), "mucking it up" (313), a nuisance even if he had not mentioned, of all things, "the antitreating league" (311)—a rhetorical outcast as well. One of his favorite phrases is "as a matter of fact" when facts are the least interesting things anyone wants to hear. He may well be right about the racial origin of Marx or Spinoza,[10] or even the Savior, but such information would fail to rouse much interest at the best of times and, at this juncture, merely reinforces the prejudices against him. It matters very little that the Citizen and his faction are contradictory and inconsistent. For all the proximity of the courts and the thematic relevance of parliament and debates at the meetings about the Irish language or the cattle traders, no one wants an objective debate with pro and con. This is a gathering for having "a great confab," as we are warned early on (295), for drolleries like "don't cast your nasturtiums" (320), for clever impersonations ("taking off the old recorder," 322), where forms of "codding" are the order of the day, or "letting on" is expected as well as variations of "doing the rapparee" (295), "the weeps" (302), "the mollycoddle" (306), etc. Rhetorical compulsion requires the translation of Bloom's straightforward "cigar" into the code expression "Give us one of your prime stinkers," or at least some minor elaboration like "knockmedown cigar" (304, 305). This minor incident of Hynes forcing a cigar on reluctant Bloom is transformed by the narrator into "his twopenny stump that he cadged off Joe" (311), a bit of a distortion and a slightly more diverting story. Occasionally clarity demands the reverse translation from the coded allusion to normal terminology. "Wine of the country" and "Ditto MacAnaspey" are put into the vernacular—"Three pints" (295). We learn that "Half one . . . and a hands up" amounts to "Small whisky and bottle of Allsop" (328).[11] Such terminological shifts within the dialogue are a realistic counterpart to the alternation of spoken (ordinary) and parodistic (written, histrionic) parts in the chapter.

Where everybody is expected to wield tropes divertingly, for the fun of it, Bloom remains, even in his most rhetorical moments, factual (whether he gets the facts right or not), sincere and truthful, devoid of Odyssean trickery. The Cyclops chapter exemplifies the free transposition of Homeric material, especially in the diversified distribution of epic roles, and it shows that many of the ill-termed "parallels" are often inverted. Homer's episode confronts the civilized Greeks with uncouth and lawless giants who rely on their muscular strength. Much of this is transferred straight. Humane Bloom is holding his own against opponents who are biased, prejudiced, or brutal. And yet it is also Bloom who does not abide by the laws of the place, and he is even, according to the criteria of the regular customers, a barbarian—he speaks a strange and different language, is not conversant with the rules and yet still speaks out. He is a spoilsport, a disquieting intruder.

Imprudently (and the reader knows why), he talks more than normally. This makes him, in an odd doubling of roles, also a Polyphemus, literally *poly-phemos,* from *pheme* (in turn derived from *phemi,* I speak; cognate with Latin *fama* and "famous"): voice, speech, word, report, renown—and rumor. In fact the whole chapter is *polyphemos,* full of voices, talk, resounding exaggeration, and rumor—with an empty biscuit tin thrown in for bad measure. Conversely, it is as though this episode of elaborate naming were also to utilize the only etymology of the name Odysseus in the whole poem: it connects him with *odyssamenos* (*Od.* 19.407), the participle of a verb "to be angry" ("in great wrath," Butcher and Lang). A surprising number of participants are angry about one thing or another, starting with the narrator, the debtor Geraghty and his contestant Herzog—"the little jewy getting his shirt out" (292), and on to Denis Breen, Bob Doran, Bloom, Garryowen, and the Citizen. Anger lends force to Bloom's two outbursts and his subliminal belligerence. Cyclops is suffused with "suppressed rancour" (312).

Straightforward Bloom is distrusted, but Lenehan (both glibly *polyphemos* and angrily *odyssamenos* about his gambling losses), whose sayings at all times would merit the least literal credibility, is believed immediately when he suspects Bloom to the the only man in Dublin to have won money by backing Throwaway. The reader knows that this *fama* primordially derives from Bantam Lyons projecting onto nongambling Bloom a rhetorical and allusive ingenuity that he neither has nor ever attempts. But it may well be that Bloom's factual bias makes it easier for the others to believe he may have had some inside knowledge, or to believe the other rumor attached to him, that he "gave the idea for Sinn Fein to Griffith" (335): he might well be the sort of person who would help the cause with pertinent specific advice. But not even that momentary patriotic halo bestowed upon Bloom by a tenuous political connection would make him any more popular.

Another interesting quasi-political parallel involves the absent hero Charles Stewart Parnell, who was not a gifted speaker either, and in his early parliamentary appearances even a notably poor one, with at times a stammer.[12] This un-Irish deficiency might have contributed to his cultivation of a pose of taciturnity and aloofness, a manner that would have stood Bloom in good stead when facing Parnell's talkative epigones.

"change the venue"

Bloom's talk, for reasons mentioned, is often cut short by the others, or else the narrator simply ignores the talk and replaces it with his own more racy paraphrases. In the narrator's opinion, Bloom would, and does, talk at length and "talk steady," monotonously so.

In the long run, this might well pall on the reader too. So, following the precedent of the nameless narrator of Cyclops, Joyce from now on does not allow Bloom—or anyone else, for that matter—to "talk steady" *in his own spoken words.* Instead he takes over more and more. The daytalk of *Ulysses* culminates in Barney Kiernan's noisy pub and then gives way to nocturnal transformations. Bloom's unappreciated miniloquence has been sufficiently established and needs no further illustration. But the novel itself becomes more and more extravagantly multiloquent; it begins to change its voices away from actual speech, even though the voices still remain a substratum that can be, on demand, dexterously extrapolated.

Direct transmission of spoken words after Cyclops becomes the exception. What is being said is translated, metempsychosed, reflected into new variations and stranger modes.

Nausicaa contains little dialogue. It is essentially silent and/or stylized according to its own laws. There is just one speech by Bloom, and reported indirectly, though still almost audible: "he said he was sorry his watch was stopped but he thought it must be after eight because the sun was set." Since his watch is not functioning at this point he cannot even do what he is best at, give accurate information, and he has to fall back on circumstantial evidence. Again the reader knows that Bloom's small audience does not really care about the facts offered. Gerty attends, not to what Bloom says, but to how a gentleman expresses himself. She registers the quality of his voice, "a cultured ring," "the mellow tones," or "the measured accents" (*U* 361). A turn like "measured accents" does not really have much denotative point to it; on the other hand, it characterizes, very literally, how heroes speak in epic poetry. Translators of Homer devoted much thought to imitating Greek *meter* by English *stress*. Gertyan diction strains to project the language back to the epic grandeur from which the realistic mode of the book deliberately removed it (note that "cultured ring," "measured accents," or "mellow tones," while wholly appropriate for any Victorian authoress, could all be equivalents of Homeric compound epithets). Bloom's simple speech is variously translated— or dislocuted. Cissy Caffrey, the most linguistically venturesome girl of the group ("jaspberry ram," *U* 353), in her report restates Bloom's words in jocular and more expressive paraphrase, "and said uncle said his waterworks were out of order." She is doing what the book is doing all along, changing the narrative key. The small paragraph is typical of all post-Cyclopian chapters, where actual words spoken tend to be submerged by translation, parody, or commentary. It is a long time till we can be certain we hear Bloom's own voice again.

In Oxen of the Sun dialogue surfaces only rarely verbatim, if at all, and is mainly refined into various literary impersonations. Only the last pages of the chapter look like a return to actual speech faithfully recorded (as if by a tape recorder), as though it were the real performance of a surprisingly articulate group of *ad hoc* orators. But we are not quite sure if this placental verbiage is meant to be the substance of what the students are really saying in precisely these words, in precisely those roles, or whether these spurts of instant ingenuity may not also be tampered with by a more and more manipulative intermediary. Even if the talk is just talk, it is of the kind that Mulligan, for one, can command, and not of the Bloomian variety. One might indeed describe the second part of *Ulysses*—all those chapters, that is, that do not conform to S. L. Goldberg's aesthetic dogmas[13]—as a taking over of the Mulliganesque features that prevailed in Telemachus.

In Circe dialogue is ubiquitous but only part of it is actually real and spoken aloud. And there is no way of dispelling doubt that anything in it might not be imaginary or at least metamorphosed by the governing magic. By now all appearances have become frankly deceptive.

Of the Nostos chapters, only Eumaeus reinstates direct speech, and plenty of it; it is a return to ground that is familiar. Bloom finally takes the opportunity to hold forth at great length, in compensation for all that has gone before. He pulls out all the stops and becomes rhetorically overambitious; he is figurative and metaphorical and engages in elegant variations—all to no avail, of course, as Stephen is only minimally interested in what Bloom says and not at all in the way he says it. But again, does Bloom really and extendedly speak like that, *verbatim?* Are the following Bloom's actual words, faithfully transcribed:

—Spaniards, for instance, ... passionate temperaments like that, impetuous as Old Nick, are given to taking the law into their own hands and give you your quietus double quick with those poignards they carry in the abdomen. (637)

There are his idioms, his recognizable cadences, and yet his diction, especially in this relentlessly concentrated form, may be tarred with the brush that is responsible for the stylistic idiosyncrasies of the whole chapter, which of course, in turn, merely exaggerate the potential of his own mind. Perhaps it just no longer makes sense to distinguish actual performance from what are no doubt oratorical aspirations and those, in turn, from the mode of the chapter. *Ulysses* also teaches us to let go—reluctantly, at times—some of those neat categories that our minds have been brought up on. In practical terms this might mean that, at this late stage, we may not even trust the dashes any longer, that typographical convention by which, so far, direct speech has been honestly set off from the rest of the narration. Sounds and speeches and dashes may be impostures in Eumaeus, a chapter of guises and subterfuges.

Clearly, both Circe and Eumaeus, in their own particular modes, hint at a distorted fulfillment of Bloom's rhetorical (and authorial) aspirations, as if in compensation for what he cannot bring off in his actual day by day performances. Yet in both chapters of wishful triumphs, Bloom's fumbles and blunders too are magnified correspondingly and grotesquely.

And again, it seems that Joyce removes the novel at this point from even these highly hypothetical excrescencies of Bloomian ambitions with their semblance of direct quotation. In Ithaca direct speech has disappeared entirely and given way to pointedly oblique report, which is catalogued deadpan along with everything else, though we can, of course, try to reconstruct Bloom's and Stephen's actual spoken words by an empirical, inductive process.

The Penel) quence of the last chapter is unspoken, though based on spoken language, and *sui generis*. It does, however, reintroduce some of Bloom's sentences to Molly, spoken with effect and remembered with relish. Bloom undoubtedly is capable, at times. Even so, without the setting of rhododendrons and romantic wooing, "the sun shines for you" and you are "a flower of the mountain" (782) are not necessarily, by themselves, evidence of remarkable rhetorical potential.

158 ON *ULYSSES:* BOOK OF MANY TURNS

"various different varieties"

In grammatical metaphor, Bloom's progress through his fourteen chapters is from the predominant indicative mood (corresponding to his acts, thoughts, and talk) into different moods like subjunctive or optative, expressing more the aspirations, imaginary achievements, fears, or wishful thinking. Much of Circe is written in a kind of conditional: *if* Bloom could get up for a stump speech, and *if* he could conjure up the right phrases on the spur of the moment, and *if* . . . , then he might undergo such rapid changes and rise to glory and also suffer such ignominies. And if he had the resources of a Mr Philip Beaufoy (or, as he seems to think, of Stephen Dedalus, poet and man of letters), then he might be able to compose such figurative, parabolic, ornate, winged, fumbling, discordant, and alert (yes, alert) prose as the one of Eumaeus.

The rhetorics and tropes Bloom lacks in everyday life are lavished on the novel as a novel, with increasing boldness. The book as an event in language plays most of the roles, along with, and above, the characters. The smooth and sweet and cunning words that Odysseus contrives when he first addresses Nausicaa (*Od.* 6.143 ff.) are never even attempted by Bloom, but they inform the first part of the softly featured and mellifluent chapter. Beyond the reaches of any one person, the book becomes mercurial, myriadminded, multifaceted, histrionic, and polytropically all-round.

The mind around which all this mainly revolves is, like most minds, relatively pedestrian. Mr Bloom's own utterances can be improved upon by a good translation. So Joyce comes to his aid and more and more conspicuously runs the show on his behalf, with transformations, transmutations, transubstantiations, and metamorphoses, with different contexts and styles and parallactic systems of correspondences. It did not occur to the detractors of *Ulysses* that even its more elaborate features, whatever else, also work against the boredom of anything that is carried on for too long. That is all done with a purpose and with consideration for the reader, believe it or not, "to cheer a fellow up" (107).

Joyce puts poor Bloom, who endures many troubles and hardships (*Od.* 1.4), at one of the greatest further disadvantages, by depriving him of a quality that Homer, the Greeks, the Irish, and most lovers of literature and talk, value highly. But he lends him his sympathy, does duty as his own personal Muse and gives assistance by metaphrasing more and more of his words and by providing him (though Bloom would never know)—and us (and we had better know it)—with a course in remedial rhetorics.

1978

Notes

1. I discuss "Chrysostomos" as narrative deviation in the essay "Metastasis," reprinted in this volume.

2. "*Polytropos*, he [Antisthenes] argues, does not refer to character or ethics at all. It simply denotes Odysseus's skill in adapting his figures of speech ('tropes') to his hearers at any particular time." In W. B. Stanford, *The Ulysses Theme: A Study in the Adaptability of a Traditional Hero*, 2nd ed. (Ann Arbor: University of Michigan Press, 1968), p. 99. See my essay "Odysseeische Metamorphosen," in *James Joyce's "Ulysses": Neuere deutsche Aufsätze*, ed. Therese Fischer-Seidel (Frankfurt: Edition Suhrkamp, 1977), p. 44; and Michael Groden, *"Ulysses" in Progress* (Princeton: Princeton University Press, 1977), pp. 91–92.

3. "Yet [Bloom] must be separated from those about him, and by the gift of expression— the highest a writer can bestow on his creature. . . . But Bloom has to speak in ordinary language . . . taking a keen pleasure in manoeuvring among common idioms, allusions, and proverbs. It is this power of speech, mostly inward speech, that inclines Bloom towards Odysseus." In Richard Ellmann, *Ulysses on the Liffey* (London: Faber and Faber, 1972), p. 30.

4. Marvin Magalaner, "Leopold Bloom before *Ulysses*," *Modern Language Notes* 68 (February 1953): 110–12.

5. But then, Bloom's first words spoken in "Aeolus" constitute the best all-time editorial advice that fits all occasions: "Just cut it out" (116).

6. The implication is that eloquence is not everything, and anyway, the Lord said, "Who hath made man's mouth" (Exod. 4:11). Intriguingly, Stephen, who has worked "mouth" into the semiplagiarized creation recalled in the chapter, speculates at length on the reverberations of this word. "Must be some" (138).

7. See also Phillip F. Herring, ed., *Joyce's Notes and Early Drafts for "Ulysses": Selections from the Buffalo Collection* (Charlottesville: University Press of Virginia, 1977), p. 146; and Groden, *"Ulysses" in Progress*, p. 133ff. To all these lists might be added the parallel that in both chapters Bloom appears twice and on his return gets worse treatment each time.

8. The Citizen's "No music and no art and no literature worthy of the name" (325) follows, roughly, a pattern set in Taylor's speech (142).

9. Hugh B. Staples, " 'Ribbonmen' Signs and Passwords in *Ulysses*," *Notes and Queries*, n.s. 13 (1966): 95–96.

10. In the roll call of great Jews in Bloom's enumeration (342), Mercadante is the odd one out, by no stretch of ethnic definition a Jew. What happened is that Bloom has been confusing two composers he likes for different reasons, Mercadante (82) and Meyerbeer (168). In "Sirens" he wrongly attributed *Seven Last Words* to Meyerbeer (290) and now, in his unrehearsed speech, seems to make up for it. He means Meyerbeer, whose opera *The Hugenots* is about religious persecution.

11. It is important to have no misunderstanding interfere with the order of one's drink, but these variations also comply to the avoidance of mere repetition in conventional rhetorics.

12. Pointed out to me by Wayne Hall, a former student at Indiana University, who mentioned this when an earlier version of this essay was presented as a talk.

13. S. L. Goldberg, *The Classical Temper: A Study of James Joyce's "Ulysses"* (London: Chatto and Windus, 1961); to this day still the best book ever written against *Ulysses*.

11

Nausicaa

The last scene of the preceding chapter transfigured Leopold Bloom and projected him skyward at a specified and ballistically advantageous angle. The ascendant curve is continued into the first part of Nausicaa, which gratifyingly exalts Bloom, at least as viewed from the favorable angle of one observer, from a particularly one-eyed, romanticized perspective. The observer, Gerty MacDowell, herself intently watched by Bloom, is in turn portrayed at her spectacular best, with fulsome touches and lavish colors. In addition, both she and Bloom are emotionally and physiologically exalted. Nausicaa is a chapter of culminations, of aspirations and high expectations, of sky-gazing and firework-gazing, of ecstatic flights and raised limbs.

The sustained flight, in Nausicaa as in Cyclops, owes much to the elevation of its language. Its heights are rhetorical. Stripped of its metaphorical props, the flight becomes no more than fleeing. The escape from the citizen's rage transforms itself into a mysterious embrace, with Bloom, lingering lovingly in a soft world slowly losing its harsh contours, seeking refuge and comfort for his afflictions in illusory fulfillment.

Like all ballistic curves, those described in Nausicaa contain a rise, a climax, a descent, and an abrupt return to the ground. The movement is paralleled in such details as the rockets of the bazaar fireworks, a ball thrown and kicked, a stick flung away, and a bat flying to and fro. Within the human body, the movement corresponds to the surge of blood that animates Gerty's cheeks with quaint blushes or a "telltale flush" (349), implicitly contributing to the underlying genital tumescence.

"branded as the lowest of the low" (354)

The protagonists' rise to unprecedented heights is counterpointed, conspicuously enough, by a converse movement of which the reader, who inevitably depreciates the various altitudes according to his own scale, is very much aware and to which Gerty MacDowell herself carefully closes her eyes. The parabola of the flight is a parable of frustration and loneliness. In the setting of all-embracing love, Bloom resorts to the most isolated form of sexual gratification, an event made more poignant by his realization that a more vital and more mutually fulfilling embrace has recently been staged at home. Gerty too has been thwarted, by the loss of the attentions of her boy, who has, of late, been distracted by an entirely different kind of "exhibition" (349, 352); and she is out to gain attention elsewhere. The way in which the two work off their disappointments would have found little sympathy in any culture that produces these frustrations, and none at all in the Ireland of 1904. Masturbation is a sin in the Catholic context, and its essential sterility made it an offence in the Judaic code. We can translate the term into more contemporary condemnatory terms, such as "self-deception" and "escapism."

In Gerty's and Bloom's brief coming together, there is no coition (they do not go together, *co-ire*); both merely linger in relative proximity, within visual range, and then continue on their lonely ways, Gerty on hers, moreover, with a limp. There is no consummation, no physical touch (only, we are told, "consummate tact," and even that is used to "pass . . . off" something unpleasant; 363), no verbal contact. Fewer words are spoken in Nausicaa than in the other chapters (except the basically silent Proteus and Penelope). Two monologues, one indirect, one direct, the one before, the other after, are its suitable expression. The cheap satisfaction is brought out in a style of cheap fiction, lacking vitality, incapable of communication.

Nausicaa then is a profitable chapter for the critic who may rise to the occasion and comment, with Cyclopean assurance, on the multiple inadequacies displayed by the two lovers, treating them, according to his inclination, with benign condescension or downright contempt. Nausicaa yields ample illustration for the marriage counsellor, the preacher, or the moral guide. The moralistic attitude first manifested itself in public through the activities of the Society for the Prevention of Vice, which instituted legal proceedings in 1920, thus stopping the book's first flight in serial publication and bringing it abruptly down to court. Sentences similar to that pronounced in the Court of Special Sessions in New York, in 1921, have been reiterated since, with some relevant fashionable modifications: nowadays the author is generally enlisted on the right side; he is in fact represented as implicitly adding his voice to those expressing righteous disapprobation of his characters.

"Look at it other way round" (380)

There is no intrinsic necessity to restrict one's views to censorious glances from superior vantage points. These may even blind us to some of the chapter's scintillating delights. One of the potential moral effects of *Ulysses* is that it can condition us, more than any previous novel, to suspend or, at any rate, postpone the moralizing tendency that consists in dispensing blame and credit, in favor of a series of constant readjustments and a fluctuating awareness of the complexity of motivation. Nausicaa at least enables us, besides the pleasures of judicial evaluation, to experience sympathy and to arrive at the kind of intricate understanding that makes the attitude of forgiveness (cf. 358) just as pointless as its opposite.

In the imperfect world of Dublin, 1904, the imperfect solution that the two characters allow themselves to be driven to, passively reactive rather than passionately active, does have some advantages. There is relief from various tensions, relief from the conflicts of aggression and prejudice, as in Barney Kiernan's, and relief also from the depressing squalor of the Dignam's household. Bloom's foreignness, usually a cause of trouble, stands him in good stead in Nausicaa, heightened as it is by some spurious effects. There is compensation for recent setbacks. Bloom knows one has to be "Thankful for small mercies" (368). For the moment he feels young again. At the end of the day, the encounter is listed positively as having been accompanied by "pleasant reflection" (722), and there have been few enough such moments. Substitute satisfactions are better than no satisfactions at all, and Bloom, for one, appreciates the benefits to be derived from the momentary shutting off of unpleasant aspects of reality: "Glad I didn't know it when she was on show" (368).

Throughout, *Ulysses* interfuses reality with illusion, and in some parts the validity of the distinction is even challenged (it seems to have disappeared entirely in *Finnegans Wake*). Nausicaa varies the theme in its own manner, ringing the changes on the mind's inventiveness in superimposing satisfactions of which reality is acutely devoid. Illusion, partly "optical illusion" (376), is one way of "smoothing over life's tiny troubles" (347). Without some tempering from the imagination, reality might well become unbearable. Belief in "intercessory power" (356) or in the curative and beautifying power of advertised goods performs such tempering functions and so does art. To afford illusory gratifications is one of the legitimate functions of fiction, of highbrow literature no less than of Gerty's favorite reading matter.

Some techniques for putting up with bothersome situations and creating compensatory patterns are compulsorily learned in our childhood: "Tommy Caffrey could never be got to take his castor oil unless it was Cissy Caffrey that held his nose and promised him the scatty heal of the loaf of brown bread with golden syrup on" (346). That sets the tone for Nausicaa, similarly coated with syrupy "sweetness" (360). When baby Boardman is deprived of his ball, his frustration is dealt with by two other mechanisms prominent in the chapter, titillation and the conjuring up of fictitious scenes from a life far higher than one's own, rendered in stylized form: "And she tickled tiny tot's two cheeks to make him forget and played here's the lord mayor, here's his two horses, here's his gingerbread carriage and here he walks in, chinchopper, chinchopper, chinchopper chin" (353).

Such escape mechanisms, basically aimed at diverting attention from disagreeable aspects of reality, also have some positive value. Bloom at least meets a being who, by virtue of whatever distorting projections, seems to accept him and to desire him. Something approaching love does, after all, take place, and a kind of rapport is established: "Still it was a kind of language between us" (372). The lack of communication in *Ulysses* is perhaps less surprising than the occasional occurrence of *some* imperfect communication. Gerty, injured and slighted, presents herself to her best advantage for one short span, at the proper distance, with just the right degree of illumination to increase her glamour (which is what the advice she gets from the fashion page amounts to). Even after the release of tension and after the effects of the stage setting have worn off, Bloom is capable of sympathizing with her. "Poor girl" is one of his first thoughts. Nor does he appear to be any more depressed or guilt-ridden than we know him to have been previously.

The pathetic climax of the two chance lovers resembles Bloom's confrontation with the citizen, an earlier blend of conviction, tumescent courage, irritation, and pulpit sentimentality, where Bloom is sublimely exalted as well as ridiculously abased—and there it would be equally hard to place him, or the events, conclusively on any evaluative scale.

After Bloom's precipitate proclamation of the gospel of love, he does embark on a tour of love in its varieties. The visit to the Dignams is an act of charity; romantic love culminates in Nausicaa (which is steeped in colors of loveliness, including even the "lovely" dog Garryowen); the depths of sexuality are charted in Circe; paternal love comes into its own from Oxen of the Sun to Ithaca. At the same time these pursuits are also patently motivated by an unwillingness to face domestic realities. As against any normative ideals, Bloom's performances fall short. Still, in his encounter with Gerty he comes within visible distance of his own definition of love as "the opposite of hatred." The abortive message that Bloom writes into the sand and effaces immediately, "I . . . AM. A." (381), happens to contain, besides himself, the latin root *ama-*, love, no doubt outside his own consciousness and yet somehow "done half by design" (382), indicative more of a wish, unfulfilled like the rest of them, than an achievement. In one respect Bloom attains the Christian aim of forgiving his most recent persecutor, the citizen: "Look at it other way round. Not so bad then. Perhaps not to hurt he meant" (380).

"matters feminine" (346)

With the Nausicaa chapter we enter, for the first time, a predominantly female world. So far Stephen and Bloom have moved in a masculine environment. No single woman was present in Cyclops, except for glimpses of wretched Mrs Breen as the servant of her master (who, through the postcard "U.P.: up," is treated to his own rise and fall). Now we are immersed in the soft cadences of feminine fiction, with three girls in the foreground dominating a triad of young males, reducing Bloom to the role of a spectator. Gerty's is the first feminine mind that is unfolded before us at any length. Before that the reader was favored with a few parenthetical flashes of the minds of the seductive barmaids in Sirens, who also provide flirtatious distractions for careworn Dubliners. Miss Douce even performs an exhibitionistic set piece for two ogling males.

An earlier mild prefiguration of Gerty MacDowell is the Miss Dunne of Wandering Rocks. Her brief succession of thoughts include "mystery," "love," and envious comments on the pictorial exhibitionism of a star of the Dublin stage, named Marie (Kendall), "holding up her bit of a skirt." She considers the fascinated stare of men and a "concertina skirt" for herself (229). Like Gerty, she has a secret in her drawer (cf. 442), she hopes (as Gerty "wishes") "to goodness" (229, 357, 361), and she uses the tumescent word "swells." Her employer, Blazes Boylan, generally better off than Bloom, is at the same moment viewing the charms of another blushing girl, while anticipating the more palpable charms of Molly.

The oblique characterization of Gerty MacDowell is the first extended delineation of a female psyche. From now on, the book moves through several female phases. The Virgin, Joyce's "symbol" for Nausicaa, is succeeded by the Mother and the Whore in the next two chapters—three traditional archetypal manifestations. In Penelope, Molly's fullness encompasses them all. On a smaller scale, the three girls in Nausicaa play all these roles, being virginal but having maternal responsibilities, as well as scortatory duties later in Circe.

"the gathering twilight" (363)

The immersion in this female world coincides with the oncoming of night. Gerty appears in twilight; at the end of the chapter darkness has descended. Bloom estimates the time by such signs as the waning of the light and the appearance of the mailboat. The sun set in Dublin at 8:27 P.M. on 16 June 1904 (as indicated in *Thom's Directory*), and lighting up time for cyclists (376) was fixed at 9 hours, 17 minutes, as the *Evening Telegraph,* sold in the streets at Sandymount a little before that time, told its readers.[1]

In most mythological representations, and in the grammatical gender of Indo-European languages, the night is female. The darker half of *Ulysses* is ushered in by Gerty and closed by Molly's ruminations in her bedroom; at the end the faint incipient luster of approaching dawn, and the remembered swelling memory of a scene steeped in the sunlight of Gibraltar and of Howth, herald a new turning toward the sun. Immediately after Nausicaa, in the first word of the next chapter, Deshil,[2] there is another metaphorical turning toward sun and son.

The second, larger part of *Ulysses* extends between opposite poles of womanhood: young, immature Gerty, lame and incomplete (she is only accorded half a chapter), and ripe, fullblown Molly. Bloomsnight is structured symmetrically, enclosed at each end by female outpourings, fluid, subjective, with orgasmic climaxes. These are accompanied by male counterparts, arranged concentrically—Bloom's sober reflective attempt at a reasoned view in Nausicaa is set off against the rationalized pseudoscientific and objective inventory of Ithaca, both down-to-earth, disillusioned stocktakings. Both chapters end, similarly, with Bloom's falling asleep and with a transition into dream language, a dissolution of narrative as masculine control gives way to uninterrupted, associative strings of words and memories (382, 737). In the *Odyssey* too, the isle of the Phaeacians is closest to Ithaca and the last stop on the return journey.

Tucked between enveloping folds of femininity, the meeting, interacting, parting of Bloom and Stephen are circumveloped by a darkness that both does and does not comprehend them. They are thus "wombed in sin darkness" (38). The image of an enfolding womb within which the most significant action takes place is more than a convenient analogy. Regression into uterine security is at the core of infantile notions of illusory escape, as in Nausicaa; the same local anatomical habitation is necessary for the more positive interpretations concentrating on birth and rebirth or for Stephen's concept of a creative womb of the imagination. A womb is included in the word "wombfruit" at the beginning of the Oxen of the Sun chapter (383), whose organ is the womb. The last page of Ithaca, which is symmetrically opposite and in which Bloom disappears, contains a corresponding image: "the manchild in the womb" (737.13).

There is an uterine quality to the darkness of the night of 16–17 June, enfolded into a female texture, and stretching from the metaphorical all-including embrace that sets the scene in Nausicaa (with an early glance at dear old Howth) all the way to the remembered real, carnal embrace on Howth Head.

"a story behind it" (355)

Gerty MacDowell is the latest avatar of the temptress in Joyce's fiction. An early incarnation is Polly Mooney in "The Boarding House," who exposes herself to a male viewer, at night, against a backdrop of candles. She first emerges in a scene full of social pretense and cliché, e.g., "the *artistes* would oblige" at one of the "reunions." She is both naively innocent and cunningly knowing; her song mentions "sham." She is explicitly referred to as "a little perverse madonna" (*D* 62–63). Her grammar, like Gerty's, is imperfect, but what, says Mr Doran—and it could have been said by Gerty or one of her authoresses—, "would grammar matter if he really loved her?" (*D* 66). Polly and Gerty know how to cry in front of a mirror (*D* 68; 351). And Polly "knew she was being watched" (*D* 63). Her seduction, however, has graver consequences. Mr Doran considers vainly and irrationally escape by flight through the roof but is brought down to reality by the confederate forces of familial and social gravity, and by Cyclopean threats. Bloom, at any rate, is more prudent than Polly's victim, who by the time of *Ulysses* has further declined to a wretched state. A handshake briefly unites the two in Cyclops, with the I-narrator putting them in the same category: "Shake hands, brother. You're a rogue and I'm another" (313).

A Portrait presents its own gallery of temptresses, leading up to the vision in chapter 4 and the villanelle of chapter 5. The girl who meets Stephen's gaze on the strand connects two otherwise separate strands of sensual eroticism and mariolatric images of purity. The similarity between this twilight scene and the portrait of Gerty MacDowell in *Ulysses* has often been remarked upon. The stage setting in both contains the beach, the dusk, the sea, weedgrown rocks, the display of thighs, pictorial representation, and elevated vocabulary. The mind is turned to higher things. The universe and the world are freely brought to bear on the situation, Stephen relating to "the heavenly bodies, . . . the earth, . . . some new world" (*P* 172), while Gerty can be just as liberal with the evocation of "worlds" (351, 357, etc.). There is neither physical contact nor any spoken word to break the spell. It takes the next section—chapter 5 of *A Portrait,* part 2 of Nausicaa—to reestablish more realistic proportions.

"Same style of beauty" (380)

To realize just how much the Nausicaa chapter metamorphoses elements of Stephen's ecstasy on the beach in *A Portrait,* it is worth collating a few images and phrases. Almost every item, for example, of the catalogue that describes the impression made on Stephen by the bird-girl has been reused. Both girls are alone, gazing into the distant sea, aware of being watched, and in both cases there is mention of waist, bosom, hair, face, softness, drawers, skirts, slenderness, touch, shame, etc. Some specific transpositions are amusing. The "magic" changing the girl into the likeness of a seabird is at work in Nausicaa too, in the "magic lure" (364) in Gerty's eyes. The seabird may have become a "canary bird" (359), but Bloom himself thinks of "seabirds" (380). The girl's legs are "delicate"; delicacy is one of Gerty's strong points, extending to her hands (348), her flush (349—flushes are part of the scenery in the *Portrait* too, p. 172), and the "pink" creeping into her pretty cheek (356). Since "from everything in the least indelicate her finebred nature instinctively recoiled" (364), she would be peeved to know that Bloom callously awards the palm of delicacy to her rival: "That squinty one is delicate" (368). The ivory of the bird-girl's thighs is part of Gerty's make-up: "ivory-like purity" (348). The term "slateblue" contains Gerty's favorite color, but Bloom uses "on the slate" (375) in quite another context. The "ringdove" (362) associated with Gerty's defiant voice may be compared to the "dove-like" bosom of Stephen's vision, or to her skirts, which are "dovetailed." The "worship" of Stephen's eyes has its counterpart in Bloom's "dark eyes . . . literally worshipping at her shrine" (361). The "faint flame" that trembled on the cheek of the girl in *A Portrait* is relit as a "warm flush . . . surging and flaming into her [Gerty's] cheeks" (356). Even the precious word "fashioned," which is used for the trail of seaweed in the earlier scene, seems to have been transferred from the literary tradition to the marketplace—to the ambit of "Dame Fashion," one of Gerty's patron saints, whose call she follows as a "votary" (350), just as Stephen devoted himself to Art.

A more detailed list of such transferences would include the cry uttered by both Stephen and Gerty at their respective raptures, a trembling of limbs, a phrase like "the palest rose" (*P* 172), which becomes "waxen pallor" in conjunction with "rosebud mouth" (348). Gerty's climax could be called, as Stephen's is, "an outburst of profane joy" (*P* 171). Etymologically, "profane" means "outside the temple" (Lat. *fanum* = fane), which is exactly where the action on Sandymount strand takes place, literally near "that simple fane beside the waves" (354).

It is, above all, one of Stephen's choicest terms, "radiant" (see *P* 169 and "radiance" *passim,* in the aesthetic theory) which, together with another thematic word of *A Portrait,* is now applied to Gerty MacDowell's showy appearance: "a radiant little vision" (360). The "pure radiance" of the Virgin (346) is one of many links.

The two visions are made up of the same touches, sometimes with a marked drop in tone and connotation. The purple tinge, noticeable in *A Portrait,* but not easily appreciated with critical nicety, had now been applied much more strongly. One's impressions of the earlier scene will now be readjusted; in the comic exaggerations of Nausicaa some traits in *A Portrait* are seen in a different light. The two episodes reflect on each other. Nausicaa continues the familiar technique of *A Portrait,* the repetition of an earlier event in a rearrangement, with a change of tone and a new slant (often amounting to a disillusionment) brought about, very often, by a reshuffling of the same verbal material with some additional twists of phraseology. The reading experience is characterized by shifts of perspective (one of the structural devices of *Ulysses*), which should also make us wary of singling out any one of the stages in the process of cognition, however convincing, as the decisive one.

"with careful hand recomposed" (370)

We know that Joyce, while working on *Ulysses,* met a live incarnation of whoever had inspired the event that had been turned into the vocational epiphany on the beach in chapter 4 of *A Portrait.* Late in 1918, in Zürich, Joyce saw and addressed a girl, Martha or (Marthe) Fleischmann, bearing a name that itself contained an alluring tangle of Ulyssean motifs, and embarked upon a liaison that was mainly an affair of looks and letters (at least until its climax, a final rendezvous of, presumably, more daring enterprise, shrouded—for us—in appropriate obscurity, but illuminated—for the participants—by candles specially and ritualistically provided; fittingly, the episode has been reported by a painter, Joyce's friend Frank Budgen, in whose studio the meeting took place).³

Whether acting on impulse or imitating Bloom's epistolary precedent, Joyce sent his Martha some letters and one postcard (this, addressed from "Odysseus" to "Nausicaa," is now lost;⁴ as it happens, Gerty received one "silly postcard," 362)—documents of a *Schwärmerei* that prove the Swiss seductress reinforced some of the attractions that were to be attributed to Gerty MacDowell. The affair, with a strong element of "studied attitude" (355) on Joyce's part, no doubt also contained its serious involvement. The letters allow us some rare glimpses into that mysterious process of distillation that turns living experience into distanced art. The situation already has about it an air of a laboratory experiment arranged with a view to literary exploitation. In real life Joyce could adopt fictional roles by comparing himself outright with Dante or Shakespeare, while playing a provincial Romeo or Tristan.

Again it is fascinating to watch Joyce using, to express private feelings for the kinetic purpose of evoking an emotional response, the same turns of phrase (though in French and German) and the same images that served him, not too much later, for the hilarious parodies of Nausicaa. He did not of course use the letters (which were out of his hands and whose preservation is accidental) as he might use the actual text of previously published works. All we can say with certainty is that concepts and analogies that were in his mind in 1918 to 1919, and which were used for practical purposes, recur in the chapter that was drafted a few months later.⁵ The artist is in full control of his material, which seems to be more than we can claim of the lover and correspondent.

In the first letter, of December 1918,⁶ Joyce gives voice to his frustration at not seeing Martha, whose name he does not yet know. His first visual impressions include her big hat, similar to the one that Gerty takes off with striking effect, and, in more detail, "la mollesse des traits réguliers et la douceur des yeux." The charm of Gerty's eyes is general all over "Nausicaa," and her "sweetness" is tied to her whole vision (360), but the softness of her face is explicitly noted: "her softlyfeatured face" (348). Joyce goes on to remark how he thought Martha was a Jewess, an illusion, but an endeavor to make life conform to fictional patterns. In the fictional refashioning, the inversion of racial roles corresponds to the shifting of the sentimentality to the female partner. In his letter, Joyce then adduces the symbolism that is central for much of his writing, and in particular for Nausicaa and Oxen of the Sun: "Jesus Christ a pris son corps humain: dans le ventre d'une femme juive." Molly, at least, has been turned into a half-Jewess.

Joyce confesses to giving in to "une espèce de fascination." Bloom is "fascinated by a loveliness that made him gaze" (361). The letter also conjures up the evening scene, "un soir brumeux." Martha has given a sign (". . . vous m'avez fait un signe"), and so does Gerty on p. 367. Joyce hints at Byronic repercussions in his life: ". . . je suis un pauvre chercheur dans ce monde, . . . j'ai vécu et péché et créé. . . ." The same instances of a dissolute but creative life figure in Stephen's visionary repertoire (*P* 172), and, accordingly, Gerty projects that Bloom "had erred and sinned and wandered" (367).

In this long first letter, with its odd confessional urge, Joyce slightly rejuvenates himself to establish a parallel with the great writers. He uses the imagery of an entry into the night: "C'est l'àge que Dante a eu quand il est entrê dans la nuit de son être." A few lines later Joyce even refers to the infantile retreat into the darkness of the womb, so basic to the nocturnal chapters in *Ulysses*: " . . . je m'en irai, un jour, n'ayant rien compris, dans l'obscuritê qui nous a enfantês tous." Joyce is paraphrasing Stephen's "darkness shining in brightness which brightness could not comprehend" (28), as well as "wombed in sin darkness . . . made not begotten" (38)—subtleties that must necessarily have been lost on a somewhat puzzled Martha Fleischmann, whose preferred reading is reported to have been sentimental novels. Joyce calls Martha "gracious" and "rêveuse," and both gracefulness and dreaminess are among Gerty's attributes.

In another letter (9 December 1918) Joyce compares Martha's suffering, brought on by illness, to his own: "moi, j'ai souffert aussi." Gerty wonders if Bloom too "had suffered" (358). In the last extant letter Joyce switches over to languishing phrases in German. He describes Martha's face: ". . . Dein Gesicht, aber so blass, so müde und so traurig!" This air of sadness suits Gerty's complexion too: her "sad downcast eyes" (349), for example, and in another passage: ". . . that tired feeling. The waxen pallor of her face . . ." (348). In a last imaginative flight Joyce soars to Gertyan heights of imagery and emotion, kitsching that note of romantic rapture to sweet perfection, though (in *this* case no doubt unwittingly) marring the effect by a grammatical lapse:

Durch die Nacht der Bitterkeit meiner Seele fielen die Küsse Deiner Lippen über meinen Herz—weich wie Rosenblätter, sanft wie Tau.

We do not know where Joyce's tongue was when he wrote those cadences. After the enchantment was over, at any rate, the dewy softness acquired a different quality. In Nausicaa the rapturous burst, "O so soft, sweet, soft," is followed by "all melted away dewily" (367). And the dew that covers Sandymount strand is more matter of fact: "Dew falling. Bad for you, dear, to sit on that stone. Brings on white fluxions" (376).

The litany of the Blessed Virgin is the source for Joyce's parting address to Martha Fleischmann: "O rosa mistica, ora pro me!" Translated into the novel, it becomes ". . . pray for us, mystical rose" (356), and again *"Ora pro nobis"* (358).

These letters show that Joyce did not have to look very far for the psychological material he was to deal with; his own *personae* proved a rich quarry. The attitudes of the pining adorer contributed more to the Nausicaa chapter than the adored girl herself. Joyce's introspective acumen and capacity to see himself from a distance must have been remarkable. An element of spite, consequence of almost inevitable frustration, may have been at play too in the malicious reversal of roles: the sentimentality and doubtful taste and languishing are projected onto the girl. Bloom (roughly of the age of Joyce when Nausicaa was being written in 1919 to 1920) appears detached and down to earth. It remains one of the mysteries of literary creation how the internal set-up that could produce such dewy epistolary prose could be transmuted, by processes of displacement and transference, into the comic portraits of Gerty MacDowell and Mr Leopold Bloom.

"Must have the stage setting" (370)

It is appropriate that Gerty's portrait is made up of strokes found elsewhere in life and fiction (Joyce's and others'). Make-up is her medium. Gerty's plumes are borrowed ones, so much so that some readers deny her any individual character. She is composed of traits assembled in a technique of collage and montage, in keeping with the chapter's art, painting.

However, Gerty MacDowell is not wholly dependent on her models. The coda of the Wandering Rocks chapter introduces her in a revelatory vignette that condenses her component traits and limitations, excepting only the posing and the artificial embellishment:

> Passing by Roger Greene's office and Dollard's big red printing house Gerty MacDowell, carrying the Catesby's cork lino letters for her father who was laid up, knew by the style it was the lord and lady lieutenant but she couldn't see what Her Excellency had on because the tram and Spring's big yellow furniture van had to stop in front of her on account of its being the lord lieutenant. (252)

Joyce exposes Gerty's preoccupation with appearance, dress, and position and her attempt to take a vicarious part in Her Excellency's excellency. The sentence has a tenseness about it which we shall notice again in Nausicaa. Its rhythm, combining a supple pace with a halting awkwardness, suggests Gerty's limp, while the imagery includes three strong primary colors. The little episode is a frustrated vision into which reality crudely interferes. The style exemplifies in a lower key the tone that characterizes Gerty. We learn, indeed, that it is possible to know "by the style."

Wandering Rocks emphasizes location in space, and Gerty's meticulously specified location indirectly reveals one of her roles, even if this is frustratingly out of the uninformed reader's range of vision. Some special knowledge of Dublin is required, in keeping with the labyrinthine technique:[7] between Roger Greene's office (referred to in Nausicaa as the site of a slightly voyeuristic scene—372), at no. 11 Wellington quay, and Dollard's big red[8] printing house, at nos. 2, 3, 4, and 5 Wellington quay, she must have passed, at nos. 8 and 9, the firm of Ceppi, Peter and Sons, picture frame and looking glass factory, and statuary manufacturers, as they are officially listed.[9] They might well furnish some of the stage property for Nausicaa: pictures, looking glass, and statuary. Bloom, who follows in Gerty's footsteps a few minutes later, notices that Messrs Ceppi deal in statuary: ". . . by Ceppi's virgins, bright of their oils" (260).[10] On her first appearance Gerty is thus tacitly juxtaposed with the Virgin Mary displayed in a shop window, done in bright oils. The bright colors will return in Nausicaa, where, in her new position on the rocks of Sandymount, she is set off against the Virgin Mary, whose Litany is part of the background.

"accidentally on purpose" (359)

It so happens that the sentence that first announces Gerty contains just two verbs in its main clause, "knew" and "couldn't see." This may give a perverse twist to the first words of the Virgin Mary when confronted with the Angel of the Lord and his announcement. She said: "How shall this be, *seeing* I *know* not a man?" (Luke, 1:34).[11] The only other words uttered by the Virgin are quoted verbatim in Nausicaa, 358.

Coincidence may play into Joyce's sacerdotal hands, but it is no coincidence that the operative words "see" and "know," with their negations, are prominent in Nausicaa, often in close conjunction. For example, ". . . Gerty could see by her looking as black as thunder . . . and they both knew that she was something aloof, . . . and there was somebody else too that knew it and saw it . . ." (363); ". . . so she said she could see from where she was . . . and she knew he could be trusted . . . there was no one to see only him . . . because she knew about the passion of men like that. . . ." (365), etc. The chapter is, in one sense, a variation on the subject of seeing (with numerous synonyms) and knowing. In the biblical sense there is no knowledge in the encounter. Cognition and vision blend and are both interdependent and complementary. Both Bloom and Gerty see things without knowing and know about what they cannot see. The reader in turn knows more than he sees. Even a limitation of one's perception ("See her as she is spoil all," 370) or of one's knowledge ("Glad I didn't know. . . ," 368) may at times prove to be an advantage.

Earlier in the day, on the same beach, Stephen contemplated the relation between knowledge and the ineluctable modality of the visible: "thought through my eyes" (37), and went on to conduct an experiment by closing his eyes. Indirectly the closing of the eyes also introduces the visually oriented Nausicaa chapter, at least etymologically. The initial "mysterious" embrace (346) suggests mystery, originally a form of gaining knowledge without the senses. The word derives from Greek *myo,* to close (said of the eyes). Bloom links the word "mystery" with perception in darkness: ". . . into a cellar where it's dark. Mysterious thing too" (374). Cognition through vision is connected with Aristotelian "diaphane" in Proteus, the sensual leering in Nausicaa with transparent stockings.

The precedent of the Virgin's own words does not necessarily justify the prevalence of seeing and knowing in Gerty's chapter. Even so it is worth noticing that the phrases singled out as examples of the bad grammar of Polly Mooney, the perverse little madonna and forerunner of Gerty, are *"I seen"* and *"If I had've known"* (*D* 66). In *Ulysses* she is known for "exposing her person" (303) and to be "open to all comers," which suggests an irreverent equivalent for a "refuge of sinners" (358).

"singular devotion" (356)

Gerty MacDowell's apposition with the Virgin Mary is transparent enough. In the nearby Star of the Sea church, the Litany of the Blessed Virgin is recited, blending with the main narrative. Stuart Gilbert pointed out that the Abbey of Howth, suggested by the references to Howth Head (especially at the beginning, 346), was dedicated to the Blessed Virgin.[12] Sandymount itself is situated in the parish of St Mary. Some of the Virgin's appellations have been assimilated to the description of Gerty's exterior. Her face is noted for its "ivorylike purity" (348); her heart is worth its "weight in gold" (355)—gold and ivory had already acquired liturgical overtones in *A Portrait.* The Virgin is undefiled, Gerty's soul "unsullied" (367). Physically Gerty remains virginally untouched, while some of Mary's spiritual attributes are also translated into physical terms: she is "full of grace," her figure and face being "graceful" (348, 365). Joyce conceives of her as wearing "immaculate" stockings: "there wasn't a brack on them" (360); "brack" is Gaelic for speck or stain.

Some of the epithets in the Litany can be related to Gerty, and not only in scathing irony, but, like everything else, with perspectival modification. Stylistically, of course, the immutable appellations of the Virgin are not far removed from the stereotypes of cliché. Gerty is, for the time being, "most powerful," and as we are told expressly at 367, she is "merciful" (354). For practical and not entirely irrelevant purposes, she proves a refuge for one sinner and a "comfortress" for at least one of the "afflicted" (358), a momentary "haven of refuge" (358) for Bloom, who has "erred and sinned and wandered" (367). If judged by the same Catholic view, of course, the refuge he finds is in sin itself. But he finds relief and forgiveness and pardon, like the faithful at the retreat (Bloom's tarrying is another form of retreat). He belongs to the "toilers for their daily bread," with "careworn hearts" (356). As a "child of Mary" (364) Gerty would be pledged to imitate the example of the Virgin as best she could in daily life. Weighed in the balance of orthodoxy, her actual conduct would not rate as very high, but in Bloom's valuation it may do. Evaluation is a tricky matter, liable to error and modification: "Remember about the mistake in the valuation" (377).

The Annunciation is explicitly referred to by way of the remembered words of the priest in the confession box. He seems to apply the Virgin's words of submission, "be it done unto me according to Thy Word," rather obliquely to the idea of obeying "the voice of nature" (358), himself establishing a somewhat mundane parallel. Gerty's thoughts immediately turn to the priest and his home, which features "a canary bird" (359). Buck Mulligan, joking joiner of the holy and the ribald, has prepared us for the Holy Family, whose *"father's a bird"* (19); Léo Taxil's dialogue about *"le pigeon"* (41) has similarly prepared us for another bird in Nausicaa, for this bird, revealed as a cuckoo.[13] The cuckoo's nine-fold cry reverberates blasphemously up toward the Holy Ghost as well as downward to Bloom's domestic situation. At the end of the chapter the clock speaks with a columbine tongue, it "cooed" (382). Gerty's own words, as she says that she can throw her "cap at who I like" (being thus blessed among women), ring out "more musical than the cooing of the ringdove" (362).

In the vision of *A Portrait*, "a wild angel had appeared" (*P* 172); in Nausicaa a bird, a bat, and a dark stranger appear, while there is inversion in the phrase "Dark devilish appearance" (369). Bloom, when he considers writing a "message" (381), comes linguistically close to being an angel (*angelos* = messenger). His message reveals him to be lonely and disappointed, though his confession remains unfinished: "I . . . AM. A." Whether we substitute ". . . a cuckold," ". . . a naughty boy," ". . . alone," or whatever, we bear in mind his earthly *fichue position,* in marked contrast to the more divine overtones contained in the "A." It suggests an incomplete half of the Christ of the Revelation (who is A *and* Ω, beginning and end). There is a faint adumbration of a Jehovean I AM THAT I AM; or, through another tangential extrapolation, we may be reminded of how, when told about the woman taken in adultery, Jesus "stooped down, and with his finger wrote on the ground, as though he heard them not" (John 8:6). Bloom, who "stooped" and "gently vexed the thick sand" (381), is often motivated by not wanting to hear about a woman taken in adultery.

Such potential divine flutters may be left in limbo or accepted in addition to the direct references to the Annunciation. At whichever elevation we prefer to place the essence of the sterile encounter between Bloom (pitiful human being set off against godlike potentialities) and Gerty, the following chapter contains the real birth of a real son, discussion of the "utterance of the Word" (422), and countless theological allusions. As the Annunciation promises, the "fruit of thy womb" (Luke 1:42) will be blessed and come to life, in the thrice repeated "wombfruit" at the beginning of Oxen of the Sun.

"Suppose there's some connection" (374)

Joyce creates, and invites us to treat, his chapters almost as individuals, with distinct idiosyncrasies and with affinities for each other. Nausicaa has some special bonds. It is certainly paired off against the preceding chapter, Cyclops, after whose noisy brawling and brute force it appears soothing and quiet. Both are climactic chapters, dealing with sentiment and passion. The men in Cyclops are concerned with politics, chauvinism, war, rebellion, execution, punishment, fighting (finding a female counterpart, too, in the three girls' malicious bickerings; the twins in Nausicaa are already engaged in strife about the power and possession of castle and ball). The girls in Nausicaa dream of love and marriage. Bloom's involvement is significant; he inclines to making love (in Nausicaa his participation is voluntary and deliberate) rather than to making war (the entanglement in Barney Kiernan's comes about mainly by accident and imprudence).

In either case the views are dimmed by prejudice, combined with hatred or with romantic notions. Stereotypes have replaced judgment and discrimination; attitudes to life fall into ready-made categories. The protagonists see what they have been conditioned to find and remain blind to the rest. Eyes are important, their use in Nausicaa ranging all the way from candid glances to blindness: "Thinks I'm a tree, so blind" (377). Identities are mistaken. In fact, Gerty's mind is almost incapable of recognizing an identity. There is a preexisting classification to which phenomena have to conform, and she, herself, seems predetermined: ". . . she was more a Giltrap than a Mac-Dowell" (348). Bloom cannot be appreciated for what he is, becoming a dark, handsome foreigner with all the trappings of the mysterious stranger of popular fiction. For Gerty, he consists of projections. Even noses are categorized in advance: ". . . but she could not see whether he had an aquiline nose or a slightly *retroussé* from where he was sitting" (357). The citizen's categories were different, but similarly fixed.

There are many oblique views. Edy Boardman, who has a squint, can be acutely and unpleasantly perceptive. Spite usually makes the observer more sharp-sighted, and even Gerty grows one-sidedly keen-eyed when it comes to criticizing her rivals, even if she never attains the terseness of the Narrator in Cyclops.

Soon after Bloom's entry, the conversation in Barney Kiernan's pub veers round to "ruling passion" and erection (304), which are suitably associated with death and execution. Bloom sets himself up as an expert and is parodied as a "scientist" (one who knows). In both chapters Bloom is exalted and humiliated. In his defiant outburst he is seen as "an almanac picture" (333), anticipating the one that Gerty keeps in an intimate place: "the grocer's christmas almanac the picture of halcyon days . . ." (355). His act is presented as a rise ("Old lardyface standing up . . . ") and a fall ("then he collapses all of a sudden"), followed by detumescent imagery: ". . . as limp as a wet rag" (333). The subsequent persiflage of the propagation of universal love thematically features our heroine: "Gerty MacDowell loves the boy that has the bicycle" (333). The whole of Nausicaa could be taken as an extension of this parodic sketch.

The style of Gerty's part could easily have found a place as one of the Cyclopean parodies.[14] The opening caress of the summer evening, which had begun "to fold the world in its mysterious embrace" (346), is lifted from such a parody, the Execution scene: "The hero folded her willowy form in a loving embrace" (309),[15] a sentence proclaiming the literary execution of Gerty MacDowell, to which loving care is devoted in Nausicaa.

Bloom's exit from the Cyclops' den is followed by the one explicit naming of the Blessed Virgin in the citizen's benediction: "The blessing of God and Mary and Patrick on you" (333). In accordance with the theme of violence, the Virgin Mary is perverted, in the imperialist's creed, into an instrument of brutal force and suppression: "born of the fighting navy" (329). In clear contrast, the Virgin offers her friendly protection to all who need it (356), while "the fighting navy . . . keeps our foes at bay" (328). Gerty, of course, is connected with the navy through her clothes, wearing a "navy threequarter skirt" (350). In Joyce's view, even the I-narrator's favorite expletive is etymologically derived from the Virgin ("by our Lady"),[16] so that "bloody" conveniently takes care both of the sanguinary aspect and the blasphemy, the I-narrator of Cyclops reversing the manner of the implied narrator of Nausicaa, choosing a register that is too low and vulgar as against one that is too elevated.

In Cyclops, Throwaway is announced as the winner of the race, and the outsider Bloom suffers innocently for a causal connection for which he is not responsible. His hasty flight is clothed in the glory of Elijah's ascension, "clothed upon," "raiment," and "fair as the moon" (345) all pointing forward to the next chapter, which celebrates the coming of this Elijah as a throwing away of seed on Sandymount strand, an onanistic waste of the potential needed for the continuation of the race.

Both chapters have a bi-polar structure, in Cyclops, as an alternating sequence of rudely clashing passages (fit expression of political strife and conflict), in Nausicaa, in evident antithetical symmetry. Even the motif of the change of name and address is continued into Nausicaa: "Might be a false name however like my and the address Dolphin's barn a blind" (372).

"Because it's arranged" (374)

Both Cyclopean war and Nausicaan love were among the chords struck in the Sirens chapter, notably in the song *Love and War,* the stanzas of which are confused by Dollard and mused upon by Bloom (270). "The Croppy Boy" prepares us for rebellion and execution, the aria from *Martha* for Gerty's lure. The opening words of the latter set off a corresponding "endearing flow" (273), and the culminating *"Come!"* with its soaring imagery and orgiastic tension (275–76), anticipates events and emotions in Nausicaa, which is after all a visual restaging of temptations manifested as aural charms in Sirens.

Bloom's voyeuristic inclination was first exposed in the Lotuseaters chapter, with its varied possibilities of escape from reality. One vicarious satisfaction is the adoration of Martha Clifford, who corresponds with a Bloom she does not know and who likes a name he does not have. Like Gerty, she goes in for thinking (77), is interested in perfume, has difficulties with her vocabulary,[17] and inadvertently blows up a disturbing word into a "world" (77), equaling the hyperbolic generosity with which Gerty, of whom everyone "thought the world" (355),[18] verbally handles whole worlds of experience. Bloom lumps the two girls together on p. 368, and Joyce's affair with Martha Fleischmann provides a cluster of links external to the text.

The chemist's assorted "ointments," "alabaster lilypots," and "lotions" toward the end of Lotuseaters (84), all recurring in Nausicaa, might furnish the cosmetic ingredients for Gerty's makeup. Her florid expressions, the "embroidered floral design" of her present (359) and of the chapter's style are a kind of "language of flowers," like the one Bloom makes up after reading Martha's letter (78). Almost two pages (374–75) may be seen as a recall of events and motifs introduced in Lotuseaters. Bloom even remembers that he has forgotten the lotion. It is Gerty, moreover, who with a Wildean touch literally approximates to the *Lotophagoi:* "often she wondered why you couldn't eat something poetical like violets or roses" (352). The "organ" of Lotuseaters, the genitals, becomes covertly central to Nausicaa, Bloom's limpness being foreshadowed in the limp and languid floating flower with which the earlier chapter closes.

The Proteus chapter shares its setting, near Leahy's terrace, with Nausicaa. Stephen, too, changes from one pose to another, but with him it is an intentional arrangement, while Gerty is determined by attitudes that she does not recognize *as* attitudes. Stephen's imitations are volitional, skillful re-creations, recalls of pretences and disguises. His thoughts are evoked in their vivid wayward fluctuations, with unique freshness and originality, at least in their startling combinations. The collage of his thoughts is conscious. Gerty, ineluctably visible, specializes in thinking too. She is "lost in thought" or, soon afterwards, "wrapt in thought" (354): this is precise; thinking for her is a becoming pose, to be used like drapery. As against the immediate contents of Stephen's thinking in Proteus, for Gerty "thinking" is often an intransitive verb (see 354), an attitude familiar from so many paintings. She too tries her hand at "reading" nonverbal phenomena: "the story of a haunting sorrow was written on his face" (357), but this is hardly to be equated with trying to read the signatures of all things (Bloom comes closer to it in "All these rocks with lines and scars and letters," 381). She would not dream of bringing anything or anyone "beyond the veil" (48). No Protean flux is caught in the sequence of essentially static pictures that constitute the first part of Nausicaa.

"there for a certain purpose" (355)

Nausicaa also looks forward to the next chapter. Its close, with the three times threefold call of "Cuckoo," leads directly into the evocation of Helios, with its three paragraphs of three sentences each. Nine is, of course, a signifi-cant number for the chapter of Birth. Holles street is associated by Bloom with the once-attentive nurse Callan (373, 385), who, along with Gerty, figures in the brief list of women attracted to Bloom on 16 June (722). The crime inveighed against in Oxen of the Sun has been committed in Nausicaa. Bloom becomes, in Joyce's comments, what he has just wasted—sperm.[19] At the other end of the sterility-fertility axis, the "A" that Bloom attributed to him-self in his writing in the sand reappears as "Alpha, a ruby and triangled sign upon the forehead of Taurus" (414).

Of all the pastiches of the Oxen of the Sun chapter, the Dickensian paragraph on pages 420–421 comes closest to the style of Gerty's meditations. It abounds in emotional adjectives ("brave woman," "loving eyes," "her pretty head," etc.). Gerty's adolescent sentimentalities are carried over into motherhood. The mother, like Gerty, "reclines," but with "motherlight in her eyes." The mysterious embrace, when domesticized, is transformed into "lawful embraces." Gerty has set the tone for "a nice snug and cosy little homely house" (352), complete with tall husband and brekky and all the rest, the details being lovingly filled in by the eulogy of father Purefoy. Through his association with Catesby's cork lino, Gerty's father suggests the comforts of the ideal home ("always bright and cheery in the home," 355), while his drinking and gout reveal the actuality.

"That's where Molly can knock spots off them" (373)

Gerty and Molly Bloom, Nausicaa and Penelope, have some traits in common, and Molly is ubiquitous in Bloom's half of the chapter. Superstition, ignorance, and faulty grammar are common to both of them, as is a splendid inconsistency. Both begin their menstrual cycle. They set great store by their appearance and their clothes; they thrive on admiration; their thoughts circle around men. Bloom is able to assess this last aspect shrewdly, and his condensation "he, he and he" (371) summarizes one salient aspect both of Gerty's gush and the gyrations of Molly's monologue. The scale is always reduced in the younger girl, who can muster fewer males than Molly. Her slim graceful figure and somewhat anaemic nature contrast with Molly's amplitude. Gerty looks away into the distance, or up at the sky, while Molly is earthy, even tellurian, stained, and, on the whole, horizontal. Gerty is only half reclined. Molly's coarseness expresses itself with gusto, even though there is a prudish streak in her too, but Gerty's finebred nature instinctively recoils from everything in the least indelicate.

For all that, their thinking and their language are often very similar. Compare Gerty's ". . . those cyclists showing off what they hadn't got" (358) with Molly's ". . . she didnt make much secret of what she hadnt" (750). They can be equally catty about members of their own sex and would feel contempt for each other. In many ways the style of Penelope is prefigured in Nausicaa, many of the sentences of which string together without pause or punctuation,[20] and with the same lack of subordination:

> . . . but those iron jelloids she had been taking of late had done her a world of good much better than the Widow Welch's female pills and she was much better of those discharges she used to get and that tired feeling. (348)

This could be translated, with few changes, into the rhetoric of the last chapter. Gerty's diction (assuming that this would be her own) is characterized by one of the cardinal words of Penelope, "because,"[21] which she uses abundantly and usually without any causal function: "But this was altogether different from a thing like that because there was all the difference because she could almost feel him draw her face to his and the first quick hot touch of his handsome lips" (366).

Molly, though attached to her own form of sentimentality, would not, however, be caught in Gerty's artificialities, having generally a good sense of what is spurious about others. She makes fun of euphemisms, prefers "a few simple words" to phrases from "the ladies letterwriter" (758), and Bloom remembers that she "twigged at once" that the man Bloom thought goodlooking "had a false arm" (372). She has a sharp eye for pretence, circumlocution, and evasive euphemisms. Her "Lord couldnt he say bottom right out and have done with it" (741) contrasts with the ripple of thrilled queasiness that even a diluted "beetoteetom" causes in Gerty (353).

"perfect proportions" (350)

At a first glance the chapter (it is one of glances) appears bipartite, with distinctly contrasting, complementary halves. Gerty's outlook is characterized by self-inflated infatuations beyond critical questioning, by hyperbole, self-deception, and a basically timid selectivity. There is an upward tendency in the first half, with altitudes as diverse as the promontory of Howth, a castle built of sand, amatory and social aspirations and pretensions, glances at the flying fireworks, at the Blessed Sacrament raised in the benediction service, at a view high up offered by Gerty. The imagery is lofty, and an accumulation of heights such as "queenly *hauteur*, . . . higharched instep, . . . a gentlewoman of high degree, . . . how to be tall increase your height" are to be found in the space of a few lines (348–49). Language is correspondingly exalted, as though it too had to be kept from touching base ground.

In Bloom's section, eyes, with language, are kept nearer the ground, over which Bloom bends, and on which he writes. He is very aware of the rocks they are sitting on as part of his present reality: "Bad for you, dear, to sit on that stone. Brings on white fluxions" (376). His monologue is interspersed with the customary objectifying qualifiers, "but," "all the same," "on the other hand," "look at it other way round." Where Gerty is unthinkingly posing, he does a lot of his usual "supposing." His mind is, of course, revealed to us after the orgasmic release, when he is again in control of his emotions. The effect is a sobering down, a reduction of things to their everyday dimension.

The boundless generalities of Gerty's wishful reveries become concrete trifles. The "infinite store of mercy," noted in Gerty's eyes (367), becomes more manageable in Bloom's gratitude for "small mercies" (368). The chapter is structured by such contrasts, as when the sweet and homely cosiness of connubial life imagined in the first section is set against Bloom's *précis:* ". . . till they settle down to potwalloping and papa's pants will soon fit Willy and fuller's earth for the baby when they hold him out to do ah ah" (373). The earthiness is unmistakable, and it is the "settling *down*" that is typical of the second half of Nausicaa. It is exemplified in the baby's "ah ah," so different from the high-pitched "O!s" that go before (367) or from the evasive terms that are used for similar bodily processes of Baby Boardman. Again, we may compare the various perfections that adorn Gerty—showing off "her slim graceful figure to perfection" (350), her "perfect proportions" (350), her rosebud mouth, "Greekly perfect" (348)—with Bloom's aside that a "defect is ten times worse in a woman" (368). The first half presents a rich palette of colors, especially blue, but with liberal daubs of scarlet, crimson, rose, coral-pink, etc., against which the second half appears gray, and Bloom "off colour" (372).

"a kind of language between us" (372)

Despite numerous contrasts of that kind, the chapter is not the simple dichotomized structure it appears to be at first blush (it is a chapter of blushes too). Not all the colors are reserved for the first half, but those toward the end of the chapter are less visualized, more abstractly thought about (376). Not all the ups are scattered over the first half. Bloom too looks up at rockets, at the stars and the moon, if with a weary mind. Conversely, Gerty's section has its downs, the "fallen women" (364) and the "fine tumble" she wishes on Cissy Caffrey (359) (significantly to dethrone her from the elevation of "her high crooked French heels"). Most poignantly, her own accident occurred "coming *down* Dalkey hill" (364—not, of course, Gerty's italics). The general pattern, then, is mirrored as a succession of smaller movements within either section, so that each part potentially contains the whole.

The two halves are also intricately dovetailed, separated by a definite break and yet joined by a gliding transition. When Gerty's gush gives way to dewy melting, there follows a quiet paragraph that temporarily blends Bloom and Gerty. Both seem painted by the same painter's brush, and he "coloured like a girl" (367). Even Bloom's physical position becomes identical with hers: "He was leaning back against the rock behind. Leopold Bloom (for it is he) . . ." (367). His identity is revealed for the first time (in a novelistic fashion reminiscent of 348), and he is judged by the morality appropriate to this kind of literature. But there is a drop in tone, and one sentence—"At it again?"—reaches down to Bloom's half. The accustomed pitch is immediately resumed and Bloom is stylistically approximated to Gerty: "A fair unsullied soul had called to him and, wretch that he was, how had he answered?"

The opposite occurs in the next long paragraph, describing Gerty's fare-well greeting, in which she briefly touches the ground of typically Bloom-esque prose: "Wonder if he's too far to" (367), one bit of direct inner monologue, with the typical trailing off. But she at once rises again, literally and stylistically: "She rose. . . . She drew herself up to her full height. . . ," and prepares her exit. Her actual movements bring her in touch with the earth, and her walk is expressed in the plainest possible language, without artificial embellishment: "Slowly without looking back she went down the uneven strand. . . ." Only when she sublimates the awkwardness of her gait into a stylized pose is there a last, short-lived ascent: "She walked with a certain quiet dignity characteristic of her. . . ," but by now the line of vision is clearly directed at her feet and Bloom's sudden realization plunks the narrative down with a final jolt: "Tight boots? No. She's lame! O!" Even the "O!" conveys a fall. From now on the language jogs along in relatively short, halting steps.

The transition has been prepared for in another interlacing counter-movement. In spite of appearances, the forced deportment of Gerty's style has been felt as essentially lame all along, and correspondingly the limping procession of Bloom's thoughts emerges as basically more dignified.

"it was all things combined" (372)

Nor is Bloom's half all of a piece. Though it would have to be read aloud with a level voice, it has its ups and downs. Even the narrative is lifted from Bloom's perspective at some points, notably when a "lost long candle [wandering] up the sky" (379) raises the point of view and brings about a sweeping motion of the camera for a survey ranging from the streets of Sandymount across the bay to Howth Head, re-personified, as in the opening shot (346). The style, too, is raised and broadened, reverting to the novelette manner, with pretty pictures and a touch of Thomas Moore's glow-worm, until the lighthouse of Kish far away, winking at Mr Bloom, brings the perspective, along with the tone of the tale, back to Bloom's level. For one paragraph the narrative has risen above Bloom's head, in a "tryst" (379) that is also stylistic.

The first postgasmic rocket (372), also widens the perspective to take in the party of girls and children in the distance, resulting in a quickening of Bloom's pulse and a little climactic flutter "Will she? Watch! Watch! See!" imitative of the central outburst of the chapter and, in its wording and rhythm, echoing the morning scene outside the Grosvenor hotel (74).

With Bloom's dozing off at the end, the style shifts again, to become unpunctuated associative alogical dream language (382). Afterwards the narrative splits up into three parallel strands, separated by the voice of the cuckoo clock, a temporal divider for an action going on in three different places. A short Bloom passage is followed by an evenly descriptive bit relating to the priest's house, before a last jerk brings the tone back to Gerty's more homely vein and a style that virtually closes the embrace indicated in the opening lines of the chapter.

"Her high notes and her low notes" (374)

Nausicaa is technically complex, numerous discordant ruptures disturbing the basic division into two main parts. Not even the style of Gerty's half is as monotonous or uniform as critics have assumed. Like Cyclops and Oxen of the Sun, Nausicaa is a compendium of moods and styles, though the spectrum is narrower. Apart from flat descriptive passages, baby talk, a sermon, a recipe, and other variants, there is Gerty's own palette, of which it may be useful to distinguish such subcategories as:

"Luxuriant Clusters" (349)

—the sweetly romantic passages that we usually consider the trade mark of the first half of Nausicaa. "Mayhap it was this, the love that might have been, that lent to her softlyfeatured face at whiles a look, tense with suppressed meaning, that imparted a strange yearning tendency to the beautiful eyes, a charm few could resist" (348). Their features are precious, elevated diction, pretentious and threadbare metaphors, ample adornment. Few nouns lack decorative epithets: "There was an innate refinement, a languid queenly *hauteur*, . . . her delicate hands and higharched instep . . ." (348). Such lines cannot simply be read aloud; they have to be declaimed.

"Endearing Ways" (346)

—a more homely sentimental vein, with less variety in its imagery, but full of feeling: ". . . he would give his dear little wifey a good hearty hug and gaze for a moment deep down into her eyes" (352).

"Sumptuous Confection" (351)

—the fashion page of the women's magazine: "She wore a coquettish little love of a hat . . ." (350).

"Madame Vera Verity" (349)

—the column of practical advice: "Then there was blushing scientifically cured" (349).

"Persuasive Power" (346)

—advertisement slogans: "the fabric that caresses the skin" (366).

"Little Tiffs" (348)

—more straightforward girlish thoughts that often move at a brisk pace with a touch of vicious directness: ". . . irritable little gnat she was" (360).

"Unmentionables" (347)

—at times Gerty's voice drops to evasive vagueness when an unpalatable or unladylike subject is bypassed in the flattest way, with phrases like "when there for a certain purpose," "that thing must be coming," "without all that other," "the other thing," "a thing like that."

Such styles and tones and other variants that we might mention could be arranged in a kind of hierarchy. The most conspicuous effusions of (what Gerty would consider) poetical (and we condescendingly classify as) *kitsch* occur as high points in the narrative rather than as a continual performance. It is difficult to remain in the upper register throughout.

"Keep that thing up for hours" (374)

Stylistically, and psychologically, there is a strenuous attempt to sustain that high tone together with repeated failures "to keep it up" (those words are also implied by Bloom's recall of the song about Mary who "lost the pin of her drawers," 78 and 368). The different stylistic elevations are juxtaposed in free and surprising discords, with comic drops and new flights. The tone keeps changing within a limited range so that the chapter is one of those characterized by the marvelously attuned wrong note. The ups and downs can be seen as sequences of tumescence and detumescence, pathos and bathos, or inflations and deflations. Bloom remembers blown-up phrases from Aeolus, "moonlight silver effulgence" (370). Nausicaa, like Aeolus, depends on airy distensions; Gerty's figure is composed of rhetorical ones.

Some of the shifts in the exposition illustrate this (significantly, Nausicaa is the only chapter that has an exposition). The opening description of the *dramatis personae*, not ostensibly lofty, still aims at a stately pace and is clearly literary: "The three girl friends were seated on the rocks, enjoying the evening air which was fresh but not too chilly" (346). Somewhere around the middle the tone flops; "seated" does not quite match the conversational "but not too chilly"; the implied situational contexts jar, if only slightly (another change from the clashing strong contrasts in Cyclops). Some readjustments will occur later in the reading, when the epithet "girl friends" will be undercut by the give and talk of girlish gall and by Edy Boardman's speaking "none too amiably" (347). Even if an identical phrase is repeated, such as "on the rocks," it can assume a baser meaning: "when we were on the rocks in Holles street," Bloom remembers (369). This sense can retrospectively modify in the opening scene. Gerty's life is on the rocks.

While the strained-after grace of the sentence quoted above is not, perhaps, decisively marred, there is nevertheless a chill. A bit of fresh air, real air, has interfered with the air of refinement. All through the chapter, natural or common things, like "stones and bits of wood," or else parts of the physical (not figurative) body (". . . but it was only the end of her nose," 351) have a way of breaking the spell.

After "chilly," the effort to elevate the diction is evident in redundancy: "Many a time and oft were they wont. . . ." A tiny drop follows, "to come there," and a gentle rise, "to that favourite nook," and another descent into a more homely strain, "to have a cosy chat," then a spurring of the poetic impulse: "beside the sparkling waves. . . ." But after this sparkle we are in for a trivialized tumble—". . . to discuss matters feminine." And so the chapter stumbles forward and tension mounts, the stylistic heights grow dizzier, and the ecstatic flights correspondingly longer. Toward the center the sentences swell and punctuation decreases (every comma or period is, after all, a stop to fetch breath and a brief touching of the ground), until we reach the magnificent sweep of the climax and are ready for the final descent and the last drop.

"Just changes when you're on the track" *(368)*

The stylistic metamorphoses, some rapid, others gliding, need not be interpreted as merely vertical shifts. The language could be recorded on a sort of oscillogram, but it would not be simple to articulate the discernment of modes of language, which we believe we can grasp intuitively. The flexibility of the style, with its odd traverses and sudden bounds, contrasts pointedly with Gerty MacDowell's inflexible fixedness and her unconscious and tacit acceptance of the several poses of which the styles are the outward and visible form. The constant refocusing obliges the reader to sharpen his sense of disparities (some inherently comical) and the perpetual clashes between illusory disguises and chilly reality. Each new attitude is apt to invalidate the previous one. But even within one given stylistic level, the metaphors often jostle each other incongruously: "that vile decoction which has ruined so many hearths and homes had cast its shadow over her childhood days . . ." (354). And Gerty is able to move unconcernedly from the "scorn immeasurable" that emanates from her eyes, to "one look of measured scorn," on the same page (362; the more liberal, unmeasured quantity, by the way, is reserved for the female rival).

Scenic changes implicit in the stylistic and metaphorical potential of this chapter's language will be taken literally in Circe, where they are grotesquely staged. Stylistic guises adapted to the current themes are, of course, the distinctive mark of *Ulysses;* in the later chapters the method is intensified by formal intricacy, and the adaptability of the style, corresponding to the mercurial assumption of expedient roles, may perhaps be understood as a reflection of Odyssean tactics. Odysseus is known for his versatility: he cunningly suits his language, form of address, and guise to the immediate purpose and has on occasion recourse to impersonation (at times divine agencies help along with a touch of transfiguration). When he appears to Nausicaa from the bushes, he is quickly considering alternative approaches to win her over and decides on sweet words and pretense that she is a goddess, queen, or bride.[22] (Gerty's presumptions are similar.)

To change one's voice according to the situation is common to Odysseus and to *Ulysses,* whose true hero is language. The language of the book is *polytropos:* ingenious, resourceful, resilient, of many turns—wiles or tropes.[23]

At the same time, the style chosen for Gerty's parts (and within the framework of her own ambitions), the cliché and the shopsoiled charms of stereotyped fiction or commercial slickness, is manifestly unable to characterize anything outside itself. It reflects only its own vacuity, it hardly illuminates or communicates, its glitter is narcissistic, its essence is self-gratification.

"all put on before third person" *(374)*

Montage helps Joyce to convey both the interior landscape of Gerty's mind and her environment. The question is whether the various items fit together. To the reader's delight, they do not. Gerty's fashions and styles do not do what articles of clothing should do—they do not "match" (which is one of the thematic words: "with caps to match," 346; "to match the chenille," 350; "blue to match," 366; "As God made them He matched them," 373). Thematic references to fashion are highly appropriate. Fashion is a matter of putting something on, of a careful array of different elements to create a type, its success depending on taste and discernment. It is also changeable. Fashion and cosmetics serve to touch up the appearance, and Gerty's appearance is put together from many little touches. We are privileged to experience her charms along with the means by which she will achieve them: "Her hands were of finely veined alabaster with tapering fingers and as white[24] as lemon juice and queen of ointments could make them" (348).

We are also treated to a close-up of Gerty's mind and, simultaneously, are made aware of the forces that helped to shape it. The first half of the chapter is a novelette conveying the de-formation of Gerty MacDowell: what she is and what made her what she is. The kind of writing here parodied would lead to that kind of thinking, which, in turn, if it could articulate itself, would produce that kind of culture. In one way, Gerty is indistinguishable from the forces that determine her. That through such a melange of set pieces and trash, she does emerge as a person in her own right, however limited, is a triumph of indirect characterization.

"piquant tilt" (353)

Part of the humor of the paradoxically slanted episode may result from reading certain phrases as though they belonged to a context different from the apparent one. Each verbal unit seems to belong to a number of situational frameworks, just as the whole of *Ulysses* can be viewed within naturalistic, psychological, symbolic, Homeric, and numerous other contexts. Some of the turns language takes are inversely appropriate. Gerty is introduced as "in very truth as fair a specimen of winsome Irish girlhood as one could wish to see" (348). She is precisely such a *specimen,* by definition something selected as typical of its class, by etymology something to look at, something that one might be content to see, as Bloom is, wishing for little other contact. There *is* "suppressed meaning" in her look (348); she has "raised the devil" in Bloom (360). The "studied attitude" of the lady in the almanac picture (355) epiphanizes Gerty's own posing and describes a scenic principle of the Nausicaa chapter. Not only does Gerty wrap herself "in thought," she is really "lost in thought" (348). It seems appropriate to offer "A penny for [her] thoughts" (360).

By expressing unmitigated disdain for the cliché, for *kitsch*, and for a victim like Gerty MacDowell (or Bloom's inept endeavors), we also, of course, are adopting a Gertyan pose, pretending to remain perpetually above their inefficacious lure. But the lure affects us too, on and off. Romantic *kitsch* in Nausicaa (or in Sirens) also serves to embody the motif of seductiveness, to which most readers are not wholly immune. There is a fascination about that glamour too, an appeal that we hesitate to acknowledge. In fact, clichés could not have become popular but for some inherent charm, however cheap. The *Portrait* expressed this lure in all its elusive complexity. That Joyce (like the rest of us) was attracted to *kitsch*, in music, in painting, and in literature is fairly obvious but less relevant than the skill with which he knew how to work on our susceptibilities, seducing us and at the same time allowing us to laugh about the tricks that are being used. Our laughter sometimes becomes a bit ostentatious and the clichés in which *we* give voice to distaste for the literary cliché testify to the intricacies of structure and tone, and, finally, to the complexity of response that is closely tied up with human motivation—difficult to trace and even more elusive of evaluation.

The axis along which we might measure our own attraction or repulsion is only one among the many subtly graduated scales that make up the network of multiple foci that is *Ulysses*. There is a Protean quality about Nausicaa too. Its simple outlines and the even-textured appearance are deceptive. The surface alone reveals itself as jagged as the uneven strand, "stones and bits of wood . . . and slippy seaweed" (367)—full of ups and downs. For *this* relief, too, much thanks.

1971

Notes

1. *Evening Telegraph*, 16 June 1904, p. 2, column 4.
2. P. W. Joyce, in *A Social History of Ancient Ireland* (Dublin: M. H. Gill and Son, 1920), has a chapter on "Turning 'Deisol,' or Sunwise" (I, 301). The word *deisol* or, in modern spelling, *deiseal, deisil,* is pronounced "deshil."
3. Richard Ellmann, *James Joyce* (New York: Oxford University Press, 1959), p. 462; Frank Budgen, *Myselves When Young* (London: Oxford University Press, 1970), pp. 189–94.
4. Heinrich Straumann, in *Letters* II, 430–31.
5. A. Walton Litz, *The Art of James Joyce* (London: Oxford University Press, 1961), writes that "*Nausicaa*, begun in Zürich in the autumn of 1919, was finished in Trieste early in 1920" (p. 144).
6. *Letters* II, 431–32. These and other parallels between Joyce's letters to Martha Fleischmann and phrases in Nausicaa were pointed out in my review of Richard Ellmann's edition of the *Letters* in *Neue Zürcher Zeitung*, 26 February 1967. Other biographical sources are to be found in the letters to Nora of 1909, available in *Selected Letters of James Joyce*, ed. Richard Ellmann (New York: Viking Press, 1975).
7. See in this regard my "Symbolic Juxtaposition" in *James Joyce Quarterly* 5, no. 3 (Spring 1968): 276–78.
8. The same words mean erection to Molly: that "big brute of a thing" (742).
9. For example, in *Thom's Official Directory* for the year 1905. (Dublin: Alex. Thom and Co., 1905), p. 1667.

10. Bloom is carrying the *Sweets of Sin*, to complete the missing traits in Gerty's presentation: seduction and cliché language. There is another inversion of roles here: it is Gerty who appears occupied with solid, down-to-earth matter, Catesby's cork lino, meant for the ordinary home, while Bloom is after illusory wish-fulfillment through the written word.

11. The Douay version does not use "seeing," but another favorite word of Gerty's: "*because* I know not man." See note 21 below.

12. Stuart Gilbert, *James Joyce's "Ulysses,"* rev. ed. (London: Faber and Faber, 1952), p. 281.

13. Also heralded by Buck Mulligan (212); it is Mulligan too who has introduced masturbation as a major theme connected with literature.

14. One passage from such a parody, indiscriminately scattering loveliness over the scenery, anticipates the style of the first part of Nausicaa: "Lovely maidens sit in close proximity to the roots of the lovely trees singing the most lovely songs while they play with all kinds of lovely objects . . ." (294)

15. Even the willow returns in Nausicaa: "Weeping willow" (377).

16. Joyce writes about the use of "bloody" to Grant Richards: ". . . it is strange that he should object more strongly to a profane use of the Virgin than to a profane use of the name of God" (5 May 1906 , *Letters* II, 134). Stuart Gilbert, perhaps prompted by Joyce, refers to it as "Our Lady's adjective" (p. 255).

17. Both mistake singular forms for plural ones: "my patience are exhausted" (78); "the perfume of those incense" (357).

18. ". . . those iron jelloids . . . had done her a world of good" (348); "she would give worlds to be in the privacy of her own familiar chamber" (351—it might be simpler just to leave and go to her chamber); "She would have given worlds to know what it was" (357); "Dearer than the whole world would she be to him" (364); "the only man in all the world for her" (365). Joyce is also parodying his own macrocosmic aspirations in writing *Ulysses*.

19. "Bloom is the spermatozoon, the hospital the womb . . ." (*Letters* I, 140).

20. Note that the sentence introducing Gerty on pp. 252–53 has little punctuation in its first part and none in its second.

21. "Penelope's four cardinal points being the female breasts, arse, womb and cunt, expressed by the words *because, bottom, . . . woman, yes*" (*Letters* I, 170).

22. *Odyssey* 6.141–85.

23. See my essay "Book of Many Turns," *James Joyce Quarterly* 10, no. 1 (Fall 1972): 29–46, reprinted in this volume.

24. The whiteness of Gerty's hands, and the "snowy slender arms" (366) may also owe something to Homer's Nausicaa: *"Nausikaa leukolenos"* (*Odyssey* 6.101), "Nausicaa of the white arms," as Butcher and Lang translate it (p. 95). A number of Gerty's traits can be traced back to Homer.

12

The Rhythm
of *Ulysses*

Rhythm is here taken in the sense in which Stephen Dedalus defines it in *A Portrait of the Artist as a Young Man*: "the . . . formal relation of part to part in any esthetic whole . . . " (*P* 206). I shall examine in some detail the formal relations of those parts of *Ulysses* that we call chapters or episodes and whose Homeric titles we retain even though Joyce decided to withdraw them. That we need these characteristic, individual titles shows how much we tend to be impressed by the uniqueness of every chapter.

There cannot be many other novels that allow us to treat their various chapters or sections separately, almost as individuals. *Ulysses* seems to ask for that kind of treatment, and the existence of studies in which each critic is assigned a different chapter will hardly surprise us. For the individuality of each chapter, we have abundant textual evidence, Joyce's schema and Joyce's words. "My intention is to transpose the myth *sub specie temporis nostri*. Each adventure (that is, every hour, every organ, every art being interconnected and interrelated in the structural scheme of the whole) should not only condition but even create its own technique. Each adventure is so to say one person although it is composed of persons . . . " (*Letters* I, 146–47).

Joyce succeeded in this. The chapters, or adventures, are different, radically different, stridently different. It does not take much textual analysis to prove this. If you open the book anywhere between its middle and its end the graphic appearance of the page alone will tell you which chapter you are looking at.

Technically, *Ulysses* is based on variety ("infinite variety," 212), variation ("exquisite variations," 663), change, mutation, alternation. No single
mode is kept up for too long; relief is sure to come. Reading *Ulysses* is a jerky
process, full of unexpected twists and turns. The chapters differ greatly in
such externals as length, and they vary considerably in the amount of difficulty they present to the reader. After a particularly complex chapter a relatively straightforward one is likely to follow and the reader is allowed to take
a breath. There is a rapid crescendo of difficulty in the first three chapters,
culminating in the incredible density of Proteus. Calypso, which follows it, is
probably the easiest chapter in the novel. And after the fairly plain sailing of
Lotuseaters and Hades, the Aeolus episode suddenly interjects confusion and
formal extravaganza. In the wake of another calm interlude, Lestrygonians,
the Library chapter challenges the reader by its allusive depth and versatile
wit, set off against the most ostentatiously shallow episode in the whole book,
Wandering Rocks. The reader is again likely to get lost in his first journey
through the polyphonic maze and technical virtuosity of the Sirens chapter.
The single and earthy voice of an old-fashioned narrator in Cyclops may come
as a relief, but the voice keeps being interrupted by heteroglossic, parodistic
passages. The tone changes again, and radically softens, in Nausicaa, so
much so that even the homely cadences of Bloom's monologue, encountered
again in the second half of the chapter, seem to have acquired a briskness
perhaps unnoticed before. Oxen of the Sun, a sequence of rapid vocal
changes, is again one of the most difficult chapters. In comparison, Circe is
almost lucid, at least in its dramatic structure, and easy to follow even if the
hallucinatory pyrotechnics present difficulties of quite another kind. Eumaeus
is anticlimactically lusterless and verbose. The abstract aridity of the vocabulary and the pedantic precision make the Ithaca chapter at times hard to
penetrate before a last, and most drastic, relief is afforded by Molly's utterly
concrete, fluid monologue. The reading experience, though invariably subjective, is extremely diverse and diversely extreme.

The various contrasts of style, mood, point of view, tone, etc., need little
demonstration. The chapters could be classified according to multiple criteria.
There are, for instance, predominantly silent and predominantly noisy chapters. The more migratory ones are interspersed with sedentary ones. The
center of the novel is characterized by an increase of the more social, communal type of episode, taking place in a public building or a public house (or a
substitute for it): Aeolus, Scylla and Charybdis, Sirens, Cyclops, Oxen of the
Sun, Circe, Eumaeus. Then the action resolves itself again into loneliness and
meditation. Or else it might be possible to distinguish male and female chapters, introverted and extroverted ones, but such distinctions might only bring
out the inherently subjective nature of all characterizations.

The changes are much more marked in the second half of *Ulysses*. A
reader may well remain unaware of formal differences from episode to epi-

sode until he works his way past the mid-hour of Bloomsday. The first half of the book appears (relatively) uniform. The multiformity of the later chapters, however, cannot be overlooked. In fact, the later chapters are remarkable for their formal complexity, and it is somewhere in the middle of *Ulysses* that some critics parted company with Joyce, Ezra Pound being an early instance, S. L. Goldberg[1] a later one. The disparity between the two halves of the book in itself constitutes a change of rhythm. The break seems to fall neatly between the first and the second ennead of chapters, between Scylla and Charybdis (difficult to read, but structurally simple) and Wandering Rocks (easy to read, structurally complex). In the second half of the book Joyce is less concerned with realistic verisimilitude, and the reader is accordingly conscious of an omnipotent author and manipulator. The exceptions—roughly equidistant from the center—seem to be, in the first half, the Aeolus chapter, with its authorial headlines, and, in the second half, part two of Nausicaa with its return to the familiar unparodistic stream of consciousness.

It is possible also to view chapter 10, Wandering Rocks, as the pivotal one, all the more so since it also functions as a small-scale model of the whole novel. It is a Janus-faced construction, symmetrically facing forward and backward. Section one, with Father Conmee, continues, and even simplifies, the technique of the first half of the book; the section is even and homogeneous. Its contrapuntal equivalent, the section describing the viceregal procession, is a replica of what is to follow: a concise sequence of rapidly changing styles, all appropriate to the characters who are epiphanized.

A study of the rhythmic changes of the eighteen chapters of *Ulysses* would be too long, and so I limit myself to an examination of three consecutive chapters and their interconnections—Scylla and Charybdis, Wandering Rocks, and Sirens. They are strange bedfellows indeed. On a first reading, they clearly clash against one another (the mythical Symplegades of course were clashing rocks), they jolt the reader into a different mood. The underlying continuity, even formal continuity, of such a discordant sequel of chapters is far less striking than the conspicuous dissimilarities and has to be worked out in detailed analysis.

The rich narrative, the imaginative transformations, the allusive style and the reverberating language of Scylla are succeeded by a disjointed group of scenes of external actions and physical movements in a solid, angular world. The language of Wandering Rocks is dry, prosy, precise; outlines are hard. Sirens is resonant, musical, vibrant, sentimental, full of overtones. Scylla and Sirens deal with an Art each, Literature and Music, and so they are abundantly orchestrated. The "art" of Wandering Rocks, Mechanics, accounts for the lines, circles, crosses of its exterior, the interactions of its many wheels. Scylla is cerebral (its organ is the brain), Wandering Rocks imitates the circulation of the blood, and Sirens is distinctly aural.

After Scylla, the reader enters another dimension in Wandering Rocks.

The Library chapter preserves the classical unities; Wandering Rocks is locally dispersed, its plots are many. Scylla is intensive, probing depths, exploring growth, development, historical changes; it is full of imaginative flights. Wandering Rocks extends in space; it is centrifugal, loose. It concerns itself with external trivia. The literary tradition speculated upon and referred to in Scylla gives way to the marketplace, where books, like other merchandise, are displayed, priced, sold, bought, hawked, or pawned. The market is real in Wandering Rocks (222, and the numerous references to shops), but merely part of a figure of speech in Scylla: ". . . genius would be a drug in the market" (195). As it happens, Stephen Dedalus, who holds forth on a man of genius with ingenuity, later on finds himself in a marketplace of shops and engines, associating "a lore of drugs" (242).

Naturally, every episode has links with the previous ones. Stephen's theory of literature and of Shakespeare has been anticipated by Bloom in Lestrygonians, also a chapter of the marketplace. Bloom speculates on Shakespeare's verse technique and misquotes King Hamlet (152). In keeping with the theme of Lestrygonians, Bloom's esthetic thesis is framed in comestible terms: ". . . symbolistic. Esthetes they are. I wouldn't be surprised if it was that kind of food you see produces the like waves of the brain the poetical. For example one of the policemen sweating Irish stew into their shirts; you couldn't squeeze a line of poetry out of him. Don't know what poetry is even. Must be in a certain mood" (166). Bloom even refers to the organ of Scylla, the brain. His metabolistic theory of literature is replaced by Stephen's more sophisticated one, a cunning maze of facts and allusions. He builds a speculative labyrinth of strange turnings that then, in Wandering Rocks will be externalized, petrified into the stones and bricks of the city. And more bricks are brought into Dublin by the threemaster with the poetical name of *Rosevean* (249). In Stephen's discourse we miss many points because of our ignorance of the bypaths of recondite apocrypha. In Wandering Rocks we are misled by ignorance of Dublin geography and by the tricky nature of surfaces. Stephen disposes freely, and not always honestly, of his material; he selects facts according to his purposes and is not above dislodging time: "Don't tell them he was nine years old when it was quenched" (210). The author of Wandering Rocks proceeds in a similar fashion in the arrangement of his material, displacing time ("Don John Conmee walked. . . ," 223), but more frequently by the characteristic interjection of displaced action.

Early in his presentation, Stephen Dedalus works in Shakespeare's itinerary; that is, an exposition in space as it might appear in any section of Wandering Rocks: "Shakespeare has left the huguenot's house in Silver street and walks by the swanmews along the riverbank" (188). This type of description is appropriate to Wandering Rocks. Stephen is deliberately following Jesuit precedent: "Composition of place" (188), which St. Ignatius Loyola explains: "the composition will be to see with the eyes of the imagination the corporeal place where the thing I wish to contemplate is found."² The contemplation of Scylla is succeeded by the actual corporeal places of things in Wandering Rocks, whose structural principle is composition of place in the most everyday meaning of those terms, a putting together of places. A top-ranking Jesuit and follower of St. Ignatius, incidentally, opens the Wandering Rocks chapter. Like Stephen's theory, Wandering Rocks is carefully pieced together, tortuous, and bewildering. Stephen is concerned with art, with artists, and the "fabulous artificer" (210). Though the presentation of Wandering Rocks is naturalistic, it is patently artificial, a Dedalian artifact of multiple joinings.³ Error is incorporated in both.

Within the variegated style of Scylla, the plain, unadorned language of the next chapter forms already one tiny strand. Bloom's entry and exit are rendered in terms of mechanical motion and mere outline. "A patient silhouette waited, listening . . . a bowing dark figure following his hasty heels" (200). "A man passed between them, bowing, greeting" (217). "A dark back went before them" (218). Operative words like "waited, listening, following, passed, bowing, greeting" all occur several times in Wandering Rocks. Bloom's "dark figure" and "a dark back" are verbally carried over into the next chapter and (in the technique of Wandering Rocks) conjoined, put together: "A darkbacked figure" (227, 233).

At the end of Scylla the corporeal surface of Dublin reemerges and prepares us for Wandering Rocks. Geometrical designs and architectural details are mentioned: "Wheelbarrow sun over arch of bridge" (217). A touch like concrete "plumes of smoke" (247), though immediately translated back into the literary tradition, is a link with the preceding episode ("a puffball of smoke plumed up," 152) and the subsequent one: "a plume of smoke" (247). Sense impressions reassert themselves: "Kind air defined the coigns of houses in Kildare street" (218). Dublin becomes concrete and specific again, and the defining of coigns and streets is the characteristic pastime of Wandering Rocks. That the lines from *Cymbeline* quoted at the end of the Library chapter can be prolonged into a foreshadowing of the representatives of Rome and Britain, Father Conmee and the Viceroy, has been noted long ago.⁴ There is an easy transition, in any case, from the final words—"*our bless'd altars*"⁵— to Father Conmee descending from the Jesuit stronghold and liberally blessing the populace as he goes along.

Buck Mulligan, in the library, is a true herald in appending both Stephen and Bloom with the appropriate epithet for the chapter to come. He calls Stephen "wandering Aengus" (214) and Bloom "the wandering jew" (217). The rocks of Scylla (Scylla is usually interpreted as a rock) are set in motion in chapter 10, a chapter of rocks and stone and clashes. The whirlpool element of Charybdis seems to be resumed in the technique of Sirens. In Joyce's schema, Scylla, the rock, corresponds to Aristotle, and so Aristotle is bound to reappear in Wandering Rocks, even if it is a pseudo-Aristotle (235). Aristotle was referred to as a "schoolboy" (185), and a group of actual schoolboys is enlisted by Father Conmee in Wandering Rocks. Stephen likes to work in Aristotle:

> God: noise in the street: very peripatetic. Space: what you damn well have to see. Through spaces smaller than red globules of man's blood they creepycrawl. . . . (186)

This anticipates themes (space, noises in the street) and the technique of the most peripatetic chapter in *Ulysses*, and even its organ, the blood and its circulation. Blood is very much in evidence throughout the discussion of *Hamlet*. Conversely, the organ of Scylla reappears, weakened, in Wandering Rocks as "brainsick" (242).

So, in a way, Wandering Rocks simply continues Scylla, but with significant transferences. The tendency is trivialization, externalization ("the throb always within you" is transferred to "throb always without you," 242), localization, and a direction toward the surface. Wandering Rocks is a superficial chapter. Wit, brilliant and accretive in Scylla, becomes shallow in the thoughts of F. Conmee or Kernan. Stephen makes good use of names. F. Conmee's use of the name of Dignam (*"Vere dignum,"* 219), or Rochford's "I'm Boylan with impatience" (232), is trite and mechanical in marked contrast. Stephen's system of symbolic equations and identifications is transferred to the surface of Dublin geography, where identity becomes a problem of not mistaking one person, or a name, for another with similar surface appearance. Emotional problems are transferred to problems of locomotion in a modern city. "A hesitating soul . . . torn by conflicting doubts, as one sees in real life" (184) is transposed, *sub specie temporis nostri,* into real life, and utterly trivialized, in the person of Mr Dudley White, B.L., M.A., who is "stroking his nose with his forefinger, undecided whether he should arrive at Phibsborough more quickly by a triple change of tram or by hailing a car or on foot through Smithfield, Constitution hill and Broadstone terminus" (252).

It so happens that Dublin's street furniture contains elements of the Library discussion, almost inevitably. That Dublin's nomenclature can oblige with such items as "Williams's row" (237), or "north William street" (222), is merely a happy coincidence after all the mental energy exerted on Shakespeare's first name, but a convenient one. What's in a name? Such candidates for authorship of Shakespeare's plays as "James I or Essex" (185) are somehow, and quite unconnected, externalized, and petrified in Essex bridge and James's Gate, and so on. Oscar Wilde, figuring as poet, critic, and wit in Scylla, is reduced to the local habitation of his father: "the corner of Wilde's" (250). Haines turns Shakespeare into a "happy huntingground" (248); that is, something topographical and spatial. And due to the accidents of language (the material Shakespeare and Joyce work with), the name of Hamlet can become externalized to its extreme: Wandering Rocks is the only chapter containing the word "hamlet" (221, 242).[6]

Literary quotations, like the "porches" of King Hamlet's ear (as on 196 and elsewhere), can be transformed into architecture: the "porch of the bank of Ireland" (228). Shakespeare is still referred to and quoted from, in Wandering Rocks, usually in a superficial manner. In this episode almost everybody is, in Bloom's simplified version, "doomed for a certain time to walk the earth" (152). After Stephen's analytic study of the "swan of Avon" (188), Wandering Rocks in its opening paragraph features "Brother Swan." The resemblance is merely superficial. The transference to the surface is most clearly brought out in Martin Cunningham, one of the first persons to be mentioned in Wandering Rocks (219), and dominating a whole section (246–48). He is the man who has a *face* like Shakespeare, as Bloom noted (96) and as Circe will bear out (558).

How trivial and external Shakespearean correspondences can become may be shown in the person of Master Patrick Aloysius Dignam, to whom one section of Wandering Rocks is devoted (250–52). He is a most peripheral non-Hamlet. Characteristically, it is the novel's surface Shakespeare who will take care of him, Martin Cunningham, with Bloom (another Shakespeare, but in the symbolic superstructure) donating a handsome sum (246). Dignam junior has just come from Mangan's, a porkbutcher's (compare 187). (The shop is situated, incidentally, at 2 *William* street.) Paddy Dignam's dawdling is emphasized, an externalized counterpart of Prince Hamlet's hesitations. His father has recently died, his mother is in mourning, and an uncle is in charge. The uncle stages a little feast ("the superior tawney sherry uncle Barney brought . . . And they eating crumbs of the cottage fruit cake"), from which Paddy absents himself in disgust and boredom. The last glimpse of his father was "on the landing," more or less in the way the dead king makes his appearance on the stage. Paddy Dignam senior will actually become a ghost in a Cyclopic parody (301–2). Like the ghost of the dead king, his father admonished Master Dignam "to be a good son to ma." The "court dresses"[7] necessary for the occasion are provided by "Madame Doyle," in front of whose window the boy stops. Outrageous fortune troubles him mainly through his collar. Like Hamlet, he considers subterfuge: "I could easy do a bunk on ma." But he is frustrated in his plan to see a prize fight, modern-day equivalent to deadly challenges in history and on stage: "Sure, the blooming thing is all over." Time, obviously, is out of joint, and repeatedly so: "One puck in the wind from that fellow would knock you in the middle of next week, man."

So the elements making up the complex themes of Shakespeare and Hamlet are displaced and dispersed throughout Wandering Rocks, in accordance with its fragmentary character. As the chapter of displacements, it is disjointed. The heterotopical interpolations are its outstanding structural feature:[8] passages lifted from one part to another indicate simultaneity and hint at some relation. The interruptions of Stephen's discourse in the library, due to external circumstances and parallel actions, have prepared us for the technique. But in Wandering Rocks the interpolations disrupt the unity of place within each scene, as they interconnect the various places.

The principle of displacement is carried over into the Sirens chapter, which is also full of heterotopic transitions. In the first phase, Bloom passages are interspersed in the action of the Ormond bar; some readers erroneously believe the barmaids are actually observing Bloom. The device of mechanically displaced passages is magnified at the beginning: the overture, or prelude, consists of nothing but sentences lifted from the succeeding chapter, though most of the sentences have been changed in the process.

Wandering Rocks is pieced together of solid blocks, neatly separated as paragraphs. Such distinct paragraphs still make up much of the structure of Sirens, but the transitions are often achieved by sound: "Yoeman cap./Tap." (285), and tonal glides like *"hie"/*"High" (266) are characteristic. This device of tonal glides also operates occasionally in Wandering Rocks. The sound of the handbell "Barang" is synchronous with the "Bang of the lastlap bell" of a distant cycle race (237). Such tonal glides soften the edges that are jutting so hard in Wandering Rocks. In Sirens, however, heterotopic items can be condensed into one paragraph, even into one sentence:

Last rose Castille of summer left bloom I feel so sad alone. (285)

The juxtapositions of Wandering Rocks turn into the orchestration of Sirens. A different order forms coincidental noises into music. The principle of composition, mechanical and artistic, links the two episodes, but Sirens has become a composition in the musical sense. We have moved from the composition of place to the composition of sound. Units are still transposed in Sirens, even literally: "Miss Kennedy with manners transposed the teatray down to an upturned lithia crate" (258). This is still the transposition in space characteristic of Wandering Rocks already; "transposed" is an ideal thematic and technical link between the chapters. In fact, Sirens transposes the contents of the previous one, by changing key, mood, and technique.

Perhaps the most artificial transposition occurs toward the end of the chapter and disrupts the otherwise realistic flow of Bloom's musings:

Want to have wadding in his no don't she cried. (288)

"No don't she cried" remains syntactically and semantically unassimilated until it is recognized as a displacement from, or an echo of, an earlier passage, well outside the ken of Bloom's consciousness:

Sweet tea Miss Kennedy having poured with milk plugged both two ears with little fingers.—No don't, she cried. (259)

Wandering Rocks and Sirens are meticulously arranged (just as Stephen's theory is), but the arrangements are different. Of course, Tom Kernan's favorite phrase—"a retrospective sort of arrangement"—has to turn up in both chapters, with minor variations (241, 277). Wandering Rocks actually ends with a retrospective arrangement: the Coda of the viceregal cavalcade subsumes most of the action of the chapter; it also integrates many of the dispersed heterotopical interpolations. Most of the *dramatis personae* are ·rearranged along the linear progress of the cavalcade. The counterpart of the Coda, the overture of Sirens, is a prospective arrangement. It sums up the entire contents of the succeeding actions, but is comprehensible only retrospectively. The Coda is a final, lucid, panoramic rearrangement; the overture an initial, confusing, panacoustic prearrangement.

Sirens is musical also in the sense of being a variation of themes that are (mainly) already familiar. So is the Coda of Wandering Rocks. It could also be considered a variation of the theme expressed at its beginning: "The viceroy was most cordially greeted on his way through the metropolis" (252). This newspaper cliché is then simply modified and transposed into different keys.

Thematically too, the Sirens chapter grows out of Wandering Rocks. The first sounds to be heard are the hoofirons of the viceregal carriages. Nearly all of the persons gathering in the Ormond hotel have been met with in Wandering Rocks. No longer concerned with the logistic precision of Wandering Rocks, the arranger of Sirens is more interested in themes and sounds. So the actual distribution of the protagonists within the localities of the bar and dining room, though helpful for an understanding, has to be laboriously deduced. The *nebeneinander* of things is apt to get lost in the *nacheinander* of sound.

The music of Sirens is abundantly prepared for in Wandering Rocks, which features many songs, a Highland band, a music hall, an earful of Molly's whistling (225), and all the *artistes* scheduled to appear in Sirens. Tom Kernan is reminded by historical sites (history having become Dublin topography) of Irish rebels, and he recalls a line from a rebel ballad: "At the siege of Ross did my father fall" (241). Characteristic for Wandering Rocks, the line contains a place reference. But the ballad is *The Croppy Boy,* and the association will have consequences, for it is Tom Kernan who is later responsible for the choice of this song from Ben Dollard's repertoire (282).

A passage in the Coda adumbrates the theme of Sirens—diversion through music as an escape. "His Excellency," seemingly disquieted by Blazes Boylan's visual charms and the "salute offered to the three ladies," "drew the attention of his bowing consort to the programme of music which was being discoursed . . ." (254). Bloom will similarly use the charms of music as a momentary way out.

Wandering Rocks ends with an escape: the last glimpse is of the disappearing trousers of Almidano Artifoni. Artifoni, who has earlier on been "holding up a baton of rolled music as a signal" (229), functions as a conductor in front of a waiting orchestra. Sirens is a chapter of orchestration, and it is dominated by sound. Taken simply as sound, Artifoni's name suggests the "*art*" of sound or voice (Greek *phone*). Sirens is an artificial and artful arrangement of sounds and many voices.

Names are still given attention in Sirens (see 259). It is appropriate that names should function as sound in the context of this chapter. Bloom has his own thoughts on names: "Hate. Love. Those are names" (285). The words are those heard from Dollard singing *The Croppy Boy,* but as it happens they actually *were* names in Wandering Rocks. "Love is the name?" (245); while "hate" is present in Haines, whose name can be taken as French *haine*. In Circe love and hate will be names again, in the Reverend Mr Hugh C. *Haines Love* (559). "Love" and "hate" are not only retrospective links, they also look forward to the next chapters. Hate and its manifestations will dominate the Cyclops chapter, where Bloom will define love as "the opposite of hatred" (333), unaware, probably, that he is remembering a patriotic song. The devious ways of love, however, will be conjugated in the Nausicaa chapter.

The simple point is that the three chapters chosen here are linked and that the interconnections are manifold. It would be possible to trace such larger themes as time (from a metaphysical concept in Scylla to clockwork time in Wandering Rocks to *Sonnez la cloche* in Sirens) or paternity through the chapters and to examine the changes. For all its diversity, *Ulysses* is very much of a piece, though its intricate, latent continuity is less in evidence than its disparities and discrepancies. Joyce's intention was to transpose, to compose, to interconnect, and to interrelate. And he did, with amazing ingenuity.

There is "infinite variety everywhere," but the poles of sameness and difference, and the process of transformation bringing them about, underlie everything, including such concepts and themes as metempsychosis, incarnation, trinity, identity, Homeric parallels, analogies, Viconian schemes, "history repeating itself with a difference," and the representativeness of Joyce's Dublin. It is the "same old dingdong always" (167), but—*mutatis mutandis*. And part of the vitality lies in the transmutations.

1972

Notes

1. S. L. Goldberg, *The Classical Temper: A Study of James Joyce's "Ulysses"* (London: Chatto and Windus, 1961). This is probably the most brilliant study written against those of Joyce's methods that are looked into here with much more favor.

2. *The Spiritual Exercises of Saint Ignatius* (London: Burns and Oates, 1893), p. 20.
3. See the discussion of *"artes"* and joining on pp. 76, 80.
4. Let
   A Roman and a British ensign wave
   Friendly together. (*Cymbeline*, 5.5.479-81)
5. Retrospectively, however, the *"bless'd altars"* also link the close of Scylla and Charybdis back to the book's opening: *"Introibo ad altare Dei"* (3). It is Buck Mulligan who lifts these words from where they belong, and soon afterwards he solemnly blesses the scenery around him. In this way the first half of *Ulysses* is thematically bracketed. Elevation seems to structure *Ulysses:* "altar" is connected with *altus,* high. The beginning is on top of a tower, the echoing *"altars"* at the end of the first half is a literary altitude. The next chapter opens on the steps of the presbytery of the Jesuit church in Gardiner street, Upper: high both geographically and hierarchically. *Ulysses* ends with memories of Gibraltar as well as Howth Head.

But we can think of alternative bisections; one obvious one would include Wandering Rocks, with its externalized realism, still within the first half, the overtly "realistic" one, of *Ulysses.* A division according to Day versus Night, or else along an axis of male against female predominance, is suggested on pp. 164-65. Ulysses is a book of more than one midway point.

6. Etymologically, "hamlet" (derived from "home") connects Hamlet with such familiar themes of *Ulysses* as home, Home Rule, *Home Sweet Home,* etc.
7. Dresses are characteristic of Wandering Rocks as contrived surfaces; "court dresses," in particular, reappear in Sirens as second-hand clothes and ornamentals for the opera (269).
8. I owe this useful term to Leo Knuth.

13

Dislocution

As the historians we cannot help being, we feel inclined to treat every work of art, no matter how unique it may strike us at first, also as something derived, something we can trace to sources or else place within a common tradition of ideas, attitudes, perceptions, techniques and—in literature—rhetorical conventions. Historical inquiries are necessary and generally feasible, justified by ample results. But we are still left with the complementary task to focus on what appears new and different as well, to determine what it might be that looks, or vaguely feels, distinct, not yet experienced before. With this polarity in view, a one-sided attempt shall be made to observe—and provisionally name—one of the features that seem to set *Ulysses* apart from whatever happened before the shock of its advent. All of such features are, of course, at least prefigured in Joyce's earlier works in perceptible graduations, and they will be magnified in *Finnegans Wake*.

A prime characteristic of *Ulysses* is its lofty reluctance to conform, its resistance to any of our categories, to any kind of methodization. It still eludes us. It is true that if you look at the assurance with which some statements about *Ulysses* are being put forth, you are likely to doubt the elusiveness claimed here, but the certainties academically announced tend to be mainly in the trustful eyes of the beholders: one of the things *Ulysses* could teach us is just *how naïve* eyes trained in tradition can be. Actually we do not even understand *Ulysses* sufficiently, on the most elementary of all possible levels, certainly not as well as some reference works blandly assert. We find ourselves faced by more questions than we thought might be there. The common professional way to deal with *Ulysses* is to bypass it with some glib generalizations, or theories never quite put to the test. Take, for example, almost any of the dissertations emerging today in German-speaking countries, and you will see that most of the quotations they contain will not be from *Ulysses,* but will instead repeat something already in print in respectful regressive reiteration. We can always have recourse to established pretense mechanisms.

Ulysses is tricky to grasp because of its volatility. Such an attestation has to be substantiated, as it seems to run counter to a first, lasting impression, that of reliable, expansive solidity, the book's foundation in the bricks, the stone, and steel of a very real, well-documented city. This city takes shape by nominal delineation, though mainly in the casual way in which an actual inhabitant might notice and recall familiar urban views. But it also arises out of our trust that somewhere outside there was a city to match the written word, and what is left of the city today still remains open to our verification. Or we have such substitutes as a topographical guide, maps, old photographs, or that stately source book, *Thom's Official Directory of Dublin,* to fall back on. In some essential manner *Ulysses* is a fictional rearrangement of such extralingual data. But it is against some assured metropolitan firmness of that kind that the book's metamorphotic fictions are played off. At some stage the illusion of specific reality will be recognized as perhaps the most cunning artifice among many. Ultimately there may be nothing but verbal imagination. In the end, as there was in the beginning, there may be nothing but the word—Joyce has a way of belaboring this point. The suggestion is here made very strongly that this *verbum in principio* is indeed a dynamic *verb,* rather than some material or abstract *noun.* It may be precisely the nominalizing tendency of our conceptualizing that gets in the way of our dealing with processes, processes that could be most appropriately served by verbs that can express voices, moods, tenses, and engage in multiple conjugations.

Again, appearances may contradict this, notably in that long, informative, stationary chapter that we have agreed to call Ithaca. It presents itself as an almost purely nominal conglomerate, in which finite verbs perform mainly menial tasks. But to read this chapter in practice amounts to releasing the verbs and the actions that have been frozen, in true occidental style, into fossils of abstraction. We translate what is on the page by the sort of mental alteration that is my subject; we unbind the emotions that the text is at such pains to put at a safe, dispassionate distance.

We might also examine the novel's opening sentence, an arrangement of qualities and objects:

> Stately, plump Buck Mulligan came from the stairhead, bearing a bowl of lather on which a mirror and a razor lay crossed.

First, two adjectives, joined into unusual companionship to herald a name, then a close-up view of some concrete items of shaving gear—a predominantly nominal splurge. We can easily lose sight of the verbs: the main one, "came," is an unmemorable syntactical necessity; the subordinate one, "bearing," stylishly singles out a solemn gesture we are likely to miss on a first reading; the final "lay crossed" seems to express more a fixed geometrical shape than the act that brought it about. The first beat is "Stately"; that is how we set off, with a steadfast, stable quality. The implicit motionless "standing" is doubled by an equally passive terminal "lay." The odd counterpart to "Stately," "plump," suggests more inert corporality.

It is interesting to compare all this to the way the book closes, and instructive to realize, right away, that a final equivalent has to be severed arbitrarily and artificially from what is basically ongoing syntactical motion, almost like the surgical vivisection of a live organism.

> . . . and first I put my arms around him yes and drew him down to me so he could feel my breasts all perfume yes and his heart was going like mad and yes I said yes I will Yes. (*U* 783)

We might bring out the difference by remarking that the book's opening could be painted, staged, or filmed, but that the ending essentially could not. The end accentuates drawing and feeling and excitement: it culminates in a mercurial will. Joyce singled out a moment in the past that affected the future and that the present of Bloomsday and Bloomsnight has qualified and yet somehow confirmed: such relations can mainly be brought out by verbs. What nouns still occur in that farewell burst are bodily organs validated entirely by their live functions, "arms . . . breasts . . . heart," or else "perfume," which, insofar as it relates to matter, refers to it at its most volatile, and in so far as it does not, expresses a sensation or else an act of olfactory seduction.

From *things* to *processes*—that indeed is a direction of *Ulysses*. It is, parenthetically, typical that a juxtaposition of the book's first and last statements may reveal something about it. But a further point is that even the apparent nominal stability of the opening was somehow specious.

That third word of the book, "Buck," already hovers momentarily between the term for an animal and an eighteenth-century label for a kind of dandy; and both meanings somehow inherent in the nickname, and probably tacitly rejected at first reading, will manifest themselves in the next pages. The shaving bowl will instantly be misused as though it were a ritual chalice in another elevation that would have to be celebrated elsewhere—in a holy edifice by an ordained priest. The mirror will soon do its proper duty as an optical tool for reflection and redirection of our perspective; it will also introduce one of the book's most startling new techniques. If all of this sounds like the belabored enunciation of general truisms, it is meant to be, for Joyce's artifices make us notice, as though for the first time, what should be trivially obvious.

In its rendering of what is also daily routine, *Ulysses* takes us very far afield, first to a highly specific, dated, Dublin, but geographically beyond it to Gibraltar, Paris, Hungary, but also into an Irish past, to Semitic roots of our culture, to a mythological Hellenic age, to a few centuries of patristic quibbling as well as through a skimpy tour of most occidental literature—to name just a few of the better-known landmarks. What sets *Ulysses* off from other novels that have done partly the same is that many shifts occur without express narrative warning. Conventional guidance for erratic displacements and abrupt jolts is lacking. At times the novel seems to proceed psychologically, associatively; then again it seems to adopt external points of view, even historical ones or some that are highly hypothetical. It may choose to imitate a newspaper in its typographical shape, or go through the motions and trappings of a play. At turns it behaves as though it could be orchestrated like music. In one weird penultimate stretch it dessicates itself into the precise mannerism of objective questions and answers, unless we reinterpret it all as a grotesque attempt to mimic the Church's catechetic habit of parceling out dogmatic truths.

Ulysses is an unruly book in its design, its surface, its architectures, its details, and its interweavings, quite apart from the constant allurement away from the tangible referents to the words themselves—signifiers, if you want—and their capricious linguistic discharges. Symptoms are numerous and, some, well-known. In order therefore to indicate, provisionally, and to help us observe some of the energetic, restive, and defiant animus of *Ulysses* in all its diversified manifestations I suggest a term that should be reasonably precise, so as to retain some denotative edge, and yet implicatively loose enough to accommodate multifarious features. *Dislocution* has the advantage of not being predefined. It suggests a spatial metaphor for all manner of metamorphoses, switches, transfers, displacements, but also acknowledges the overall significance of speech and writing, and insinuates that the use of language can be less than orthodox. The prefix should alert us to a persistent principle of *Ulysses,* evinced in a certain waywardness, in deviations, in heretical turns, but also in multiple errors and miscommunications. In a merely negative meaning, the term might even serve as a convenient blanket for all subgroups of transmission errors in the book's chancy progress from one stage to the next, due to understandable clerical inadvertence.

Some methodical typology of *dislocution* would be a natural next step, but even if it were feasible, the gains of systematic neatness would not make up for the intrinsic falsification. For dislocutions are not so much isolable qualities as they are entangled processes that defy administrative classification. Even so, the following representative samples will hint, though vaguely, at some elementary differentiation.

At one extreme of the scale, on the surface level, there are obvious instances of transformations in space, as in Bloom's experience of "the alterations effected in the disposition of the articles of furniture," when he reenters his drawing room. A sofa has been "translocated," a table been "placed opposite the door," a sideboard "moved from its position" (*U* 705). This experience is concrete and, as we know, painful; the redisposition of furniture suggests an actual domestic change. But it is analogous to various rearrangements within the whole book. The Wandering Rocks chapter could be cited as a further example: it disrupts the pretense of linear chronology by offering a collocation of disparate scenes, but it also tries to dovetail the heterotopical actions by fragments of dislocated narrative. In its transversal interlockings the chapter has left the tracks of the previous nine, which, for all their diversity, were still basically sequential. The Cyclops chapter also has unmistakable displacements, interpolated passages, which, in tone, style, attitude, and angle of vision, contrast markedly with the personal narration that they interrupt. It is the conspiciuous dislocations that set off the later chapters from those of the first half (which are *relatively* uniform): we experience these later chapters as jarring deviations from what looked like reliable narrative practices.

The most startling dislocutory performance for first readers is the medley of phrases that opens the so-called Sirens chapter. These phrases, hardly understood on their own in any conventional sense, turn out to be a prospective arrangement of fragments from the pages to follow, both a thematic preparation *for* and a variation *of* the composition they precede. This unique overture frankly displays itself as a verbal artifact of juxtapositions; coincidentally, it also exaggerates that the whole of *Ulysses* is a redisposition of its material, a matter of internal transferences, of kaleidoscopic diversion. *Ulysses* reshuffles its elements, and with a difference.

Stephen Dedalus, for example, in his Shakesperean argument, makes a point about Helen of Troy and Penelope of Ithaca:

—Antisthenes, pupil of Gorgias, . . . took the palm of beauty from Kyrios Menelaus' brooddam, Argive Helen, the wooden mare of Troy in whom a score of heroes slept, and handed it to poor Penelope. (*U* 201)

This is simply the adaptation of some classical learning that Stephen picked up a few hours earlier when he himself, with his bitterness, was compared to that cynic philosopher. That version was shorter:

Antisthenes, a disciple of Gorgias. . . . He wrote a book in which he took away the palm of beauty from Argive Helen and handed it to poor Penelope. (*U* 148–49)

Stephen has varied a few terms and added embroideries of his own. In a doubling of tropes, Helen has become, first, "Kyrios Menelaus' brooddam," then "the wooden mare of Troy in whom a score of heroes slept." A transformation into animal imagery becomes noticeable. It seems to be Stephen's own misogynist streak that turns the most beautiful of all women into a "brooddam." Surely her breeding proclivities were the least emphasized by the ancients or, for that matter, the painters. And it looks like an affront to equate her with the "wooden mare of Troy," even though we know that she, in her vanity, once nearly frustrated the Greeks' stratagem to capture the city (*Od.* 4:266–89). The horse becomes a mare in Stephen's imagination only, and the reader knows that here some recollection of history "as a nightmare" may have interfered—though that was a different kind of "mare," of course, but already one thought capable of giving him "a backkick" (*U* 34). We may also have an echo of "Madeline the mare" from an untraced song (*U* 37). "Mare" has become one of those many words that in the course of the book have acquired a semantic karma. If printed on paper, the word looks like a Latin term for the sea;[1] if sounded, it comes close to a French word for the sea derived from it, or else to the word for mother. We know that in Stephen's mind "sea" and "mother" have been painfully brought together in the intense brooding of that same morning. In this context it might even be fitting that a "wooden mare" was a term for a military instrument of torture; somehow, by causing a war with untold casualties, Helen of Troy did indeed become a cause of punishment and pain. If, incidentally, we were to isolate from the phrase under inspection just three words and merely say them aloud, "mare of Troy" might misleadingly suggest some ancient municipal ruler, a town "mayor." Of such philological unruliness the context takes instant care (though not always), but the point here is simply that a sentence modifying its source is full of potential turbulences.

Chances are that most readers will hardly devote much attention to "Kyrios Menelaus' brooddam," but this incongruous apposition is in itself a minor node of dislocutions. "Kyrios Menelaus," an anachronistic hybrid, joins a Latinized Homeric name to a proper Greek honorific that is not to be found in Homer, but entirely depends on later Christian usage. The early Christians needed a term for what in Hebrew was "Jehovah," and *kyrios* was substituted in the Septuagint as the beginning of a venerable career. *Ulysses* highlights it, for Stephen's phrase also echoes the words of the same person who introduced Antisthenes, Professor MacHugh, who held forth in the newspaper office on these very appellations and compared Latin *Dominus* with English *Lord,* and both—to their disfavor—with

> —The Greek! *Kyrios!* Shining word! The vowels the Semite and the Saxon know not. *Kyrie!* . . . I ought to profess Greek, the language of the mind. *Kyrie eleison!* (*U* 133)

This polyglot collation entails four cultures: each one is refracted in *Ulysses* and in turn set off against local Irish observances. They all throw some oblique light on Stephen's quotation. Since professorial authority insists on the unmatched quality of Greek vowels, which neither a Hebrew nor an English tongue can manage, we may be entitled to wonder just how Stephen

Dedalus, in his condensed recall, actually pronounces the shining word—
"kyrios, kurios, kiirios?". With his characteristic disregard for the range of
his audience (his listeners, after all, were not present at the discussion in the
newspaper office), he might well say something to be fleetingly misunderstood as "curious"; curiosity could reasonably be attributed to a husband in
the situation of Menelaus (in *Finnegans Wake* such a phonetic sweep would be
a routine shift and *is* instanced at least once: "our hagious curious encestor,"
FW 95.34). As the whole discourse in question is devoted to a speculative
view of Shakespeare, it is curious to find that Shakespeare, in the one play
linking him with the *Odyssey, Troilus and Cressida,* uses the address "Lord
Menelaus" (5.1.74), which here Stephen appears to have rendered into some
Greek contamination. While on the subject of Shakespeare, whose vocabulary
suffuses the whole chapter, we might also mention, for what it is worth, that
in *The Tempest* (which Stephen also works into his theory) Caliban calls his
mother "my dam" and has the word followed by "brood" a few lines later
(3.2.101-5). Stephen might well have fused these two nouns into his one
composite. It happens that "dam" derives from Latin *domina,* so that even
within a brief cluster, the etymological divarications of one word across
linguistic borders span the whole scale from divine to human to animal usage.

It is, of course, the oddity of "brooddam" or the incompatibility of
"Kyrios" with "Menelaus" that invites conjecturing of the kind given here.
We might imagine a translator of Homer—and they are usually hard-pressed
about the original appellatives—to try a form like "Lord Menelaus," as
Shakespeare did for other reasons. As against this elevated usage, the word
kyrios in modern Greek has socially descended and become a most ordinary
term for Mister, such as Mr Bloom, who in the modern Greek translation is
treated in general exactly as King Menelaus is specifically rendered in this
passage, by *Kyrios.* Not that we need, naturally, such a circuitous bypass by
means of a later translation to bring together a mythological hero with an
unfaithful wife and Mr Leopold Bloom, cuckolded husband of Molly. Again
we might be struck by some pertinent similarities in this ironic conjunction, or
even more by the blatant disparities: while Helen was abducted by her lover
and a gigantic and heroic war had to be waged in order to remedy the damage,
the household of the Blooms is characterized by passivity and connivance. So,
to sum up what must appear like an excessive glossing of a few almost
mechanical dislocutions, what inevitably emerges is a multiple amalgamation
of personal memories, psychological pressures, and variegated cultural
sources. The shifts involved—but never quite spelled out—range from an Old
Testament Jehovah to the present, from high to low, and in order to follow up
all ramifications one would have to unravel the whole novel.

In its particles and as a whole, *Ulysses* makes us aware of cultural
changes and erratic expansions, of how, for example, Christianity was grafted
onto an earlier religion with attendant modifications, so that the Latin quota-

tion from the beginning of the Mass also evokes—but lifts out of its primary context—an ancient Psalm in Hebrew. A reverend term like "Messiah" was transplanted and deflected into what in Greek is "Christos"; both words occur in *Ulysses,* and both roles are among those we are meant to try out on Leopold Bloom. Bloom, obligingly, is of Jewish descent, a baptized Protestant, and a converted Roman Catholic, and yet skeptically aloof from those and all other institutionalized forms of religion. A peripheral tangle like "Kyrios Menelaus" among other things also points back to Jewish and Greek roots. It is no wonder that Joyce found the theories of a French scholar serviceable for his purposes. Victor Bérard had reread Homer's *Odyssey* as a Hellenic adaptation of the nautical empirical know-how of the Phoenicians; the *Odyssey,* in this view, is an idiosyncratic assimilation of former sailing reports. It was only in keeping then to metamorphose the epic once more, into a parochial Irish version with further radical departures: this only reflects the arbitrary course of what we call civilization. History, Irish history in particular, is a checkered stratification of successive invasions, a city like Dublin consists of superimpositions and changes of names. Literature, as well, resembles a palimpsest. Our understanding of *Ulysses* as a contrived and doctored offshoot of the *Odyssey* has unfortunately been dominated too long by the deceptive term "Homeric *parallels"*—deceptive because parallelism is only one among many possible relations. The term's dominance has tended to occlude the evident fact that Joyce's Homeric dislocations were often oblique, or reversed, or diversified, not in a tidy attributive order, but in a criss-cross of mutually disruptive patterns.

Perhaps the chaotic, associative orders within our own psyches are somehow analogous. The so-called stream of consciousness is also a dislocutionary sequence. There is always some latent continuity, but tracks are switched all the time. From any one point reached, all possible directions are open. The resulting imprevidibility becomes also a characteristic of the text. On the first page, the vivid depiction of Buck Mulligan's antics comes to a halt in a frozen moment of his "white teeth . . . with gold points," and we are suddenly confronted with an unanticipated, foreign, one-word sentence: "Chrysostomos." We have shifted into a different world, ancient Greece, conjuring up a Homeric type of compound. We can account for this metastatic shift somehow, recalling oratorical saints or classical authors, eponymous customs or proverbial golden silence, which here paradoxically heralds a new rhetorical device. What we cannot overlook is that *some* accounting, *some* mental redirection, is called for.

Eccentric items like "Chrysostomos" can be labeled quotations or allusions. Those abound in *Ulysses,* all the way from conspicuously paraded, often italicized, famous words to fading and tricky echoes. All of the numerous quotations function as—in fact almost literally *are*—dislocutions, especially when the original wording is modified. A quip at Stephen Dedalus as "the loveliest mummer of them all" (*U* 5) transports the present-day situation into a stylized scene in Roman history and so incites us to detect similarities between Brutus, an ancient tyrannicide and suicide, and Stephen Dedalus—it may be that both are acting inflexibly on principles too rigid, and at too high a cost? We are also prompted to register differences. Whatever the possible relations between noble Brutus and jejune Stephen, the historical incident has been refracted by the attitudes as well as the artistic strategies of an Elizabethan playwright, who condensed it into memorable lines aimed at dramatic effect, lines now twisted and adapted again by a witty young Irishman to taunt—or woo—a cautious friend. At least three periods and three places have been conflated. Within the quotation, "loveliest mummer" has displaced "noblest Roman" and caused further unrest. In the narrow sense of Catholic, Stephen is, of course, no longer a Roman. In Shakespeare's play, all Romans were "mummers"—that is, actors. And in *Ulysses* it happens to be the liveliest actor of them all, Buck Mulligan, who has warped the words into a shape that tilts at Stephen's roles and poses. Oddly enough, a mummer used to be an actor in a dumb-show, one who "mummed," was "mum," silent, so that we might wonder if maybe Stephen's former development from a believer in the Roman faith into his well-proclaimed program of "silence, exile and cunning" is somehow touched upon remotely. Stephen Dedalus *is* gloomily silent at this particular instant, and his verbal reserve contrasts with Mulligan's eloquent histrionics. That mummery also suggest disguises and masks fits well into the book's initial display of character transformations, which prepares for all the multiple roles to come. And, in yet another twist, it is intriguing to find that Shakespeare used "mummers" just once, but applied to another Brutus, in another play, *Coriolanus* ("you make faces like mummers," 2.1.75), as though to add more unsettling texturings to those already intimated. Of course none of the interlacings instanced here as possible is as vital as the wry agitation a literary echo has imparted to the context, an echo that can be energized further if brought in line with a later variation of the same matrix: "the bravest cattle breeder of them all" (*U* 399).

To depart from the phrasing of a quotation may be due—on the realistic level—to defective memory or inner compulsions, but it is usually the author's jujitsu strategy to exploit original semantic energy for deflected intrinsic ends. From a normative point of view, such deviations are mistakes. *Ulysses* is full of errors and faults, lapses, slips, misprints, false analogies. They may arise from preconceptions, as when a racing fanatic bends a casual, impatient remark—that the intruder may keep the newspaper Bloom was "going to throw away"—into a tip on the outcome of an impending horse race. This race, the Gold Cup at Epsom on 16 June 1904, was actually won by the outsider Throwaway, and the consequent rumor of Bloom as a fortunate but stingy gambler seriously disturbs the course of his afternoon. Rumors and conjectures help to shape, in particular, the third part of *Ulysses*, the Nostos, so that a distrust for any kind of verbal report is likely to result. Bloom's humanitarian concern for Stephen translates the mumbled name of a Celtic minor god, Fergus (from a poem by Yeats), into a putative lady friend, Miss Ferguson, of the pointedly celibate companion (*U* 608). A misunderstanding thus perverts what for Stephen Dedalus is an expression of Love's Bitter Mystery into some mysterious, gratifying, but nonexistent love affair. There is a strong suggestion that history itself consists of chance memories, misrepresentations, and accidentally fixated legends.

One could conceivably specify a variety of temporal disruptions: in the experience of reading, in the narrative action, and in the book's language viewed historically. At their narrowest, they simply revive more obsolete meanings of words. The "crazy glasses" of a carriage window (*U* 87) do not of course indicate some mental oddity but hark back to a dormant meaning of "cracked" or "broken." A passage in Ithaca formally attests that Bloom was "baptised . . . three times," first by a Protestant minister soon after his birth, the last time when he joined, for matrimonial reasons, the Catholic Church. The odd, anomalous baptism was conducted, we read, "by James O'Connor, Phillip Gilligan and James Fitzpatrick, together, under a pump in the village of Swords" (*U* 682). It may be that three classmates played a trick on him and called the submersion, perhaps in a burst of anti-Semitism, his baptism; but the ascription is made possible by a regression to a pre-Christian meaning of the Greek verb *baptizo* in the secular sense of "to dip, immerse." The Ithaca chapter's priorities impassively ignore jocular or historical uses of language.

Such temporal shifts within the language can condition a whole passage or, with excessive consistency, whole sections. The notorious Oxen of the Sun chapter artificially recaptures historical opportunities that have been superseded by contemporary literary customs. The episode pretends to disguise itself in successive past modes of perception, or description, with the vocabularies and styles of certain periods of English literature. But it also frankly flaunts the whole sequence as a masquerade and dispels illusions through incongruities and anachronistic checks. In the following chapter, Circe, the process is reversed, and everything takes place in one protracted present. Stagey changes of costumes and roles occupy the foreground. In this treatment the entire contents of the book are dispersed and re-locuted in associative and extrapsychic configurations, without any regard to those probabilities that still dominated the earlier chapters.

Dislocution would be a convenient blanket term for the characteristic of *Ulysses* that in recent times has received most scholarly attention—each chapter reprocesses its ingredients according to different and, on occasion, highly deviant preferences. In their entirety, these serial approaches, or perspectives, also become a polytropic endeavor to comprehend all possible modes of being. This is not to say that we can ever pinpoint, to any satisfactory degree, the exact programing of each individual chapter. Of particular interest is the

Library episode. In the presentation here it has rather one-sidedly been seen as an incidental attempt to recycle words from Shakespeare's works into unfamiliar new patterns. One of its main interests is that it focuses on the interpretation of an artist's work and life, and by implication draws the novel's author into its meshes as well as all of us as interpreters.

The cases in point, meant to be instructive, that have been adduced so far were also misleading in their emphasis on what may be understood merely as the propensities of a stubbornly dislocutory text. What has been neglected—or, more precisely, taken for granted—is our own vital cooperation. In the last two decades or so we have discovered ourselves, with pride and embarrassment, as active participants in a complex process; and it is again provocations like *Ulysses* that have enabled us to realize such a platitude. It is, of course, the reader who—potentially—executes all the mental shifts. *Ulysses* intrigues us to dislocute according to our temperaments and our schooling, and Joyce gives us exceptionally wide scope, though never total free-associative license. We need no telling that the results are sometimes laboriously ludicrous—that is a programmatic hazard. In our interpretative distensions we have been anticipated by the text itself.

The reader of *Ulysses* may be reluctant, refuse to play the game, and soon drop out. Or else the reader tends to be amazingly sportive and willing to fall into line. Take the thematic tinge that Joyce has given to each individual chapter; it may be figurative windiness, food imagery, connotations of death, or skeletal objectivity. But it is also we who, while habitually taking little notice of everyday adjectives like "flat" or "sharp," allow them—either because of schematic compliance or some textual contagion—to set free their musical potential when they occur within the Sirens chapter. We do this by selective collusion. Joyce seems to enlist *us* to enlist "bar" as a secondary musical reference in Sirens, whereas in Cyclops we may readily recall some elongated object for potential aggression. Such docile lectoral assistance may at least alert us to the mental involvement Joyce has made hard to overlook.

Joyce gave us something to dislocute: that is one reason why we are so busy. *Ulysses,* the work in the center, shows this most clearly, but the inherent techniques already began with the gnomonic hints, the narrative nuances, or the symbolic alternatives in *Dubliners. A Portrait* boldly dislocuted Stephen's changing attitudes and, more boldly, the language through which they are evoked. But of course all previous dynamisms are escalated in *Finnegans Wake,* which demands even more active cooperation. It takes only a superficial glance to realize that *Finnegans Wake* is dislocutory throughout in all possible senses. It tampers with persons, places, and times; identities are optional. Its language is everything implied in the Latin prefix *dis-*. We tend to transform the heterographic dissensions into proper speech, not always successfully. The first stage of any honest reading of the *Wake* is still an attempt to change—transmute, metaphrase, "translout" (*FW* 281F2), rectify—the signs on the page into those forms that we imagine to have been approximated. "Murnane and Aveling are undertoken to berry that ortchert" (*FW* 613.30) is not left untouched by any reader. We are drawn into guessing at the identities of the two apparent names. In our embarrassment we are grateful if some Gaelic speaker tells us that *"muirnin"* means sweetheart, or darling, and *"aoibhinn"* means delightful or perhaps lovely (the previous line offers "lovleg"), so some Irish endearment may be voiced, not too accurately (the distance between the sound and the spelling of most Irish words gives ample scope for Joyce and considerable leeway for the interpreter). One dislocutory possibility ("undertaker" and "bury," both not literally present, but mutually corroborative) takes us in the direction of death, an opposite one toward living, growing things ("berry," "orchard"). Peace after conflict is suggested by the interred phrase "bury the hatchet" (transferred from ritual practices of North American Indians and therefore displaced), but within an orchard a hatchet will always remain a potential danger. Similar conflicts are dormant again in "Murnane and Aveling": what each word alone would not permit is achieved by their pairing—a translation into morning and evening. "Dis-locution" is accurate for what has been exemplified: the various phrasings (locutions) go in different directions (*dis-*; remember Joyce's appropriation of Ovid's *"animum dimittit,"* discussed on p. 75). The sorting out of micro-meanings, while a necessary first step toward "understanding," is not to be confused with it; note that some disturbing oddities like the suffix "-ling" and an unaccounted "token" have refused facile, rational dislocution. That even in such elementary falsification we fail more often than we succeed does not mean that such basic matching is not perversely necessary.

Finnegans Wake is a dazzling event in letters through which ordinary things like "morning" have been translated into shapes like "Murnane," and in reading it we try to reverse the process. Dislocution is an illustrative synonym for translation: in translating everything is displaced into another culture and speech. Its ambition is that, while every single part is being changed, the whole ought somehow to be preserved. Oddly enough, such improbabilities work quite often fairly well: "Good day" is "Bonjour" or "Guten Tag." We need not worry when, due to different usages of salutation, Bloom's greeting to O'Rourke, "Good day," and to Dlugacz, "Good morning" (*U* 58, 60), have to be given identical treatment in French, "Bonjour" (F 57, 59). But what about a parallel, simple, "Soft day" (*U* 31)? It becomes "Schöner Tag" (Wo 45) and "Beau temps" (F 34), and we may feel a bit uneasy. Irish weather, it seems, does not travel too well—or should we say a local greeting habit or, perhaps more to the point, a historical caricature, for nineteenth-century stage Irishmen were supposed to say "Soft day"? "Schöner Tag" and "Beau temps" take the moisture out of a greeting, but they also deprive it of a historical accretion, a stereotype, or national prejudice. A related expression, "Soft morning," sets off Anna Livia's final monologue and is echoed toward the end: "So soft this morning" (*FW* 619.20, 628.8). In a French rendering by Philippe Lavergne this becomes "Moujour . . . Il est si doux notre matin."[2] Day may have to substitute for morning in the essentially substitutive activity of translation (an earlier French version has "Doujour" and "Si doux ce matin"[3]). While an identical English morning may turn to "jour" or "matin," on account of inviolable French usage, an outlandish configuration of letters like "Murnane" mentioned above has been treated as though it were a single dislocation. Lavergne's version of "Murnane and Aveling are undertoken to berry that ortchert" is a somewhat streamlined: "Matin et Soir se sont mis à leur compte pour ensevelir ce verger d'Eden."[4] This has become a tidier story with fewer unsettling undertokens of meaning. The orchard has been specified as the garden of Eden (a clue was no doubt seen in "Aveling" as some elaboration of Eve).

The purpose of these comparisons was to show that even translating a straightforward "morning" may be tricky, but an intraWakean translation like "Murnane" is impossible to translate: just try to imagine how further metamorphoses like "moning—mourning—mournin—Moorning—moarning—moaning—morkning—modning—warning—Mahnung" and many more might be both metamorphosed *and* distinguished. As it happens, we have three rival attempts at "the moaning pipers" (*FW* 23.31) to play off against one another. The Wakean phrase foregrounds something audible that we can dislocute into reading matter (in pertinent self-contradiction the eye spells out what we can hear, the ear hears something we can see; but maybe, as a grace note, it is something we can put in our pipes and smoke as well). Such semantic miracles cannot be preserved in another language. One translator opts for "les vielleux dolents"[5] (suggesting plaintive lyres), another for simple morning papers ("les journaux du matin"[6]), without any jarring note. The Italian translator, as usual, tackles his task squarely: "i piffernali mattingementi"[7]; there is both morning and moaning, but no longer the original's effortless show of simplicity. What are least translatable are translations, like the switch from "moaning" to "morning": how can dislocutions be dislocuted?

Some terms are interchangeable, especially if they defy definition. I am aware of a temptation to replace some earlier terms for analogous processes by *dislocution*. It could be used, after all, for redescribing or (Joyce's cue) "transluding" (*FW* 419.25) what was provisionally verbalized as metamorphoses, alienated readings, an auto-corrective urge, metastasis, the disrupted pattern principle, or polytropy. . . . It might even stand for all those effects that make us respond, spontaneously, with laugher. Humor may be a matter, yet to be determined, of dislocution. The term seems to fit so generally that it ought to make us suspicious.

If anything, dislocution is an expediently blurred trope, a catalytic aid for discerning, a trifle more readily, the variants of that Protean energy that, while no single one of its symptoms may be entirely new, in its pluralistic, mercurial impact does set Joyce's later work off from its many predecessors and from most of the works that have followed in its wake.

1983

Notes

1. The graphic shape "mare" as a *word* in Latin once indirectly affected young Stephan (*P* 47); see pp. 42 and 54 n. 6.

2. *Finnegans Wake*, trans. Philippe Lavergne (Paris: Gallimard, 1982), pp. 641, 649.

3. *Finnegans Wake*, fragments trans. by André du Bouchet (Paris: Gallimard, 1962), pp. 49, 54.

4. Lavergne, p. 635.

5. Du Bouchet, p. 81.

6. Lavergne, p. 30.

7. *"Finnegans Wake"* H.C.E., trans., with glossaries, by Luigi Schenoni (Milan: Arnoldo Mondadori Editore, 1982), p. 23bis.

Bibliography
of the Writings of Fritz Senn

I. On Joyce's Early Works

"He Was Too Scrupulous Always: Joyce's 'The Sisters.'" *James Joyce Quarterly* 2, no. 2 (Winter 1965): 66–72.

"Reverberations." *James Joyce Quarterly* 3, no. 3 (Spring 1966): 222.

"Latin me that." *James Joyce Quarterly* 4, no. 3 (Spring 1967): 241–43.

"Not too scrupulous always." *James Joyce Quarterly* 4, no. 3 (Spring 1967): 244–45.

"Der grosse Joyce in kleinem Massstab." *Neue Zürcher Zeitung*, no. 123 (25 February 1968): 49–50.

"Some Further Notes on *Giacomo Joyce.*" *James Joyce Quarterly* 5, no. 3 (Spring 1968): 233–36. Translated into German by Klaus Reichert as "Ergänzung der Anmerkungen zu *Giacomo Joyce,*" pp. 73–82. Frankfurt: Suhrkamp Verlag, 1968.

Stephen D, "Nawoord." Translated from German by John Vandenbergh, pp. 91–108. Amsterdam: De Bezige Bij, 1968.

"An Encounter." In *James Joyce's "Dubliners,"* edited by Clive Hart, pp. 26–38, 171. London: Faber and Faber; New York: Viking Press, 1969.

"Nawoord" in *Giacomo Joyce.* Dutch translation of Joyce's work by Gerardine Franken; "Afterword" and "Some Further Notes" translated from German by John Vandenbergh, pp. 85–98, 67–82 passim. Amsterdam: De Bezige Bij, 1969.

"Goodness Gracious." *joycenotes,* no. 3 (December 1969): 13.

"The Challenge: *ignotas animum:* An old-fashioned close guessing at a borrowed structure." *James Joyce Quarterly* 16, nos. 1–2 (Fall 1978–Winter 1979): 123–34.

"Bibliographical Vagaries of Dublin(er)." *James Joyce Quarterly* 16, no. 3 (Spring 1979): 359–61.

"A Rhetorical Account of James Joyce's 'Grace.'" *Moderna Sprak* 74, no. 2 (1980): 121–28.

II. On *Ulysses*

"The Duke of Beaufort's Ceylon." *James Joyce Quarterly* 1, no. 4 (Summer 1964): 64–65.

"When one reads. . . ." *James Joyce Quarterly* 1, no. 4 (Summer 1964): 65.

"Esthetic Theories." *James Joyce Quarterly* 2, no. 2 (Winter 1965): 134–36.

"Mullingar Heifer." *James Joyce Quarterly* 2, no. 2 (Winter 1965): 136–37.

"Cabbage Leaves." *James Joyce Quarterly* 2, no. 2 (Winter 1965): 137–38.

"Ulysses in Zürich." *Zürcher Woche* (20 August 1965): 15.

"Seven against *Ulysses.*" *James Joyce Quarterly* 4, no. 3 (Spring 1967): 170–93.

"Tiens, tiens." *James Joyce Quarterly* 4, no. 3 (Spring 1967): 201.

"Wilderness." *James Joyce Quarterly* 4, no. 3 (Spring 1967): 245.

"Ex ungue Leopold." *English Studies* 48, no. 6 (December 1967): 537–43.

"Symbolic Juxtaposition." *James Joyce Quarterly* 5, no. 3 (Spring 1968): 276–78.

"*Ulysses* in der Übersetzung." *Sprache im technischen Zeitalter,* no. 28 (October–December 1968): 346–75.

"Breslin's Hotel." *joycenotes,* no. 1 (June 1969): 6.

"The Short and the Long of It." *joycenotes,* no. 1 (June 1969): 20–21.

"James Joyce en zijn *Ulysses.*" *Utopia* 6 (Netherlands) (June 1969), pp. 23–26 (translated from German by B. Wijffels).

"Zeven tegen *Ulysses.*" Translation of "Seven against *Ulysses*" by B. Wijffels. *Raam* 63 (March 1970): 6–35.

"Quoint a quincidence." *James Joyce Quarterly* 7, no. 3 (Spring 1970): 210–17.

"Chaste Delights." *James Joyce Quarterly* 7, no. 3 (Spring 1970): 253–54.

"No Trace of Hell." *James Joyce Quarterly* 7, no. 3 (Spring 1970): 255–56.

"Seven against *Ulysses:* Joyce in Translation." Reprinted from *James Joyce Quarterly* 4, no. 3 (1967) in *Levende Talen* 270 (1970): 512–35.

"*Ulysses* in Translation." In *Approaches to Ulysses,* edited by Thomas F. Staley and Bernard Benstock, pp. 249–86. Pittsburgh: University of Pittsburgh Press, 1970.

"James Joyce, der Verfasser des *Ulysses.*" *Der Landbote* (Winterthur, Switzerland) (4 February 1972): 3–4.

"Book of Many Turns." *James Joyce Quarterly* 10, no. 1 (Fall 1972): 29–46. Reprinted in *Ulysses: Fifty Years,* edited by Thomas F. Staley. Bloomington: Indiana University Press, 1974.

"The Rhythm of *Ulysses.*" In *Ulysses: cinquante ans après (Etudes anglaises* 53), edited by Louis Bonnerot, pp. 33–42. Paris: Didier, 1974.

"Nausicaa." In *James Joyce's Ulysses: Critical Essays,* edited by Clive Hart and David Hayman, pp. 277–311. Berkeley and Los Angeles: University of California Press, 1974.

"Metastasis." *James Joyce Quarterly* 12, no. 4 (Summer 1975): 380–85.

"Trivia Ulysseana I" ("All Too Familiar," "Frauenzimmer," "Bayed About," "That's the Word," "Touring Whom?" "Alas, Poor Bloom," "Rats: Vats," "How Poets Write," "A Pun-Gent Chapter," "Hard of Hearing," "Hellenize It," "Wallpaper," "Tip from the Stable," "Schiffe brücken"). *James Joyce Quarterly* 12, no. 4 (Summer 1975): 443–50.

"Trivia Ulysseana II" ("French Dressing," "Well pared," "Sneaky Phrase," "Dress the Character," "Last Farewell," "Hi Hung Chang," "Nation once again," "Where the boose is cheaper"). *James Joyce Quarterly* 13, no. 2 (Winter 1976): 242–46.

"Odysseeische Metamorphosen." In *James Joyces Ulysses: Neuere deutsche Aufsätze,* edited by Therese Fischer-Seidel, pp. 26–57. Edition suhrkamp, no. 826. Frankfurt: Suhrkamp, 1977.

"Trivia Ulysseana III" ("History is . . . ," "Having Eglinton's Cake," "hed say its from the Greek"). *James Joyce Quarterly* 15, no. 1 (Fall 1977): 92–93.

"Die fruchtbare Illusion der Übersetzbarkeit: Bemerkungen zur *Ulysses*-Übersetzung." *Akzente* 25, no. 1 (February 1978): 39–52.

"Das Abenteuer *Ulysses:* Beschwichtigung von Fritz Senn," Beilage zur einmaligen Sonderausgabe (inserted in the one-volume edition of *Ulysses*). Frankfurt: Suhrkamp, 1979. Reprinted as "Wer hat Angst vor dem *Ulysses?*" *Börsenblatt* 9 (30 January 1979): 193–200.

"Bloom among the Orators: The Why and the Wherefore and All the Codology." *Irish Renaissance Annual* 1, pp. 168–90. Newark: University of Delaware Press, 1980.

"Scareotypes: On Some Trenchant Renditions in *Ulysses.*" In *James Joyce: New Glances* (Modern British Literature Monograph Series), edited by Edward A. Kopper. *Modern British Literature* 5, nos. 1-2 (1980): 22-28.

"Gogarty and Joyce: Verbal Intimacy." *Cahiers Victoriens et Edouardiens* (Montpellier) 14 (October 1981): 103-9.

"Trivia Ulysseana IV" ("Brood of Tempters," "Taxilonomy," "Chap in the Paybox," "Lost Cause," "Frozen Wit," "Sophist Wallops," "Strange," "Episcopal Moves," "High Stakes," "Ramifications," "Dilapidated Conditions," "Classical Idiom," "The Kitty O'Shea Touch," "Aquiline Flutter," "Electricity in Horticulture"). *James Joyce Quarterly* 19, no. 2 (Winter 1982): 151-78.

"*Ulysses* von James Joyce." *Radio DRS Programmhinweise,* no. 24 (14 June 1982): 1-2.

"Righting *Ulysses.*" In *James Joyce: New Perspectives,* edited by Colin MacCabe, pp. 3-41. Sussex: Harvester Press, 1982.

"Six Notes for Joyce" ("Reader in Search of a Name," "Tried, like another Ulysses," "If I Had a Name like Her," "Far Cries," "Leivnits," "The Doubling of Sosie"). *SCRIPSI* 2, no. 1 (James Joyce Issue) (November 1982): 113-24.

"*Ulysses,* ou le changement." *James Joyce: Centenary Issue, Etudes Irlandaises,* James Joyce Special Number, edited by Patrick Rafroidi and Pierre Joannon (1982): 47-49.

"The Fretted Resonances of *Ulysses.*" *Eigo Seinen* (Tokyo), James Joyce Special Number (June 1983): 62-69.

"Foreign Readings." In *Work in Progress: Joyce Centenary Essays,* edited by Richard F. Peterson, Alan M. Cohn, and Edmund L. Epstein, pp. 82-105. Carbondale: Southern Illinois University Press, 1983.

III. *On* Finnegans Wake

"Early Russian History in *Finnegans Wake.*" *James Joyce Review* 2, nos. 1-2 (Spring-Summer 1958): 63-64.

"James Joyce über das Schweizer Frauenstimmrecht." *Die Tat* (Zürich) 31 (January 1959): 15.

"Schweizerdeutsches in *Finnegans Wake.*" *DU* (Zürich) 20 (May 1960): 51-52.

"Some Zürich Allusions in *Finnegans Wake.*" *The Analyst* 20 (September 1961): 1-23.

"Dublin Background." *A Wake Newslitter,* no. 2 (April 1962): 5-8.

"Every Klitty of a scolderymeid: Sexual-Political Analogies." *A Wake Newslitter,* no. 3 (June 1962): 1-7.

"Borrowed brogues." *A Wake Newslitter* no. 8 (December 1962): 4-6.

"rheadoromanscing." *A Wake Newslitter* no. 2 (March 1963): 1-2.

"A Test-Case of Overreading." *A Wake Newslitter* 1, no. 2 (April 1964): 1-8.

"Pat As Ah Be Seated." *A Wake Newslitter* 1, no. 3 (June 1964): 5-7.

"A Touch of Manichaeism." *A Wake Newslitter* 1, no. 3 (June 1964): 9-10.

"One White Elephant." *A Wake Newslitter* 1, no. 4 (August 1964): 1-3.

"First Words and No End." *A Wake Newslitter* 2, no. 3 (June 1965): 17-20.

"Ossianic Echoes." *A Wake Newslitter* 3, no. 2 (April 1966): 51-54.

"The Aliments of Jumeantry." *A Wake Newslitter* 3, no. 3 (June 1966): 51-54.

"Old Celtic Romances." *A Wake Newslitter* 4, no. 1 (February 1967): 8-10.

"Insects Appalling." In *Twelve and a Tilly,* edited by Jack P. Dalton and Clive Hart, pp. 36-39. London: Faber and Faber, 1966.

"The Tellings of the Taling." *James Joyce Quarterly* 4, no. 3 (Spring 1967): 229-33.

"Tellforth's Glory." *A Wake Newslitter* 4, no. 2 (April 1967): 42.
"'Bitterness' and Other Notes." *A Wake Newslitter* 4, no. 2 (April 1967): 44–45.
"Litterish Fragments." *A Wake Newslitter* 4, no. 3 (June 1967): 52–55.
"'Indecent Behaviour' and Other Notes." *A Wake Newslitter* 4, no. 3 (June 1967): 55–56.
"Loose Carollaries." *A Wake Newslitter* 4, no. 4 (August 1967): 78–79.
"Universal Word." *A Wake Newslitter* 4, no. 5 (October 1967): 108–9.
"Every Klitty of a scolderymeid: Sexual-Political Analogies" (revised version). *A Wake Digest* (1968): 27–38.
"Reading in Progress: Words and Letters in *Finnegans Wake*." *Leuvense Bijdragen* (Louvain) 57, no. 1 (1968): 2–18.
"An Irish Hudibras." *A Wake Newslitter* 6, no. 2 (April 1969): 27.
"Charting Old Ireland." *A Wake Newslitter* 6, no. 3 (June 1969): 43–45.
"Some Conjectures about Homosexuality in *Finnegans Wake*." *A Wake Newslitter* 6, no. 5 (October 1969): 70–72.
"Buybibles." *James Joyce Quarterly* 7, no. 3 (Spring 1970): 257–58.
"In het struikgewas von *Finnegans Wake*." Translation of "Im Dickicht von *Finnegans Wake*" by B. Wijffels. *Levende Talen* 269 (June–July 1970): 456–61.
"A Reading Exercise in *Finnegans Wake*." *Levende Talen* 269 (June–July 1970): 469–80.
"We've Found Remembrandtsers." *A Wake Newslitter* 7, no. 4 (August 1970): 61–63 (with Rosa Maria Bosinelli).
"Anmerkungen zu Goyerts Übersetzung." In James Joyce, *Anna Livia Plurabelle*, pp. 164–66. Frankfurt: Suhrkamp, 1970.
"The Localisation of Legend." *A Wake Newslitter* 8, no. 1 (February 1971): 10–12.
"Cattermole Hill." *A Wake Newslitter* 8, no. 2 (April 1971): 32.
"Terminals Four." *A Wake Newslitter* 8, no. 3 (June 1971): 46.
"Bush Abob." *A Wake Newslitter* 8, no. 3 (June 1971): 46.
"His Pillowscone Sharpened." *A Wake Newslitter* 9, no. 6 (December 1972): 109–10.
"All Agog." *A Wake Newslitter* 9, no. 6 (December 1972): 110–11.
"Dutch Interpretation." *A Wake Newslitter* 11, no. 3 (June 1974): 54.
"Thou Art Pebble," *A Wake Newslitter* 11, no. 4 (August 1974): 76.
"New Bridges for Old." *A Wake Newslitter* 11, no. 5 (October 1974): 76.
"Far Beyond." *A Wake Newslitter* 12, no. 1 (February 1975): 9.
"Fiery River." *A Wake Newslitter* 12, no. 2 (April 1975): 33.
"Noble Tree." *A Wake Newslitter* 12, no. 2 (April 1975): 33.
"Free Leaves." *A Wake Newslitter* 12, no. 2 (April 1975): 33.
"Silent Sister." *A Wake Newslitter* 12, no. 2 (April 1975): 33.
"Entzifferungen & Proben: *Finnegans Wake* in der Brechung von Arno Schmidt." *Bargfelder Bote* 27 (February 1978): 3–14. Reprinted in *Der Übersetzer* 17, nos. 11–12 (November–December 1980): 1–5.
"A Collideorscape!"*A Wake Newslitter* 15, no. 6 (December 1978): 92–93.
"Seeking a Sign." *A Wake Newslitter* 16, no. 2 (April 1979): 25–29.
"Erigenating." *A Wake Newslitter* 17, no. 2 (April 1980): 24.
"Semenal Rations." *A Wake Newslitter* 17, no. 6 (December 1980): 103.
"Finnegan neckt." *Neue Zürcher Zeitung* (30 January 1982): 67–68.
"Leivnits." *A Wake Newslitter*, Occasional Paper 1 (August 1982): 6.
"The Doubling of Sosie." *A Wake Newslitter*, Occasional Paper 1 (August 1982): 7.
"Encore *Finnegans Wake:* Comment traduire une traduction?" *La Quinzaine littéraire* 385 (1–15 January 1983): 17–18.

IV. On Joyce (General)

"Zur Deutschen Ausgabe" and "Bibliographie und Diskographie." In Richard Ellmann, *James Joyce*, pp. 9–10 and 763–70. Zürich: Rhein Verlag, 1961.

"Joyce im Gespräch." *Neue Zürcher Zeitung* (15 March 1964): 59.

"James Joyce: Eigenheiten im Werk des grossen Iren." Literary Supplement, *Zolliker Bote* (Zollikon), no. 24 (June 1966): 9–11.

"Hier wohnte Joyce." *DU-atlantis* (Zürich) 26 (September 1966): 735–36.

"Letters of James Joyce" (on volumes II and III). *Neue Zürcher Zeitung*, no. 814 (26 February 1967): 61–63.

"The Issue Is Translation." *James Joyce Quarterly* 4, no. 3 (Spring 1967): 163–64.

"Joyce, das Sechseläuten und der Föhn." *Zürcher Woche*, no. 24 (17 June 1967): 17.

"Every Word Is Right: Umgänge in Joyces Werk." *Neue Zürcher Zeitung*, no. 426 (14 July 1968): 49–50.

"In That Earopean End." *James Joyce Quarterly* 6, no. 1 (Fall 1968): 91–95.

"A Throatful of Additions to Song in the Works of James Joyce." *joycenotes*, no. 1 (June 1969): 7–17.

"Der neue Joyce: Zur Neuübersetzung des Gesamtwerks im Suhrkamp Verlag." *Die Weltwoche* (Zürich), no. 6 (6 February 1970): 27.

"In That Earopean End II." *James Joyce Quarterly* 7, no. 3 (Spring 1970): 274–80.

"Vorwort" and "Anmerkungen" (Foreword and Notes). In James Joyce, *Briefe an Nora*, pp. 5–34 and 147–72. Frankfurt: Suhrkamp, 1971.

"Joycean Translatitudes: Aspects of Translation." In *Litters from Aloft: Papers Delivered at the Second Canadian James Joyce Seminar*, edited by Ronald Bates and Harry J. Pollock, pp. 26–49. Tulsa: Tulsa Monograph Series, University of Tulsa Press, 1972.

"It Teaches Me Better to Love." *Neue Zürcher Zeitung*, no. 541 (19 November 1972): 50–52.

"The James Joysymposium." *Hawaii Review* 5 (Spring 1975): 2–17.

"The Fifth International James Joyce Symposium" (Photographic Essay). *James Joyce Quarterly* 13, no. 2 (Winter 1976): 133–42.

"Voorvoord." In *Brieven aan Nora*, pp. 5–26. Translated from German by John Vandenbergh. Amsterdam: De Bezige Bij, 1976.

James Joyce Pub Zürich. Zürich: Schweizerische Bankgesellschaft, 1978.

"James Joyce: Sprache als Modell einer verzweifelten Welt." In *Die Grossen der Weltgeschichte* 10, pp. 80–89. Zürich and Munich: Kindler Verlag, 1978.

"7. Internationales James Joyce Symposium." *Englisch Amerikanische Studien* 1, no. 3 (September 1979): 439–40.

"Joycean Workshops." *James Joyce Broadsheet* 1 (January 1980): 4.

"The Distant Dubliner: James Joyce." *Swissair Gazette* 5 (1980): 23–28.

"Dogmad or Dubliboused?" *James Joyce Quarterly* 17, no. 3 (Spring 1980): 237–61.

"James Joyce in Zürich." *Turicum* 4 (December 1980–February 1981): 75–79.

"A Modest Proposal." *James Joyce Broadsheet* 7 (February 1982): 7.

"James Joyce—Ein Überfremder" and "Spuren nach Basel." *Basler Zeitung* (30 January 1982): 6–7.

"James Joyce—Meister der Verstellungen." *Tages-Anzeiger* (Zürich) (30 January 1982): 47–48.

"Ein einheimischer Fremder." *Die Welt* (Hamburg), no. 27 (2 February 1982): 19.

"Weaving, unweaving." In *A Starchamber Quiry*, edited by E. L. Epstein, pp. 45–70. New York and London: Methuen, 1982.

"A Dublimad Replique to Nathan Halper's Letter." *James Joyce Quarterly* 19, no. 2 (Winter 1982): 219–20.

"Critical Files: A Project, Maybe." *James Joyce Quarterly* 19, no. 2 (Winter 1982): 223–24.

"James Joyce: *Ulysses* und *Finnegans Wake*—Zumutung und Chance." *Börsenblatt* 38, no. 36 (28 April 1982): 1096–99.

"Afterword." In *Nordic Rejoycings 1982—in Commemoration of the Birth of James Joyce*, edited by Johannes Hedberg, pp. 137–40. James Joyce Society of Sweden and Finland, 1982.

"James Joyce—vertraut und fremd." In *James Joyce 1882-1982: Gedenkfeier in der Aula der Universität Zürich* (commemorative booklet), pp. 13–19. Zürich: Max-Geilinger-Stiftung, 1982.

"Joyce in Zürich." *kruispunt* 85—literair kwartaalschrift (December 1982): 47–52.
"Ein Wunder in sanften Augen" (Lucia Joyce's Death). *Neue Zürcher Zeitung*, no. 292 (15 December 1982): 37–38.
"Dynamics of Corrective Unrest." In *James Joyce: A New Language—Actas/Proceedings del Simposio Internacional en el Centenario de James Joyce*, edited by Francisco Garcia Tortosa et al., pp. 231–42. University of Seville, 1982.
"Joyce, alors!" *Der Rabe*, no. 2 (1983): 196–205.
"Und gleich noch einmal *Ulysses* auf deutsch." *Der Rabe*, no. 2 (1983): 245–46.

V. *Collections of Essays*

James Joyce: Aufsätze. Preface by H. U. Rübel. Zürich: Max-Geilinger-Stiftung, 1972. (Contains: "James Joyce über das Schweizer Frauenstimmrecht," "Schweizerdeutsches in *Finnegans Wake*," "Hier wohnte Joyce: Ulysses in Zürich," "Das Besondere an Joyce," "Joyce, das Sechseläuten und der Föhn," "Der neue Joyce: Zur Neuübersetzung der Gesamtwerkes," "James Joyce, der Verfasser des *Ulysses*—zu seinem neunzigsten Geburtstag.")
Nichts gegen Joyce: Joyce versus Nothing. Edited by Franz Cavigelli. Zürich: Haffmans Verlag, 1983. (Contains: "Enzyklopädisches Stichwort: James Joyce," "Ein Überfremder," "Lese-Abenteuer *Ulysses*," "Korrespondenzen," " 'Meine arme kleine einsame Nora,' " " 'Ein Wunder in sanften Augen,' " "Umgang mit Anfängen," "Durch ein Glas," "Dynamics of Corrective Unrest," "Variants of Dislocution," "The Challenge: 'ignotas animum,' " "Paratektonik oder Nichts gegen Homer," "Homeric Afterwit," "Finnegan neckt," "Wortgeschüttel," "A Reading Exercise in *Finnegans Wake*," "*Ulysses* in der Übersetzung," "Übersetzerwehen," "Die fruchtbare Illusion der Übersetzbarkeit," "Entzifferungen und Proben," "Die erste Kreuzung," "Auf der Suche nach einem Titel," "Ein hoher Preis," "Erstarrte Phrase," "Keusche Freuden," "Keine Spur von der Hölle," "Versetzt," "Skeptimismus.")

VI. *Reviews*

"A Question of Modernity." *James Joyce Quarterly* 4, no. 2 (Winter 1967): 131–32.
"The Bloomsday Book." *James Joyce Quarterly* 4, no. 4 (Summer 1967): 347–48.
"James Joyce—Chronik von Leben und Werk." *Neue Zürcher Zeitung* 165 (16 March 1969): 51.
"James Joyce—Chronik von Leben und Werk" by Daniel von Recklinghausen. Edition suhrkamp, no. 283. *James Joyce Quarterly* 6, no. 3 (Spring 1969): 279.
"Umgang mit *Finnegans Wake*." (Commentaries on books by Anthony Burgess and Arno Schmidt.) *Neue Zürcher Zeitung*, Literary Supplement 7, no. 714 (International Edition 336) (December 1969): "Sprache als Spielraum," p. 49; "Lesbarmachen und Interpretation," p. 50.
"*Sprache und Spiel im 'Ulysses.'* " *Neue Zürcher Zeitung*, no. 63 (International Edition 38) (8 February 1970): 49–50.
"*Sprache und Spiel in 'Ulysses'* von James Joyce by Eberhard Kreutzer." *James Joyce Quarterly* 7, no. 3 (Spring 1970): 269–70.
"Der Triton mit dem Sonnenschirm by Arno Schmidt." *James Joyce Quarterly* 7, no. 3 (Spring 1970): 271–73.
"*Epic Geography*, by Michael Seidel." *James Joyce Quarterly* 14, no. 1 (Fall 1976): 111–13.
"*A Bibliography of James Joyce Studies*, by Robert H. Deming." *James Joyce Quarterly* 16, nos. 1–2 (Fall 1978–Winter 1979): 181–88.
"James Joyce: *Ulysses: A Facsimile of the Manuscript*" and "Hugh Kenner: *Joyce's Voices*." *English Amerikanische Studien* 2, no. 1 (March 1980): 154–56.

"From 'a' to 'zyngarettes.'" (On Bauerle's *A Word List to Joyce's Exiles* and Füger's *Concordance to James Joyce's "Dubliners."*) *James Joyce Broadsheet* 7 (February 1982): 7.
"A 'Ulysses' Phrasebook." *James Joyce Quarterly* 19, no. 2 (Winter 1982): 216–18.
"James Joyce: A Guide to Research (by Thomas Jackson Rice)." *James Joyce Broadsheet* 11 (June 1983): 3.

VII. On Other Authors and Topics

"Carola Giedion-Welcker." *James Joyce Broadsheet* 1 (January 1980): 3.
"P. G. Wodehouse." Afterword for Wodehouse, *Lustige Geschichten*, pp. 393–99. Zürich: Diogenes Verlag, 1980.
"In Memoriam: Jack P. Dalton." *James Joyce Quarterly* 18, no. 4 (Summer 1981): 459–60.
"Auch einer: Einem Klassiker zum 100. Geburtstag [P. G. Wodehouse]." *Tintenfass*, no. 3, pp. 206–17. Zürich: Diogenes Verlag, 1981.
"Wer liest, ist immer selber schuld." *Tintenfass*, no. 3, pp. 235–42. Zürich: Diogenes Verlag, 1981.
"Von 'Aftersenkung' bis 'Zungenkuss'—Ärger mit der Duden-Sinnverwandtschaft." *Der Rabe*, no. 4 (1983): 237–39.
"Zur Zürcher Ausgabe: Ein Duftauszug." Afterword to the third edition of *Über Schopenhauer*, edited by Gerd Haffmans, pp. 315–22. Zürich: Diogenes Verlag, 1981.
"Was denkt Penelope?" *Der Rabe*, no. 6 (1984): 205–8.

VIII. Edited Volumes

A Wake Digest. With Clive Hart. Sydney: Sydney University Press; University Park: Pennsylvania State University Press; London: Methuen and Co., 1968.
James Joyce, *Frankfurter Ausgabe.* With Klaus Reichert. Vol. I: *Dubliner* (1969); Vol. II: *Stephen der Held, Ein Porträt des Künstlers als junger Mann* (1972); Vol. III, nos. 1 and 2: *Ulysses* (1975); Vol. IV, no. 1: *Kleine Schriften* (1974); Vol. IV, no. 2 *Gesammelte Gedichte* (1981); Vol. V–VII: *Briefe* I, II, III (1969, 1970, 1974). Frankfurt: Suhrkamp Verlag.
Materialien zu James Joyce's "Dubliner." With Klaus Reichert and Dieter E. Zimmer. Edition suhrkamp, no. 357. Frankfurt: Suhrkamp, 1969.
Programme for the Second International James Joyce Symposium, 10–16 June 1969. Zürich: Carta Druck AG.
James Joyce, *Briefe an Nora.* Frankfurt: Suhrkamp, 1971.
New Light on Joyce from the Dublin Symposium. Bloomington: Indiana University Press, 1972.
A Conceptual Guide to "Finnegans Wake." With Michael H. Begnal. University Park: University of Pennsylvania Press, 1974.
Materialien zu James Joyce "Ein Porträt des Künstlers als junger Mann." With Klaus Reichert. Edition suhrkamp, no. 776. Frankfurt: Suhrkamp, 1975.
Arthur Schopenhauer, *Werke in zehn Bänden*, Zürcher Ausgabe, 10 volumes. Zürich: Diogenes Verlag, 1977 (With Claudia Schmölders and Gerd Haffmans).
James Joyce, *Die Toten*, with "Nachwort," "Nachträgliche Vorbemerkungen zum Hades-Kapitel." Zürich: Diogenes Verlag, 1979.
Das George Orwell Lesebuch (George Orwell Reader) with "Afterword," pp. 337–42. Zürich: Diogenes Verlag, 1980.
Briefe von William Faulkner. Zürich: Diogenes Verlag, 1980.
Über Patricia Highsmith: Zeugnisse von Graham Greene bis Peter Handke. Zürich: Diogenes Verlag, 1980 (with Franz Cavigelli).
Denken mit Orwell. Zürich: Diogenes Verlag, 1982.

IX. Translations

James Joyce, *The Cat and the Devil. Die Katze und der Teufel.* Illustrated by Richard Erdoes. Zürich: Rhein Verlag, 1966.
Die Katze und der Teufel. Illustrated by Jan de Tusch-Lac. Frankfurt: Insel Verlag, 1976. Reprinted in: *Die besten klassischen und modernen Katzengeschichten,* pp. 97–99. Zürich: Diogenes Verlag, 1973; *Gruss und Kuss Dein Julius: Eine Briefologie für Kinder und für alle, die gern Briefe bekommen,* edited by Hildegard Krahé, pp. 64–67. Munich: Verlag Heinrich Ellermann, 1974; *Samt und Krallen,* edited by Sybil Gräfin Schönfeldt, pp. 228–30. Würzburg: Arena Verlag, 1982.

August Suter, "Some Reminiscences of Joyce." In *Portraits of the Artist,* edited by Willard Potts, pp. 61–66. Seattle: University of Washington Press, 1979.

P. G. Wodehouse, *Im Westen kaum Neues. Tintenfass,* no. 3, pp. 218–24. Zürich: Diogenes Verlag, 1981.

Edward Gorey, *The Chinese Obelisks/Die chinesischen Obelisken.* Zürich: Diogenes Verlag, 1981.

James Abbott McNeill Whistler, *Die feine Art sich Feinde zu machen.* Zürich: Haffmans Verlag, 1984.

Index

Fritz Senn is the European editor of the *James Joyce Quarterly* and was, until 1983, the coeditor of *A Wake Newslitter*. His books *James Joyce: Aufsätze* and *Nichts gegen Joyce: Joyce versus Nothing* have appeared in German.

THE JOHNS HOPKINS UNIVERSITY PRESS

Joyce's Dislocutions

This book was composed in Times Roman text and Weiss Roman display type by BG Composition, Inc., Baltimore, Maryland, from a design by Cynthia Hotvedt.

It was printed on 50-lb. Glatfelter Offset and bound by Thomson-Shore, Inc., Dexter, Michigan.